Economics Made Fun

Best-selling books such a *Freakonomics* and *The Undercover Economist* have paved the way for the flourishing economics-made-fun genre. While books like these present economics as a strong and explanatory science, the ongoing economic crisis has exposed the shortcomings of economics to the general public. In the face of this crisis, many people, including well-known economists such as Paul Krugman, have started to express their doubts about whether economics is a success as a science. As well as academic papers, newspaper columns with a large audience have discussed the failure of economics to predict and explain ongoing trends. The emerging picture is somewhat confusing: economics-made-fun books present economics as a method of thinking that can successfully explain everyday and 'freaky' phenomena. On the other hand, however, economics seems to fail in addressing and explaining the most pressing matters related to the field of economics itself.

This book explores the confusion created by this contradictory picture of economics. Could a science that cannot answer its own core questions really be used to explain the logic of everyday life?

This book was originally published as a special issue of the *Journal of Economic Methodology*.

N. Emrah Aydinonat is an Associate Professor of Economics at Bahçeşehir University, Istanbul, Turkey. He is also a part-time Lecturer at Bogazici University, Istanbul, Turkey, and a Research Associate at the Academy of Finland Centre of Excellence in the Philosophy of Social Sciences, University of Helsinki, Finland. He is the author of *The Invisible Hand in Economics* (Routledge, 2008) and *What is Economics?* (in Turkish, İletişim, 2014).

Jack Vromen is Professor of Theoretical Philosophy at Erasmus University, Rotterdam, the Netherlands. He is also Academic Director of the Erasmus Institute for Philosophy and Economics. Since the publication of his book, *Economic Evolution* (Routledge, 1995) he has researched theoretical and meta-theoretical issues in economics and evolution. Recently he also developed research interests in neuroeconomics, in social mechanisms and in the booming 'Economics Made Fun' genre.

Economics Made Fun

Philosophy of the pop-economics

Edited by

N. Emrah Aydinonat and Jack Vromen

LONDON AND NEW YORK

First published 2015
by Routledge

2 Park Square, Milton Park, Abingdon, Oxon OX14 4RN
711 Third Avenue, New York, NY 10017, USA

Routledge is an imprint of the Taylor & Francis Group, an informa business

First issued in paperback 2017

British Library Cataloguing in Publication Data
A catalogue record for this book is available from the British Library

ISBN 13: 978-1-138-90267-1 (hbk)
ISBN 13: 978-1-138-08540-4 (pbk)

Typeset in Times
by RefineCatch Limited, Bungay, Suffolk

Publisher's Note
The publisher accepts responsibility for any inconsistencies that may have arisen during the conversion of this book from journal articles to book chapters, namely the possible inclusion of journal terminology.

Disclaimer
Every effort has been made to contact copyright holders for their permission to reprint material in this book. The publishers would be grateful to hear from any copyright holder who is not here acknowledged and will undertake to rectify any errors or omissions in future editions of this book.

Contents

Citation Information

The following chapters were originally published in the *Journal of Economic Methodology*, volume 19, issue 3 (September 2012). When citing this material, please use the original page numbering for each article, as follows:

Chapter 1
The paradox of popularity in economics
Diane Coyle
Journal of Economic Methodology, volume 19, issue 3 (September 2012) pp. 187–192

Chapter 2
A less-is-more approach to introductory economics
Robert H. Frank
Journal of Economic Methodology, volume 19, issue 3 (September 2012) pp. 193–198

Chapter 3
Finding the right levers: the serious side of 'economics made fun'
Jack Vromen
Journal of Economic Methodology, volume 19, issue 3 (September 2012) pp. 199–218

Chapter 4
On the philosophy of the new kiosk economics of everything
Uskali Mäki
Journal of Economic Methodology, volume 19, issue 3 (September 2012) pp. 219–230

Chapter 5
Economics is a serious and difficult subject: Paper prepared for Conference at EIPE, Rotterdam, December 10-11, 2010
Roger E. Backhouse
Journal of Economic Methodology, volume 19, issue 3 (September 2012) pp. 231–241

Chapter 6
The two images of economics: why the fun disappears when difficult questions are at stake?
N. Emrah Aydinonat
Journal of Economic Methodology, volume 19, issue 3 (September 2012) pp. 243–258

Chapter 7

Inland empire: economics imperialism as an imperative of Chicago neoliberalism
Edward Nik-Khah and Robert Van Horn
Journal of Economic Methodology, volume 19, issue 3 (September 2012) pp. 259–282

Chapter 8

The unbearable lightness of the economics-made-fun genre
Peter Spiegler
Journal of Economic Methodology, volume 19, issue 3 (September 2012) pp. 283–301

Chapter 9

The evolving notion of relevance: an historical perspective to the 'economics made fun' movement
Jean-Baptiste Fleury
Journal of Economic Methodology, volume 19, issue 3 (September 2012) pp. 303–316

Chapter 10

Economic page turners
Björn Frank
Journal of Economic Methodology, volume 19, issue 3 (September 2012) pp. 317–327

The following chapter was originally published in the *Journal of Economic Methodology*, volume 19, issue 4 (December 2012). When citing this material, please use the original page numbering for each article, as follows:

Chapter 11

Economics made fun, and made fun of: how 'fun' redefines the domain and identity of the economics profession
Erwin Dekker and Paul Teule
Journal of Economic Methodology, volume 19, issue 4 (December 2012) pp. 427–436

Please direct any queries you may have about the citations to
clsuk.permissions@cengage.com

Notes on Contributors

N. Emrah Aydinonat is an Associate Professor of Economics at Bahçeşehir University, Istanbul, Turkey. He is also a part-time Lecturer at Bogazici University, Istanbul, Turkey, and a Research Associate at the Academy of Finland Centre of Excellence in the Philosophy of Social Sciences, University of Helsinki, Finland. He is the author of *The Invisible Hand in Economics* (Routledge, 2008) and *What is Economics?* (in Turkish, İletişim, 2014).

Roger E. Backhouse is the author of *The Puzzle of Modern Economics* (2010), as well as the co-author of *Capitalist Revolutionary: John Maynard Keynes* (with Bradley W. Bateman, 2011), and *Transforming Modern Macroeconomics: Exploring Disequilibrium Microfoundations, 1956–2003* (with Mauro Boianovsky, 2012).

Diane Coyle runs the consultancy Enlightenment Economics, and is the author of numerous popular economics books, including *The Economics of Enough* (2011) and *The Soulful Science* (2009).

Erwin Dekker is currently working as a PhD candidate and Lecturer in Cultural Economics at Erasmus University, Rotterdam, the Netherlands. His PhD project is about economics and civilization, and more specifically how these themes come together in inter-war Austrian liberal thought. Previously he also lectured at the European Studies Department at the University of Amsterdam, the Netherlands.

Jean-Baptiste Fleury is Associate Professor at the University of Cergy-Pontoise, Paris, France, and a member of the THEMA research centre. His scholarly work focuses on the history of what has been labelled 'economics imperialism', that is, the expansion of the scope of economics outside its traditional boundaries. Recent publications include "Wandering Through the Borderlands of Social Sciences" (*History of Political Economy,* 2012), a history of the writing and reception of Gary Becker's 1957 book on discrimination; and "Drawing New Lines: Economists and Other Social Scientists on Society in the 1960s" (*History of Political Economy,* 2010), which deals with the relationship between the social policies of the Johnson administration and the work of economists outside their traditional domain of expertise.

Björn Frank is a certified creative writing trainer and holds a professorship for Applied Microeconomics at the University of Kassel, Germany. His main areas of research are cultural and media economics, and experimental economics. His previous affiliations include Clausthal University of Technology, Germany, and the German Institute for Economic Research, Berlin, Germany.

Robert H. Frank is the Henrietta Johnson Louis Professor of Management and a Professor of Economics at the Samuel Curtis Johnson Graduate School of Management at Cornell University, Ithaca, New York, USA. He contributes to the "Economic View" column in *The New York Times*. He is the author of *Passions Within Reason* (1988), *The Economic Naturalist* (2007), *The Darwin Economy* (2011), and many other books.

Uskali Mäki is Professor of Philosophy and Director of TINT – Academy of Finland Centre of Excellence in the Philosophy of the Social Sciences, based at the University of Helsinki, Finland. He was previously Professor and Academic Director at EIPE (Erasmus Institute for Philosophy and Economics) in Rotterdam, the Netherlands. He is a former editor of the *Journal of Economic Methodology*, the editor of *The Handbook of the Philosophy of Economics* (2012) and *The Methodology of Positive Economics: The Milton Friedman Legacy* (2009), and the former Chair of the International Network for Economic Method. He has published in economics and philosophy journals such as *Economics and Philosophy*, *Erkenntnis*, *Synthese*, *History of Political Economy*, *Journal of Economic Literature*, *Kyklos*, and the *Cambridge Journal of Economics*. Much of his current work is focused on models, realism and interdisciplinarity.

Edward Nik-Khah is Associate Professor of Economics at Roanoke College, Salem, Virginia, USA, and (2011–12) Research Fellow at the Centre for the History of Political Economy, Duke University, Durham, North Carolina, USA. He has published on the political economy of market design and the history of the post-war Chicago School. His current research focuses on the history of neoliberal pharmaceutical science and (with Philip Mirowski) the public role of economists during the Great Recession.

Peter Spiegler is Assistant Professor of Economics at the University of Massachusetts, Boston, USA. He is an Editorial Board member of *Forum for Social Economics* and the *Strategies of Social Inquiry* book series. He received his PhD from Harvard University, Cambridge, Massachusetts, USA, in 2005.

Paul Teule is a Lecturer in Political Economy in the Department of European Studies at the University of Amsterdam, the Netherlands. His PhD research focuses on the institutional 'strength' of the gross domestic product (GDP) statistic.

Robert Van Horn is Assistant Professor of Economics at the University of Rhode Island, Kingston, RI, USA. His research has primarily focused on the history of the post-war Chicago School. He is co-editor, along with Philip Mirowski and Thomas Stapleford, of *Building Chicago Economics* (2011). Journals such as *History of Political Economy* and the *Journal of the History of the Behavioral Sciences*, among others, have published his work.

Jack Vromen is Professor of Theoretical Philosophy at Erasmus University, Rotterdam, the Netherlands. He is also Academic Director of the Erasmus Institute for Philosophy and Economics. Since the publication of his book *Economic Evolution* (Routledge, 1995), he has researched theoretical and meta-theoretical issues in the area of economics and evolution. More recently, he also developed research interests in neuroeconomics, social mechanisms and the popularizing 'Economics Made Fun' genre. He publishes regularly in philosophy and economics journals.

The paradox of popularity in economics

Diane Coyle

Enlightenment Economics and IPEG, University of Manchester

This special issue collects papers presented at the EIPE Conference 'Economics Made Fun in the Face of the Economic Crisis' held on 10–11 December 2010 in Rotterdam. The central theme of the conference was the tension between the bold claim in Economics Made Fun books that economics can explain the hidden side of everything and the apparent failure of economics to foresee, let alone prevent the financial crisis. Economics is understandably unpopular as a subject because of the financial crisis, and yet the popular appetite for economics seems only to have increased in recent years. In this Introduction to the special issue I want to explore some reasons that might explain this paradox.

These thoughts on the genre of 'fun' economics are offered from the perspective of someone who has published six popular economics books (Coyle 1996, 1999, 2001, 2002, 2009, 2011). This genre has certainly been enjoying a period of success, with increasing numbers of titles available and increasing sales. However there is a paradox of popularity, in the sense that this success in the book-buying market has come at a time when the subject itself is in some disrepute because it is quite widely perceived to have contributed to the financial and economic crisis. In this note, I will first explore this paradox of popularity. Second, I will consider what impact the increased general audience for economics might have on economists, and on the public and public debate. Will the incentive to write for the mass audience improve economics? Will the increased supply of comprehensible economics improve their understanding – and indirectly therefore public policy? My tentative answer will be yes to both, suggesting that the pop economics phenomenon is to be welcomed.

The unpopularity of (popular) economics

Economics is held in low esteem by many people, even by some economists. It is one of the many culprits blamed for the financial crisis, especially as economics is perceived to be wholly about the advocacy of the deregulation of markets. There have always been some critics of the methodology of economics. There are books forming a 'critique of economics' genre, albeit fewer than in the 'pop economics' genre. There is a 'post-autistic' economics movement, now renamed Real World Economics.[1] There is an Institute for New Economic Thinking.[2] Some of the critics express their views in quite emotional terms. For example, Buchan (1995) has described the subject scathingly as the 'science and gospel of money':

> [Economists] should take credit for the deteriorating quality of existence. For it is their philistine notions of personal and national welfare that have helped ruin the natural world; confused technology with culture; reduced art to money, time to interest, sexual relations to pornography, friendship to advantage and liberty to shopping.

He says dismissively that there are only three short passages – a few paragraphs of Keynes, a footnote in Marshall's *Principles* and Book V of *The Wealth of Nations* – 'that attempt to describe the world you and I live in'.

Some criticisms are better founded than this kind of outburst. For example, one *Financial Times* journalist wrote of economics:

> It worships mathematical technique but pays little attention to the behavioural and institutional forces at play in the real world – which is too messy to model with tidy equations. It has lost relevance by trying to pretend economics is a 'hard science' totally divorced from related subjects such as politics, psychology and sociology. (Prowse 1993)

This was never true of the best economists, as the varied list of Nobel memorial prize-winner shows. Economic historians and institutionalists, behavioural economists and practical econometricians have featured in significant numbers as winners. The charge is also decreasingly true of most economists of any calibre. The high tide of the kind of abstraction referred to in the *Financial Times* was in early 1980s. Nevertheless, there is a grain of truth in the criticism. In both the curriculum and the kind of economics practised in financial markets by all those graduates of the late 1970s and early 1980s, the elegance of some types of model trumped the genuine insight that the study of institutions and economic history would have given.

Economics itself has been changing substantially in recent years (as I describe in *The Soulful Science* 2009), with focus on institutions, information, game theory, behavioural economics, innovations in data and econometrics. It has become much richer in its assumptions and methods. These new approaches have become well embedded, especially in applied microeconomics of the kind practised by most non-academic economists, although it has not yet reached the economics curriculum in universities.

But, in a second paradox, although the core of the subject itself has been moving firmly away from a narrow modelling approach that was dominant among economists in the 1980s, the popular perception of economics has worsened due to crisis. Economists themselves have joined the chorus of criticism. In one prominent article, 'How Did Economists Get It So Wrong?', Krugman (2009) wrote:

> The central cause of the profession's failure was the desire for an all-encompassing, intellectually elegant approach that also gave economists a chance to show off their mathematical prowess. Unfortunately, this romanticized and sanitized vision of the economy led most economists to ignore all the things that can go wrong. They turned a blind eye to the limitations of human rationality that often lead to bubbles and busts; to the problems of institutions that run amok; to the imperfections of markets.

Many economists would agree with him, while others would see this as an exaggeration, claiming that some of their number had got it right, in fact, but were ignored. Whatever the truth, the profession is currently undergoing a period of serious reflection about its methodology and the validity of mainstream views. And yet – and here is my main paradox – we can observe the phenomenon of popular economics books despite the low esteem in which the profession is held.

Explaining the pop economics phenomenon

Book publishing is in good health in general, providing a positive context for the sales of any individual genre.[3] There have also always been some economists who reached the mass market. *The Worldly Philosophers* by Heilbroner (1999) would be one example, alongside anything by J.K. Galbraith. Nevertheless, there does seem to be a definite expansion in pop economics, with new sections in bookstores and a large number of best-selling titles. There are both supply-side and demand-side factors explaining the phenomenon.

The supply-side factors are:

- Publishers' interest in expansion out of other successful 'pop' genres, such as science and history;
- The maturity of economics itself, providing ample material for books based on empirical research, experiments, behavioural research, etc.;
- The astonishing success of *Freakonomics* in 2005, leading publishers to try for the same again as the business model of publishing relies on cross-subsidy from big hits to the long tail.

Demand-side factors include:

- Consumer demand for novelty and variety, from a better-educated population;
- A secular increase in number of students of economics;[4]
- The economic crisis itself, leading to a demand for understanding of economic and financial phenomena.

There may be a parallel in the Left Book Club in the 1930s:[5] some titles in this series of 'pop' books about a wide range of academic subjects sold over 100,000 copies (out of smaller UK population of 45 million; Overy 2009). Serious times create serious tastes.

There are several sub-categories of pop economics books, as Vromen (2009) has set out:

- about economics as a subject – both pro and anti;
- about the content of economics;
- about an author's own new research;
- about using economic methods to analyse everyday life.

One of the most popular areas has been behavioural economics, which is studied by serious economists of course, but may be so popular because in many people's minds it 'disproves' economics. This may partly resolve the paradox of popularity.

The impact of economics made popular

On economists

Popular writing, such as teaching, can force the writer to understand the subject better. It is hard to communicate effectively something that one does not fully understand. So writing for a popular audience is a good discipline.

It would be a mistake, however, to think of popular communication and formal models as being in conflict with each other. Edgeworth (1881) said formalism is like scaffolding: you need it to construct the building, and then when the building is finished, you can take it down. Modelling is central to economics. It simply describes a disciplined analysis that can be confronted with data. We are used to the precision we get from models. Lucas (2004) described this when he talked about getting a note from his colleague Ed Prescott with just an equation on the piece of paper: 'Normal people would ask for some words to explain the equation. Economists ask for an equation to explain the words'.

But normal communication occurs through words and narratives. The prism of natural language is almost always a vital test of meaning. As McCloskey (2000, p. 138) puts it: 'Better writing gets read'. For some academics this is the problem – they do not want to engage with non-experts. Academic status and progression may depend on successes as defined within the profession, and success outside it may even count against career progress. As McCloskey (2000, p. 267) also notes, quoting Sir Isaac Newton: 'To avoid being baited by little smatterers in mathematics, I designedly made the *Principia* abstruse'. Academics are used to the conventions of academic writing, which is partly for precision but also meant to keep others out and demonstrate expertise. It is not meant to be understood.

Many academics are not equipped to write for the popular audience. Writing is a craft skill, which one has to do a lot to do it well. However, it would be healthier if more academics were to look to the external audience as well. Universities are a part of society, and all the more important in complicated modern societies. The academy's dialogue with the public is an important responsibility. For, importantly, economists are best placed to understand the economy. As Stein (1986, p. 17, also quoted in McCloskey 2000, p. 269) argues, 'If somebody is going to talk about economics on TV, it's probably better done by economists than by politicians, columnists, sociologists or clergymen'.

Perhaps the success of some pop economics books will provide an incentive to communicate better with the wider public, an incentive likely to be important to the kind of people who self-select into economics. The funding of economic research in the UK will in future depend more on 'impact', which is likely to be assessed in part by effective communication. This may also encourage the evident trend for more academic economists to try to bring their work to a wider audience.

On the public realm

Until about 10-years ago, few of the leading academic economists bothered with popularising their subject. Additional deadlines are onerous, there were no obvious rewards (either financial or status), and it takes a lot of work to write a successful book. The result was that the economists most people saw and heard were for the most part those who worked in financial markets. These people have two roles: talking their firm's book; and public relations. Their prominence helps explain the predominant view of economics as being about finance and obsessed with free markets. While economists know that finance is a small professional niche, and 'free' markets are an abstraction, that is not the popular impression.

Does it matter what most people think economics is about? Post-crisis, it is clear that it does. For example, one of contributory factors to the financial crisis was a political climate that prioritised the financial sector. Regulation and bank governance were ineffective. Efficient markets, a strong hypothesis about financial market outcomes under certain conditions, came to be regarded as a general hypothesis about the operation of the economy in actuality. The idea that the economy does best if markets are deregulated and left to their own devices came about in part because of a specific political agenda, but also in part because a group of economists with a certain profile said so and their views prevailed in public discourse.

The concept of 'performativity' may also be relevant. MacKenzie (2006) argues that financial markets demonstrate this characteristic: that if theory says people act as selfish rational agents, then reality shapes itself as if they were. The options market is entirely a construct of economic models because there was no way to price options before the model existed. Even if the concept cannot be taken to cover non-financial markets, many other economic phenomena have a self-fulfilling nature. Although economists know that financial markets do not constitute financial economics, and financial economics is not the whole of economics, what the wider public and political agents believe and say about economics has consequences for what happens in the economy.

It is therefore an important time for economists to publicise their work, even if it sometimes has to take the guise of being anti-economics, such as behavioural literature. Just as numeracy and scientific literacy is important for a healthy democracy, so is economic literacy. In particular, the correct application of statistics to public policy is essential, and this falls to economists (at least in the UK, where other social sciences are largely non-quantitative). Society can only combine the populist pressures of democracy with the scientific and technological complexity of modern societies if public becomes more aware of the technicalities. Pop economics has a contribution to make in this respect. It can give us better economics and a better-informed public too.

Acknowledgements

I would like to thank Jack Vromen, N. Emrah Aydınonat and participants at the Rotterdam symposium for helpful comments.

Notes

1. http://www.paecon.net/PAEReview/ (accessed 13 February 2012).
2. http://ineteconomics.org/ (accessed 13 February 2012).
3. In the US, 2010 saw a huge increase in digital books and also a 5% increase in traditional book output to over 316,000 new titles and additions. In the UK, the same year saw a 14% increase to nearly 152,000 new titles. http://www.thebookseller.com/news/number-us-physical-books-printed-increases-despite-digital.html (accessed 13 February 2012).
4. See for example the UK figures on the number of sixth form economics students: http://tutor2u.net/blog/index.php/economics/comments/a-level-economics-continues-to-grow/ (accessed 13 February 2012).
5. http://www.gla.ac.uk/services/specialcollections/collectionsa-z/leftbookclub/ (accessed 13 February 2012).

References

Buchan, J. (1995), 'The Poverty of Economics', *Prospect*, Issue 3 (20 December), http://www.prospectmagazine.co.uk/1995/12/thepovertyofeconomics/ (accessed 13 February 2012).
Coyle, D. (1996), *The Weightless World*, Oxford: Capstone.
——— (1999), *Governing the World Economy*, Cambridge: Polity Press.
——— (2001), *Paradoxes of Prosperity*, New York: Texere.
——— (2002), *Sex, Drugs and Economics*, New York: Thomson Texere.
——— (2009), *The Soulful Science: What Economists Really do and why it Matters*, Princeton, NJ: Princeton University Press.
——— (2011), *The Economics of Enough: How to Run the Economy as if the Future Matters*, Princeton, NJ: Princeton University Press.
Edgeworth, F.Y. (1881), *Mathematical Psychics: An Essay on the Application of Mathematics to the Moral Sciences*, London: C.K. Paul & Co.
Heilbroner, R.L. (1999), *The Worldly Philosophers: The Lives, Times And Ideas Of The Great Economic Thinkers*, New York: Touchstone.
Krugman, P. (2009), 'How did Economists Get it so Wrong?', *The New York Times Magazine*, September 2. http://www.nytimes.com/2009/09/06/magazine/06Economic-t.html (accessed 13 February 2012).
Lucas, R.E. (2004), *Lives of the Laureates: Eighteen Nobel Economists*, (4th ed.), eds. W. Breit and B.T. Hirsch, Boston, MA: MIT Press, pp. 273–298.
MacKenzie, D. (2006), *An Engine, Not a Camera: How Financial Models Shape Markets*, Boston: MIT Press.
McCloskey, D. (2000), *How to be Human, Though an Economist*, Ann Arbor: University of Michigan Press.

Overy, R. (2009), *The Morbid Age*, London: Allen Lane.

Prowse, M. (1993), 'A Wake Up Call From Laura Tyson', *Financial Times*, January 18.

Stein, H. (1986), *Washington Bedtime Stories: The Politics of Money and Jobs*, New York: The Free Press.

Vromen, J. (2009), 'The Booming Economics-Made-Fun Genre: More Than Having Fun, But Less Than Economics Imperialism', *Erasmus Journal for Philosophy and Economics*, 2(1), 70–99.

A less-is-more approach to introductory economics

Robert H. Frank

Johnson Graduate School of Management, Cornell University, Ithaca, NY, USA

Studies have shown that when students are tested about their knowledge of basic economic principles six months after completing an introductory economics course, they score no better, on average, than those who never took the course. That remarkable failure is explained in part by the fact that many professors try to teach their students far too much, and in part because many employ excessive mathematical formalism. This paper describes an alternative approach inspired by evidence that the human brain absorbs new ideas most efficiently when they are expressed in narrative form. It describes an extraordinarily effective pedagogical device–the economic naturalist– writing assignment, in which the student is asked to pose an interesting question based on personal observation or experience, and then use basic economic principles in an attempt to craft a plausible answer to it.

Cartoons are data. If one makes you laugh, that is almost always because it calls attention to some interesting aspect of life that you had previously failed to observe, or that you had observed only subconsciously.

In 1974, I had been teaching economics at Cornell for two years when friends in several different cities sent me copies of the same *New Yorker* cartoon by Ed Arno. It depicted a woman introducing a middle-aged man to another woman at a cocktail party, saying 'Mary, I'd like you to meet Marty Thorndecker. He's an economist, but he's really very nice.'

Long before I saw that cartoon, I had been well aware of people's skepticism about economists. At gatherings for new faculty members, I had come to expect the look of disappointment that almost always appeared on the face of a new acquaintance upon learning what department I was in. Curious, I eventually began asking people why they seemed so disappointed when I revealed that I was an economist.

To their credit, most did not try to deny their reaction. After a few moments' reflection, most would say something like, 'I took an economics course many years ago, and there were all those horrible equations and graphs!'

Indeed there were. Since their inception, introductory economics courses typically have been taught out of encyclopedic texts that cover thousands of topics, many of them enshrouded in forbiddingly complex algebra and graphs.

These courses are astonishingly ineffective. In one study, students were given tests that probed their knowledge of basic economics principles six months after having completed an introductory course. They scored no better than students in a control group who had never taken an economics course at all.[1] Hundreds of millions of person hours are devoted to introductory economics courses annually. This is waste on a grand scale.

When doctors or lawyers perform below reasonable professional standards, their clients often sue them. Why do not parents sue their children's universities for charging tens of thousands of dollars for courses that add no measurable value? My guess is that if graduates received frequent and clear negative feedback about the ineffectiveness of their economics training, such lawsuits would be common. But since most people are as ignorant of economic principles as the students we teach, there is little effective feedback. Perhaps few complain simply because few are in a position to notice.

Why are introductory economics courses so ineffective? I believe the two main problems are that most of them simply try to cover far too much material, and they present it in a way that normal human brains find difficult to absorb.

On the first point, learning theorists have long known that the key to effective mastery of any idea is to use it repeatedly. The human brain appears to have evolved to include a rule of thumb that states roughly, 'if you see or hear something only once, ignore it.' Trillions of bits of information bombard us each day, far too much to absorb and process. Unless we ignored most of it, we'd go mad. But once we hear something a second or third time, we begin paying closer attention. The brain starts laying down new circuitry for dealing with it. Courses that try to cover hundreds or even thousands of topics cannot hope to spend more than fleeting moments on each of them. But if repetition is essential for learning, that is a recipe for failure. In the end, each idea went by in a blur.

A second difficulty is the typical introductory course's heavy reliance on equations and graphs. To be sure, the brain is a remarkably flexible organ that can absorb information in many different forms. But it does not process all forms of information with equal efficiency. Our species evolved as storytellers, and when early hunter-gatherers had an idea they wanted to communicate, their impulse was not to reach for a twig to start sketching equations and graphs in the dirt. They told stories. And because the listener's attention was always a limited resource, the most effective ones were those with interesting characters and plots that made sense while conveying at least some new information.

Well-crafted narratives are absorbed effortlessly by the human brain, just as a key slides effortlessly into a lock.[2] To be sure, certain kinds of information can be more efficiently summarized in the form of equations and graphs than in narrative form. Students who major in math, engineering or other subjects that emphasize mathematical discourse can absorb information relatively easily in this form. But most students are considerably less technically sophisticated and find it much easier to absorb new ideas in narrative form.

In these simple observations lie the seeds of promising reforms for the introductory economics course. The two most important steps, I believe, are to limit topic coverage substantially and make more extensive use of narrative structure in presenting ideas.

Regarding topic coverage, the good news is that there are really only a handful of basic principles that underlie most of what economists have discovered about the world. If we asked a thousand different economists what those principles were, we'd get a thousand different lists, but there would be substantial overlap among them. In any event, it is less important that everyone agree on what constitutes the best possible short list of principles than that instructors begin with a plausible short list, and then hammer away at each of its items repeatedly.

As for the format of presentation, my claim is that economic principles are more easily mastered, even for students with a technical bent, if they are encountered in ecologically familiar examples than in the more formal abstract form in which they are often presented. Consider the cost-benefit principle, which holds that we should take an action only if its benefit exceeds its cost. Stated in that way, the principle sounds too obvious to be interesting. But figuring out which costs and benefits are relevant turns out to be a formidable challenge in many settings. One effective way to introduce this principle is by asking students to consider some simple questions that require its use.

In my own course, I first ask them to imagine that they are about to purchase an alarm clock for $20 at the nearby campus store when a friend tells them that the same clock is available for a price of $10 at a store several miles away. Except for price and location, the two stores are identical in all respects. Where would they buy the clock? Most say they would buy it at the more distant store.

Next, I ask them to imagine that they are about to buy a laptop computer from the nearby campus store for $2020 when a friend tells them that the same computer is available for a price of $2010 at a store several miles away. Where would they buy the computer? This time the overwhelming majority say the campus store.

Students are surprised when I then tell them that this pattern of responses violates the cost-benefit principle, which I then state formally and identify as the most important of all basic economic principles. Its prescription in the context of the example is that you should purchase something at the more distant store only if the benefit of doing so exceeds the cost. In each case, the benefit of going to the more distant store is $10, the amount saved by purchasing the item at the lower price. And in each case, the cost of purchasing from the more distant store is the same amount, no matter which product someone might buy. An obvious problem is that there is no readily available monetary estimate of that cost.

Conceptually, it is the implicit value of whatever time, hassle and other sacrifices are associated with the journey to the more distant store. One practical way to estimate that value is by means of the following thought experiment. Imagine that someone offered you a dollar to travel to the more distant store and back. Would you do it? Almost everyone says no. Then, imagine that the offer is raised to $2. If the answer is still no, raise the offer by another dollar, and repeat until the answer is yes. The first offer that elicits an affirmative response in the respondent's implicit cost of the journey to the more distant store. For example, the cost would be $7 for a student for whom this mental auction concluded at $7. And since that is less than the benefit of the trip – which, again, is $10 in each case – that student should make the journey to the distant store for both purchases.

But now consider someone for whom the mental auction concludes at $13 – that is, for someone who would refuse to make the trip for less than that amount. This person should make both purchases at the nearby campus store, because the $10 benefit of the journey to the more distant store is in each case less than its $13 cost. In short, the correct answer depends on the cost of the trip to the distant store, but if the decision maker is rational, it must be the same for both purchases. A rational person would not buy the clock at the distant store and the computer at the campus store.

On first exposure, many students resist this reasoning. When pressed, they argue that it makes sense to buy the clock from the distant store but not the computer because the percentage savings is so much greater for the clock. But the percentage savings simply is not relevant. The benefit of the journey to the more distant store in each case is exactly the $10 saved on the relevant purchase price. For those who still think that percentages are relevant, I then pose a follow-up question that no one answers incorrectly: which would you prefer to receive? One percent of $1 million, or 10% of $100? Focusing on percentages makes sense in some contexts, but not this one.

The examples just described are based on the pioneering work of Amos Tversky and Daniel Kahneman, the founding fathers of behavioral economics.[3] Such examples are effective as devices for introducing students to the theory of rational choice because it is such a jarring experience for students to discover that their intuitions prompt irrational decisions in some contexts. Most people do not like to think of themselves as irrational. And experiences that surprise us generally command much closer attention than ones that do not.

Students often tell me that they pose these same questions to their friends and take great delight in being able to explain why their friends' answers are not rational. Such conversations help root the cost-benefit principle more firmly in students' minds. To learn any new idea or skill, after all, practice is essential. Just as the only way to become proficient in tennis is to spend many hours on the practice court, the only way to master economic ideas is to use them actively and repeatedly.

Describing examples you have seen explained by an instructor is a useful exercise. But the real leap in understanding comes from using an idea to explain something new on your own. I believe that most of the learning that occurs in my own introductory economics course is attributable to my 'economic naturalist' writing assignment. Students must submit two brief papers during the semester – one at mid-term, the other at term's end – in which they are asked to pose an interesting question about something they have observed or experienced personally and then try employ basic economic principles to answer it.

One of my favorite examples was submitted by my former student Greg Balet. He asked why regulations require that toddlers be secured in a safety seat for even a two-block drive to the grocery store, yet can sit untethered on a parent's lap on a transcontinental airline flight. Many are quick to respond that it is because most passengers would be killed in a plane crash whether they were strapped in or not. But Mr. Balet argued that this cannot be the explanation, because the main purpose of seatbelts in planes was never to protect passengers against extremely rare events like crashes; rather, it was to protect them during all-too-common episodes of violent turbulence. In support of that claim, he noted that seatbelts were required in airplanes long before they were required in cars.

The upshot, he reasoned, was that the difference in regulation couldn't be explained by differences in the benefits of safety seats. Differences on cost side appear far more promising. Once a parent has installed a safety seat in the car, the cost of strapping an infant into it is negligible. But using a safety seat on a full flight would require purchasing an extra seat, which in some cases would cost more than $1000. So, while the benefit of a safety seat is probably at least as great in a plane as in a car, the cost is dramatically greater in a plane – and hence the regulatory difference.

Some students object that people do not really take monetary costs into account when making decisions about life and safety. But that objection does not withstand scrutiny. If costs do not matter at all, you should get your brakes checked every time you drive your car, since there is always some chance an imminent failure might be detected. But if an inspection revealed your brakes to be in good working order yesterday, most people would think it foolish to get them checked again today. Doing so would consume time and money that could be more usefully spent on other things. So, although many parents might feel uncomfortable saying so, the reason that a safety seat is not required on airplanes is that it would be too costly. Rather than paying for an extra seat, most find it prudent to cling firmly to their toddlers and hope for the best.

The economic naturalist writing assignments are short. I tell students that their answers cannot exceed 500 words and that many of the best submissions are less than half that length. (My description of Mr. Balet's paper, for example, consumed 241 words.) I instruct students not to use equations, graphs or technical jargon in their papers and urge them to imagine that they are talking to someone who has never taken a course in economics.

Above all, I urge them to come up with the most interesting question they possibly can – ideally, one that will spur me to knock on a colleague's door to tell him about it. Do not ask, for example, why students are more likely to order out for pizza after having been up late studying for an exam the previous night. It would be correct to say it is because it is more difficult to cook for yourself when you are tired, but that is just too obvious to be interesting.

I warn students that it is not easy to come up with examples as interesting and persuasive as Greg Balet's. But a determined search for such an example pays big dividends for several reasons. First, because it is unlikely that the first question that pops into mind will be genuinely interesting, it is generally necessary to consider many options before finding one that measures up, and the more attention this assignment receives, the more the students learn. Second, students who succeed in posing an interesting question are likely to be far more motivated to come up with a plausible answer. A third benefit is that students who have posed interesting questions immediately want to tell others about them. And every such conversation deepens their mastery of basic economic principles.

In the week before the first assignment's due date at mid-semester, students often drop by my office to ask whether the questions they have posed seem interesting. Some of them do. More often, however, I tell students they have got a few more days and might want to keep thinking a little longer.

My student conferences about the second paper have a very different flavor. By term's end, few of them seem worried about whether their questions are interesting. More commonly, they announce that they have got several interesting ones and want to know whether it is acceptable to submit a medley. Absolutely, I tell them. But their space limit is still 500 words.

The average quality of the submissions is substantially higher for second papers than for the first ones. I view that difference as clear evidence that students' brains have become rewired during the course. Most students began the term without having had any real exposure to basic economic principles, much less any facility for using them to help explain and understand patterns of behavior they see all around them. Yet by term's end, a substantial majority of them can not only identify interesting behavioral patterns from everyday experience, but also suggest plausible economic explanations for them. That is a striking contrast to the experience of most alumni of introductory economics courses – who, as noted, score no better on tests about basic economic principles than others who had never taken any economics.

My first exposure to the less-is-more approach to teaching came shortly after I graduated from college. I had taken four years of Spanish in high school and three semesters of German as an undergraduate. In those courses, we spent a lot of time on the pluperfect subjunctive tense and other grammatical arcana that instructors thought important. But we did not learn to speak. When I traveled in Spain and Germany, I had great difficulty communicating even basic thoughts in those languages. Many friends have described similar experiences.

My first inkling that there was a more effective way to learn languages came during the instruction I received before leaving to serve as a Peace Corps volunteer in Nepal. The program lasted only 13 weeks and was completely different from my earlier language courses. It never once mentioned the pluperfect subjunctive or other obscure tenses and made no attempt to teach us any formal grammatical rules. Its task was to teach us to speak Nepali, and mastering technical grammatical details was simply not on the critical path to that goal. The method of instruction was to mimic the way children learn to speak their native language.

Our instructor began with the simplest of sentences and had us repeat them multiple times. The first was 'This hat is expensive.' Since one has to bargain for everything one buys in Nepal, it was a useful sentence. The next step was to announce a different noun – say, 'long socks' – and we would have to respond on the fly with the Nepali sentence for 'These long socks are expensive.' The goal was to get us to be able to respond without even thinking about it.

In brief, they started with a simple example from a familiar context, had us drill it several times, then had us do slight variations on it, drilling again. Once we could function on our own at the current level – but not before – they would push us a little further.

The program's responsibility was to make sure we were proficient in Nepali after 13 weeks. My fellow volunteers and I had to teach science and math in that language shortly after arriving in the country. And starting from zero, we did it. The process itself created a sense of empowerment I had never experienced in traditional language courses.

Learning economics is much like learning to speak a new language. The keys in both cases are to start simple and drill intensively, focusing on examples from familiar contexts.

The approach that proved so effective in my Peace Corps language training program was discovered because people who needed to be able to speak a foreign language to function effectively got forceful and immediate negative feedback when they could not do it. Learning economics is important, too, but few employment settings provide the negative feedback that stimulates improvement when a teaching approach fails.

People may not be complaining about the inadequacy of their economics instruction, but we have enough evidence to be confident that our massive investment in introductory economics courses currently yields a pitifully low return. The less-is-more approach promises a big improvement. And given the abysmal performance of the current approach, little would be risked by trying it.

Notes

1. See Hansen et al. (2002).
2. See, for example, Doyle and Carter (2003) and Bruner (1985).
3. See Tversky and Kahneman (1974).

References

Bruner, Jerome (1985), 'Narrative and Paradigmatic Modes of Thought', in *Learning and Teaching the Ways of Knowing* (84th Yearbook, pt. 2 of the National Society for the Study of Education), ed. E.W. Eisner, Chicago, IL: University of Chicago Press, pp. 97–115.

Doyle, Walter, and Carter, Kathy (2003), 'Narrative and Learning to Teach: Implications for Teacher-Education curriculum', http://faculty.ed.uiuc.edu/westbury/JCS/Vol35/DOYLE.HTM

Hansen, W.L., Salemi, M.K., and Siegfried, J.J. (2002), 'Use It or Lose It: Teaching Literacy in the Economics Principles Course', *American Economic Review* (Papers and Proceedings), 92(2), 463–472.

Tversky, Amos, and Kahneman, Daniel (1974), 'Judgment under Uncertainty: Heuristics and Biases', *Science*, 185, 1124–1130.

Finding the right levers: the serious side of 'economics made fun'

Jack Vromen

EIPE, Faculty of Philosophy, Erasmus University, Rotterdam, The Netherlands

The serious side of the Economics Made Fun genre stems from its mantra that people respond to incentives. As Levitt and Dubner put it, economists typically believe they can solve virtually all problems by designing a proper incentive scheme. What is not always sufficiently appreciated is that Levitt and Dubner argue that economists nowadays grant the existence of social and moral incentives, besides the standard economic ones. A glance at the relevant literature in academic economics confirms this. Although there is an ongoing debate in academic economics about the necessity and desirability of introducing social preferences in utility functions and also about the relative strengths of various sorts of preferences, economists increasingly take the existence of various sorts of incentives and motivations into account. The recognition of non-monetary incentives and of non-economic motivation makes the economic approach to policy making more comprehensive and flexible. But since there might be various kinds of interaction effects between different sorts of incentives and different sorts of motivations, it also vastly complicates devising optimal policy schemes. What Levitt and Dubner say almost in passing about the "strange nature" of incentives also reflects the present state of art in academic economics: while it is increasingly acknowledged that different sorts of incentives and different sorts of motivations might interact in various ways, little is still known about when, under what conditions, the one or the other interaction effect obtains. Yet knowledge of the latter is required to devise optimal incentive schemes. Thus even though Levitt and Dubner might be right that economists are quite confident that they can solve virtually all problems by devising optimal incentive schemes, it seems the limited understanding of incentives, motivations and their various interaction effects in present-day academic economics falls short of bolstering this confidence.

1 Introduction

Books in the 'economics made fun' genre spread the message that applying basic economic principles to resolve all kinds of puzzles can be great fun. This can be fun, it is argued, in the following three senses (Vromen 2009). First, there is no need to go through all the tedious formal modeling that is typical of much of current economics to access the insights that economic theory harbors. Simple informal reasoning on the basis of basic economic principles often suffices to grasp these insights. Second, the principles can be brought to bear on more exciting and sometimes outright freakish subjects than the sorts economists are traditionally preoccupied with. Economic theory does not only shed light on worn out subjects such as economic growth, business cycles and inflation, but it can also illuminate outlandish subjects such as what estate agents and the members of the Ku Klux Klan have in common. Third, the sorts of insights that economic theory yields typically contradict conventional wisdom. Readers are supposed to share the 'devilish fun' that economists have in undermining received views.

Not everything in the genre is supposed to be fun, however. Practitioners of the genre are dead serious about the truth of the contrary insights that economic theory engenders. These insights are supposed to provoke not just an experience of amusement or entertainment in readers; they are also meant to provoke a 'Eureka' feeling. Economic theory can reveal the hidden side of everything, as some of the (sub)titles of the books in the genre promise (Levitt and Dubner 2005; Harford 2008). Practitioners of this genre agree that if there is one basic insight to be singled out that economic theory provides into how things actually work, it is that people respond to incentives. Change incentives and you will see that the behavior of people will follow suit. You want to increase the contributions that people make to the provision of public goods? Make it more attractive for them to increase their contributions, either by increasing the benefits of contributing or by decreasing the costs of contributing. It is believed that this basic insight gives us an effective handle on how to change behavior for the better. Devising the right kind of incentive structure provides the key to solving all problems, it is maintained, not only economic ones such as how to secure provision of public goods but also non-economic ones such as how to promote safer sex (Landsburg 2007). Find out what levers to pull, implement them and the problem is fixed.

One wonders whether all problems can be solved in this way. Is simply raising the stakes for people really a panacea? Will raising rewards for the type of behavior you want to encourage (or raising penalties for the type of behavior you want to discourage) always lead to the intended result, no matter the sort of problem you are trying to solve? More than any other book in the genre, Levitt and Dubner's books *Freakonomics* (2005) and *Superfreakonomics* (2009) capitalize on the insight that people respond to incentives. Indeed, Levitt and Dubner go as far as to proclaim that:

> a question like 'Are people innately altruistic?' is the wrong kind of question to ask. People aren't 'good' or 'bad'. People are people, and they respond to incentives. They can nearly always be manipulated – for good *or* ill – if only you find the right levers. (2009, p. 123)

Levitt and Dubner furthermore argue that economists tend to believe they can find the right levers for any kind of problem: 'The typical economist believes the world has not yet invented a problem that he cannot fix if given a free hand to design the proper incentive scheme' (2005, p. 16). True to the spirit of the books, I will take these assertions totally seriously in this paper. Is it really true that economists believe that they can solve any kind of problem whatsoever by devising an optimal incentive scheme? If so, what are the ingredients of such a scheme? How are incentives supposed to affect behavior? And what guidance does current economic theory provide to devising an optimal incentive scheme for some particular problem? These are the questions I will try to answer in this paper.[1]

2 Incentives in Freakonomics and Superfreakonomics

The idea that 'Incentives are the cornerstone of modern life' (2005, p. 11) is ranked by Levitt and Dubner as the first fundamental idea in their worldview. Indeed, as some commentators observed (DiNardo 2007), the contribution of economic theory to the stories and analyses in the books seems to be limited to this message. When Levitt and Dubner start discussing how a focus on incentives and their impact on behavior allow us to see 'the hidden side of everything', they immediately make clear that there are more sorts of incentives than just economic (or monetary) ones. Social and moral incentives are the two other flavors of incentive they recognize (2005, p. 17). People are said to respond to *social* incentives because people do not want to be seen by others as doing something wrong. People abstain from doing certain things if they believe that doing those things would provoke disapproval and blame in onlookers. People would feel ashamed of themselves if they nevertheless were to do these things. People are said to respond to *moral* incentives because they do not want to do something they consider wrong (2005, pp. 17–18). In this case people abstain from doing certain things if they themselves deem doing these things morally wrong. People would be plagued by feelings of guilt (or bad conscience) if they nevertheless were to do those things.[2]

Levitt and Dubner argue that incentive schemes often comprise all three flavors of incentives. They give the example of the anti-smoking campaign. The introduction of a 'sin tax' is an economic incentive not to buy cigarettes. The banning of smoking in bars and restaurants on top of that is a social incentive to reduce smoking, Levitt and Dubner argue. Finally, disclosing the information that terrorists earn money by selling black-market cigarettes complements all this as a moral incentive (2005, p. 17).

In the case of the anti-smoking campaign the three sorts of incentives mutually reinforce each other.

Another example that Levitt and Dubner (2005) discuss makes it clear that this is not always the case. In an experiment with 10 Israeli day-care centers conducted by Gneezy and Rustichini (2000), the introduction of a fine of $3 for parents who picked up their children too late did not decrease but increase the number of latecomers. Before the fine was introduced there were on average 10 late pickups. After the fine was introduced the average number of late pickups doubled. The introduction of an economic incentive clearly backfired. In the case of the day-care center fine, the economic and moral incentive did not mutually reinforce each other in reducing the number of late pickups. Levitt and Dubner suggest that introducing the fine effectively silenced the moral incentive of parents to pick up their children in time. Before the fine was introduced, the number of latecomers was held in check because parents felt guilty when picking up their children too late. After the introduction of the fine, now that the parents could pay their debt in monetary terms, they felt no guilt anymore when they picked up their children late and paid the fine. As Levitt and Dubner argue, it seems that in this case the economic incentive replaced the moral incentive. Rather than economic and moral incentives being complements, as in the case of the anti-smoking campaign, economic and moral incentives here seem to be substitutes.

The day-care center fine case shed light also on other aspects of ' ... the strange and powerful nature of incentives' (Levitt and Dubner 2005, p. 19). Levitt and Dubner suggest that if the fine had been set at $100, instead of $3, this probably would have put an end to the late pickups. But they also note that this probably would have engendered a lot of ill will with the parents. Parent would be inclined to take their children to another day-care center, for example. This could cost the day-care center dearly in terms of revenues foregone. The trick, they argue, is to find the right balance. Unfortunately, however, they do not tell how to find the right balance.

Yet another aspect of the strangeness of incentives Levitt and Dubner draw our attention to is that they might encourage dishonest behavior and cheating. Levitt and Dubner follow W.C. Fields in quipping that a thing worth having is a thing worth cheating for. In the case of late coming at day-care centers the opportunities for parents to cheat might be relatively few. It is relatively easy for people at the day-care center to expose and punish parents who say (or pretend) they pick up their children in time but who are in fact latecomers. But in other cases opportunities for cheaters to get away with their cheating (without anyone noticing that they are cheating) might be considerably larger. Think, for example, of making payments of schoolteachers dependent on the proportion of students that pass the examination. Instead of putting more effort into bringing the knowledge and skills of student to the desired level, schoolteachers might lower the standards for passing the exam. Or consider shirking in team production or contributing nothing in the provision of public goods. Especially if the teams or groups in question are large, monitoring whether everyone has put in their fair share is difficult. This makes it tempting for people to shirk, cheat and free ride on the efforts of others. As Levitt and Dubner put it, cheating is a primordial economic act. Instead of incurring costs to reap benefits, successful cheaters economize on costs while reaping the same benefits.

Changing incentives might thus backfire and bring about adverse unintended effects. But what are incentives exactly? Levitt and Dubner do not say much on this. They are not very precise in particular in specifying what exactly social and moral incentives are. Sometimes it seems they argue that feelings of shame (2005, p. 45) and guilt are themselves social and moral incentives, respectively. At other times it seems they call incentives the things that might incite these feelings. In the example of the anti-smoking campaign, they argue, for example, that the banning of cigarettes in bars and restaurants is a social incentive. The idea apparently is that after the ban is installed, just the prospect of smoking will fill smokers with shame (more on this below). Here the smoking ban, the thing that is supposed to somehow incite smokers with shame, is called the social incentive, not the thing (i.e., shame) it is supposed to incite. Likewise, Levitt and Dubner argue that providing people with the factual information that terrorism is sponsored by the revenues of cigarette sales can act as a jarring moral incentive. Here it is the information provided, rather than the feeling of guilt that it is supposed to incite, that is called a moral incentive. In short, it seems Levitt and Dubner do not distinguish between the 'internal' motives people might have and the sorts of external circumstances or stimuli that might attend to them.[3] It seems they call all of them incentives.

Levitt and Dubner also do not say much about the relative strength of economic, social and moral incentives. When we are looking for optimal incentive schemes, we might want to know which sort of incentive (and what mix of incentives) is most effective and powerful. Levitt and Dubner leave us in the dark here. They do assert, however, that helping and giving is more often the result of impure or warm-glow altruism, than of pure altruism: 'You give not only because you want to help but because it makes you look good, or feel good, or perhaps feel less bad' (2009, p. 124).[4] Levitt and Dubner follow Becker (1996) in suggesting that people who give money to panhandlers do so because the uncomfortable sight of beggars makes them feel bad or guilty. Why else would people tend to cross a street to avoid a panhandler, while they rarely cross over to meet one? Calling this impure altruism suggests that in principle there could also have been a form of 'pure altruism' underlying the act of giving to panhandlers, which apparently would not be driven by guilt but, for example, by some ethical principle.[5] It is not clear whether Levitt and Dubner would only call the latter a purely moral 'incentive'. If impure altruism is a matter of doing good in the eyes of others (such as the panhandler), or at the least of not being in the position to be blamed by others, then impure altruism seems to be closer to what Levitt and Dubner call social incentives than what they call moral incentives. If so, it seems Levitt and Dubner would hold that social incentives are more powerful in directing behavior than moral incentives.

On closer inspection, more things are unclear about what Levitt and Dubner call social and moral incentives. Reconsider the banning of smoking in bars and restaurants. Assuming that this regulation is effectively implemented and monitored, it will eliminate smoking in bars and restaurants. If there are no offsetting effects of more smoking in other places, aggregate smoking will decrease. So much is clear. But why is the ban called a *social* incentive? The foregoing discussion suggests that there should be a link with social (dis)approval and shame. We could perhaps say that the implementation of the ban signals disapproval of smoking in public settings by the policy maker. But it is not clear that this should be called social rather than moral disapproval. Social disapproval seems to involve the responses of 'peers' (i.e., other agents) rather than that of the policy maker. Will the banning of smoking by some policy maker contribute to the disapproval of smokers by other agents? That does not seem to be clear. If agents see this ban as an illegitimate intrusion by the policy maker and if they are strongly averse to this kind of 'coercive' control, social disapproval of smoking might remain the same or might even decrease rather than increase.

Levitt and Dubner (2005) argue that presenting information to agents that terrorism is sponsored by revenues of cigarette sales acts as a moral incentive to stop smoking. In what sense is presenting this information introducing a *moral* incentive? There is not anything inherently moral in this supposedly factual information, it seems. Instead, it seems to charge smoking, something that is initially seen as an amoral activity, with moral content.[6] The implicit assumption seems to be that initially it is not smoking as such, but terrorism that agents deem morally bad. By providing the factual information that smoking supports terrorism, they start linking smoking to supporting terrorism and the perceived moral wrongness of terrorism derivatively carries over to a perceived moral wrongness of smoking. In a process of practical reasoning, the act of smoking comes to be seen as instrumentally morally bad. The 'moral incentive' here appeals to pre-existing moral norms of agents, norms that do not pertain to the activity to be discouraged, but to something further down the practical reasoning chain.

When Levitt and Dubner argue that if given a free hand the typical economist believes he can solve any problem by designing an optimal incentive scheme, they add that the incentive scheme might not always be pretty in the sense of being coercive or violating civil liberties. It is interesting to see that in their own examples, Levitt and Dubner do not go very far in contemplating such not-so-pretty schemes. If we want to reduce smoking, why not think of rewiring the reward systems in the brains of addicted smokers, for example? Levitt and Dubner also do not consider changing the social and moral norms of agents. One reason might be that in the case of smoking they do not see a reason to do so. They assume that the social and moral norms already in place can be attended to attain the desired result. Indeed, also in the late coming case at the day-care center they simply assume that all individuals involved, agents and policy maker alike, agree on what sort of behavior is 'prosocial' behavior (i.e., behavior with agreeable social consequences that should be promoted). Levitt and Dubner state that 'An incentive is simply a means of urging people to do more of a good things and less of a bad thing' (2005, p. 17). In their examples, Levitt and Dubner implicitly assume that there is already a broad agreement among agents and policy makers on what things are good and what things are bad. No need, therefore, for the policy maker to directly interfere with the agents' social and moral norms.

Levitt and Dubner (2005) argue they base most of their freakish stories on serious academic work in economics, often done by the 'maverick' (or 'rogue') economist Levitt himself. So it seems fair to ask to what extent their discussion of incentives and of how people respond to them finds a basis in the academic literature in economics. Is it customary in the academic literature not to distinguish clearly between incentives and the motives they supposedly attend to? And is it common in current economic theory to recognize social and moral incentives, alongside economic incentives? If so, what is their relative strength in affecting behavior? Does current economic theory shed more light on the strange nature of incentives and how they affect behavior? In particular, is there a consensus among economists about when different sorts of incentives complement each other and when they substitute each other? Are these things well understood in current economics? It seems economists would need to know about all these things if they are to find out what incentive scheme, if any, is optimal in solving a particular problem.

3 Different sorts of incentives and different sorts of motivation?

In this section, I want to address the questions stated at the end of the preceding section one by one. The leading question is whether the views by Levitt and Dubner (2005) on the strange nature of incentives and on how incentives affect behavior reflect the present state of the art in the academic literature in economics.

Let us start with the very meaning of 'incentives'. Levitt and Dubner do not distinguish clearly between feelings of shame and guilt and the sorts of things external to agents that typically incite them. Is this characteristic also of the academic literature in economics? The short answer is that it depends. It depends on which papers one looks at. There are papers in economics such as Kaplow and Shavell (2007) that also do not distinguish sharply between 'internal' feelings and motivations, on the one hand, and 'external' things attending to them, on the other. Like Levitt and Dubner, Kaplow and Shavell explicitly recognize the existence and significance of moral incentives. They follow Adam Smith in stressing on the motivational importance of moral sentiments such as guilt: '... feelings of guilt and of virtue along with their external correlates, disapprobation and praise' (2007, pp. 494–495). The issue that Kaplow and Shavell examine in their paper is '... how a social planner would design a system of morality to maximize social welfare, that is, how a social planner would associate moral feelings with acts so as to induce behavior that fosters social welfare' (2007, p. 495). The general idea is that a social planner could in principle use the motivational force of the moral feelings of guilt and virtue in its attempts to maximize social welfare. The way to go, Kaplow and Shavell suggest, would be for the social planner to establish that the higher the negative external effects of some act (such as lying or shirking), the more intensely people exhibiting the act (or contemplating exhibiting it) would be plagued by the moral feeling of guilt. As guilt is supposed to be a direct source of disutility, the more intensely people are plagued by feelings of guilt, the more they would be disinclined to exhibit the act in question.[7]

It seems Kaplow and Shavell (2007) go much further in fathoming not-so-pretty incentive schemes than Levitt and Dubner. What Kaplow and Shavell in effect consider is to change the moral norms of agents so as to maximize social welfare. Kaplow and Shavell's proposition is likely to meet ethical objections. One need not be a staunch libertarian to object to intrusive government interference with its citizens' morals. It seems Kaplow and Shavell also feel free to disregard practical obstacles to implementing their proposed policy. They argue that moral rules are at least to some extent malleable. Societies devote efforts to inculcating moral views, they note, and these views tend to vary across societies and over time. That might be true, but that does not imply that a social planner is able to inculcate social welfare-maximizing associations between acts and moral feelings in people. Parents and peers probably are much more influential in inculcating particular moral views in people than social planners. And it surely does not give social planners the moral right to try to instill particular moral views in people. Thus both the practical feasibility and ethical admissibility of Kaplow and Shavell's optimal moral incentive scheme can be called into question. This seems to make Kaplow and Shavell's policy proposal a purely theoretical exercise. The free hand given by Levitt and Dubner to an economist in devising the optimal incentive scheme seems to be taken here to its extreme.

More pertinent to our present purposes is that like Levitt and Dubner, Kaplow and Shavell call feelings of guilt, virtue, blame and praise incentives. But in Kaplow and Shavell's paper there is at least the beginning of an understanding that a distinction is to be made between things external to agents such as social disapprobation (or blame) and social approbation (or praise), and things internal to agents that they supposedly attend to. They make the rather obvious but important observation that praise and blame only work as incentives if agents care about being praised or blamed by others. People must care about their social image and reputation, for example, or they must try to avoid feelings of shame.[8] These concerns, which are internal to agents, can be called *social motivation*. Praise can be seen as a social benefit and blame as a social cost for some agents only if the agent has such social motivation.

Note that this depiction of social motivation and how it can be attended to from the outside is similar to a standard depiction of how economic motivation can be attended to from the outside by changing taxes or subsidies (as paradigmatic examples of economic incentives). In this standard depiction, changing taxes or subsidies change the monetary costs and benefits of options. This is supposed to affect behavior because it is assumed that people care about their own wealth. If people lacked such economic motivation, changes in monetary costs and benefits would not lead to the intended behavioral responses.[9] On this account, just as external things such as taxes and subsidies are seen as economic incentives, external things such as praise and blame would be seen as social incentives rather than the internal motivation and the associated feelings of shame and pride that they are supposed to attend to.

Thus in Kaplow and Shavell (2007) there is some understanding not only that external rewards and punishments can (and perhaps should) be distinguished from the internal motivations they are supposed to attend to, but also that particular internal motivations should be in place for external rewards and punishments to have their intended effects on behavior. In the academic literature in economics, other economists are much more explicit and straightforward about this than Kaplow and Shavell. Bénabou and Tirole (2006) is a case in point. Next to standard economic motivation ('greed'), Bénabou and Tirole explicitly acknowledge the presence of social and moral motivation in agents. The utility function posited by them has three arguments: extrinsic economic motivation, social image motivation (also called reputational motivation) and intrinsic motivation (also called values). What Bénabou and Tirole call social image motivation seems to correspond roughly to what I call social motivation. The idea is that they want to be regarded and approved of by others as fair, intrinsically motivated people. Intrinsic motivation seems to correspond roughly to what I call moral motivation. Intrinsically motivated people are not led by expectations of external rewards such as monetary or social rewards. They want to do things they consider virtuous; things that accord with their own moral norms. Virtue is its own reward, as the saying goes. We could say that if they nevertheless were to do things they consider morally wrong, they would incur moral costs. Doing these things would 'tax their conscience'. They would feel guilty.

It is not uncommon anymore in the academic literature in economics to explicitly take social and moral motivation into account. Andreoni and Bernheim (2009), who develop a similar model as Bénabou and Tirole (2006), is another case in point. Andreoni and Bernheim suggest that social motivation is characteristic of what Andreoni (1989, 1990) called impure altruism. Although they also make room for intrinsic motivation in their utility function, they clearly suggest that impure altruism is a more potent force than 'pure' moral motivation.[10] On this matter, they clearly side with Levitt and Dubner (2005) and also with Kaplow and Shavell (2007), who suggest that 'pure' moral motivation is relatively rare. Not all economists agree with this, however. Consider, for example, the so-called social preference models advanced by behavioral economists. On the basis of a host of experimental findings, behavioral economists have argued (starting with Fehr and Schmidt 1999 and Bolton and Ockenfels 2000) that room should be made for moral preferences such as inequity aversion, fairness and altruism as separate arguments in the utility function. Behavioral economists maintain that people care about equity, for example, not instrumentally or extrinsically; that is not because they believe it furthers their own interests or boosts their social image, but intrinsically; that is in their own right and for their own sake. These behavioral economists clearly disagree with the suggestion that it is primarily the expectation of external rewards that entice people to behave prosocially.

4 Social and moral incentives?

Thus there is an ongoing debate in academic economics about the relative strength of different motivations. What about social and moral *incentives*? Is there a consensus among the economists who distinguish between 'external' incentives and 'internal' motivations on what can be called social and moral incentives? Not surprisingly, Bénabou and Tirole (2006) argue that economic incentives (also called monetary incentives) attend to extrinsic economic motivation. Analogously, they argue that the degree to which behavior is publicly visible attends to social image motivation. In the limiting case when behavior is publicly invisible, people will not be socially motivated to behave prosocially. Thus one way for a policy maker to boost prosocial behavior is to see to it that prosocial behavior by one agent will not go unnoticed by others. Public visibility can be called a *social* incentive. Just as changes in taxes and subsidies can change the monetary costs and benefits of options, changes in public visibility can change the social costs and benefits of options. Although public visibility is almost never called a social incentive explicitly (but see Ariely, Bracha and Meier 2009), it seems that this is not an idiosyncratic view entertained only by Bénabou and Tirole (2006). Many economists seem to share the view that the degree to which behavior is publicly visible greatly affects the degree to which socially motivated agents behave prosocially.

What could be called *moral* incentives? If morally motivated persons are not led by expectations about external rewards, what sort of incentives could change their behavior? It seems changes in economic (monetary) and social incentives could have no effect on their behavior. Bénabou and Tirole (2006), for example, assume that the intrinsic motivation to behave prosocially does not respond to changes in monetary incentives and also not to changes in public visibility. Barring the impracticable and intrusive sort of mental engineering proposed by Kaplow and Shavell (2007), is there anything at all external to persons that could be changed and could attend to their moral motivation to behave prosocially?

Occasionally economists speak of *moral suasion* as a possible way in which policy makers could try to increase prosocial behavior. Romans (1966) is a case in point (see also Goodin 1980; Dal Bó and Dal Bó 2011). Romans argues that a pure case of moral suasion would be to use already existing desires in agents to promote public welfare. Impure moral suasion occurs when such an appeal to what Romans calls altruism in agents is backed by credible threats and promises of punishments and rewards. An appeal made by a policy maker in times of crisis to bankers to voluntarily abstain from cashing bonuses might perhaps be a good example of pure moral suasion. Note that such an appeal might have the desired effect also if the appeal does not attend to the bankers' moral principles, but to their social concern about their own social image. Romans also seems to note this when he argues that 'A glare of publicity can increase the power of persuasion *ex ante* (by increasing the expected cost of noncompliance) and the degree of censure of non-compliers *ex post*' (1966, p. 1223). If so, it would arguably be more appropriately called social rather than moral suasion. Note also that, unlike the mental engineering of new moral rules by Kaplow and Shavell (2007), the conception of moral suasion assumes (and appeals to) already existing moral principles. If bankers really believed that there is nothing morally wrong with cashing bonuses in times of crisis, the appeal would have no effect. What the appeal is supposed to do, presumably, is to make the moral principle a more potent force in comparison to greed.

Using already existing moral principles is what moral suasion has in common with Levitt and Dubner's moral 'incentive' to reduce smoking (2005). Telling people that terrorism is sponsored by sales of cigarettes in black markets only works as a deterrent against smoking if people already believe that supporting terrorism is morally bad. Smoking, which was seen as an amoral activity before the information was provided, becomes morally charged after people realize that smoking might support terrorism. The moral salience of cashing bonuses is similarly supposedly increased by the moral appeal not to cash bonuses. Thus, what moral suasion is supposed to do is to either increase the moral salience of options for agents, or heighten the agents' perception of the moral salience of the options.

So there might be a way after all to increase the moral motivation to behave prosocially, even though expectations of external rewards are assumed to play no role in it. This need not involve changing the moral beliefs and norms of agents. It draws on the insight that we can avoid feeling guilty by shutting our eyes for particular consequences or by downplaying (in their own eyes) the moral salience of options. Appealing to moral principles of agents from the outside might make it more difficult for agents to shut their eyes to the moral ramifications of their actions.

Summing up now, one can find a basis for most of the things Levitt and Dubner say about incentives and about how they affect behavior in the recent academic literature in economics. Levitt is not the only economist who calls incentives both 'external' circumstances to agents and the 'internal' motivations and feelings that they supposedly attend to, as the above discussion of Kaplow and Shavell (2007) shows. Yet there are also economists who try to distinguish these and reserve 'incentive' for 'external' circumstances only. Economists have started to make room for social and moral motivations in the utility function, alongside the standard economic motivation. Agents are socially motivated to behave prosocially if they believe that by behaving prosocially they look good in the eyes of others. Expectations by agents of such external rewards are characteristically lacking in moral motivation. In the absence of such expectations, morally motivated individuals still behave prosocially because this is prescribed by their own moral norms (or values).[11] Quite a few economists seem to believe that social motivation ('impure altruism') is more potent than moral motivation in determining behavior, even though this is challenged in social preference models of behavioral economists. Economists seem to agree that public visibility of behavior is a powerful social incentive. Moral suasion is sometimes discussed in academic economics as a moral incentive. Moral suasion does not involve changing the moral norms of agents. It rather uses their pre-existing moral norms in increasing the moral salience of options.

5 Crowding out?

Let us now turn to the issue of when different sorts of incentives are complements and when they are substitutes. In their discussion of the aversive effects of the day-care center fine, Levitt and Dubner (2005) suggest that the introduction of a fine meant the substitution of a moral incentive by an economic one. Parents felt that they no longer needed to feel guilty when they picked up children too late. Instead they just needed to pay $3 each time they picked up their children too late. On the basis of the discussion above, I think it is fair to say that based on Levitt and Dubner's own understanding, the introduction of a monetary incentive did not so much replace a moral *incentive*, as Levitt and Dubner suggest, it reduced, if not annihilated, the moral *motivation* of parents to pick up their children in time. The introduction of the fine effectively discharged late coming from its moral content. Late coming, which was seen as a morally bad thing before the fine was installed, transformed into some amoral thing to be paid for in monetary terms after the fine was installed.

If this analysis is correct, it suggests two things. First, that Levitt and Dubner believe that attempts to control behavior via monetary incentive can have hidden costs (sometimes called 'hidden costs of rewards' or 'hidden costs of control'). Introducing or changing monetary rewards and punishments need not have the effects on prosocial behavior that are predicted by standard price theory. As the day-care center fine case indicates, fining antisocial behavior might backfire; antisocial behavior might increase rather than decrease. Second, the reason for this is that moral motivation is diminished by extrinsic economic incentives. Introducing monetary rewards or punishments might reduce the moral motivation of people to behave prosocially.[12]

Both things are remarkable. Not everyone in the economics profession is convinced that 'hidden costs of control' is a significant phenomenon in the real world. For example, Landry, Lange, List, Price and Rupp (2011) do not find evidence that it is a robust phenomenon in the real world. Landry et al. conducted a field experiment with solicitors in a door-to-door fund-raising campaign. Solicitors turn out to perform considerably better if conditional payments (rather than unconditional payments, or no payments at all, in the baseline treatment) are introduced.[13] They suggest 'hidden costs of control' might be an artifact of laboratory experiments. It is to be noted that John List, one of Levitt's favorite 'co-rogue' economists, is one of the authors of the Landry et al. (2011) paper. In an influential joint paper, Levitt and List (2007) warn that findings of lab experiments in economics should not be taken at face value. Thus one could have expected Levitt and Dubner (2005) to side with the skeptics who doubt that 'hidden costs of control' (or non-standard price effects) also exist outside the artificial settings of laboratory experiments. Levitt and Dubner's explanation of the phenomenon, that the introduction of the fine diminished the moral motivation of parents to pick up their children in time, is also remarkable. For it seems to run counter to the view of moral motivation as intrinsic motivation that is impervious to any change in external circumstances. If expectations about monetary benefits and costs do not play a role in the moral motivation to behave prosocially, how then could it be affected by the introduction of a fine?

Levitt and Dubner (2005) seem to side here with behavioral economists who view moral motivation as intrinsic motivation, but who nonetheless believe that intrinsic motivation can be *crowded out* by extrinsic incentives. 'Crowding out' was introduced by

Deci (1971, 1975) and others in social psychology, and found its way into economics via the work of Bruno Frey (Frey and Jegen 2001). Deci and others suggested several mechanisms via which crowding out might occur. One of them is overjustification (Lepper, Greene and Nisbett 1973). Overjustification occurs when an agent, who already has sufficient reason to behave prosocially before a monetary reward is introduced, gets an additional reason to behave prosocially after the monetary reward is introduced. If so, the agent's sense of autonomy might be reduced. The agent might come to feel that attempts are made to control his behavior from the outside. If the agent is 'control-averse', his net motivation to behave prosocially might not change. Or it may even decrease rather than increase.

Bénabou and Tirole (2006) identify a different mechanism via which rewards might have hidden costs. They argue that the introduction of monetary rewards might decrease the social motivation of agents to behave prosocially. The intuition is simply that after the introduction of a monetary reward, onlookers might think that people displaying prosocial behavior do it just for the money (or they might be at a loss figuring out why prosocially behaving agents behave the way they do). Agents contemplating whether to behave prosocially will take this into account and this in turn will reduce their social motivation to behave prosocially. Again we have overjustification. But now it is not moral but social motivation to behave prosocially that is assumed to decline. Ariely et al. (2009) confirm Bénabou and Tirole's hypothesis in an empirical test. They find that agents put more effort in a good cause when their behavior is publicly visible (public treatment) than when their behavior is not visible for others (private treatment). They also find that the agents' efforts increase when monetary rewards are introduced in the private treatment. However, when monetary rewards are introduced in the public treatment, the agents' efforts are substantially lower than when monetary rewards were absent. On the basis of these findings, Ariely et al. (2009) advise policy makers to subsidize prosocial behavior that is less publicly observable. Subsidizing hybrid cars would be less effective than subsidizing energy-saving water heaters, for example.

The model by Bénabou and Tirole (2006) alerts us to the possibility that a particular sort of motivation to behave prosocially might attend to several external factors. In their model, the social motivation to behave prosocially does not only depend on the degree to which the agents' behavior is publicly visible, but also on the value of monetary rewards and punishments. Thus far I implicitly assumed there is a one-to-one correspondence between a particular sort of motivation and its associated sort of incentive. Monetary rewards and punishments would appeal only to economic motivation, social approval and disapproval only to social motivation, and moral suasion only to moral motivation. But Bénabou and Tirole's model shows that things might be more complex. In fact, once one starts thinking along these lines, things might turn out to be even much more complex than Bénabou and Tirole suggest. Monetary rewards might also have a positive effect on the social motivation to behave prosocially, for example, especially if it is assumed that people do not (or do not only) ultimately, but also instrumentally, care about their own social image. Indeed, the common theme in economic theory arguably is that people want to earn a good reputation because they expect to benefit later from that in monetary terms. A favorable social image might help them in engaging in profitable transactions in repeated games in the future, for example. If socially motivated agents ultimately (also) care about future monetary rewards, it is easy to understand why their social motivation to behave prosocially would respond positively to the introduction of monetary rewards.[14]

Likewise, the economic motivation to behave prosocially might also attend to social approval and disapproval. This might happen if people value monetary gains and losses not ultimately, but instrumentally, for example, because they believe wealth buys them prestige, status and social esteem in their community. Thus, a banker might choose not to cash a bonus because he believes it would cost him dearly in terms of massive social disapproval in society. Even the moral motivation to behave prosocially might be responsive to changes in monetary costs and benefits. Note that strictly speaking, saying that morally motivated agents behave prosocially also if there are no (expectations of) external rewards does not imply that their behavior does not respond to changes in (expectations of) external rewards. Indeed, it might be compatible with the view that morally motivated agents respond to monetary incentives as predicted by standard price theory, as Bowles and Gintis argue:[15]

> The fact that other-regarding preferences support price-responsive behaviors conforms to our representation of social preferences as distinct motivations within the framework of transitive preferences rather than some *sui generis* irrational or non-rational mode of behavior requiring a special model of decision-making. The fact that for many experimental subjects virtue is its own reward is perfectly consistent with the fact that, as in the case of people with self-regarding preferences, they would consider the price. (2011, p. 33)

Bowles and Gintis (2011) suggest that people who were solely led by moral motivation would cease to behave prosocially if the monetary costs of doing so become too high.

What I also implicitly assumed thus far is that agents perceive changes of economic incentives by policy makers as attempts to attend to their economic motivation. This might also be too simplistic. Masclet, Noussair, Tucker and Villeval (2003) discuss how morally motivated peers might incur monetary costs to punish cheaters. Here monetary punishment is meant to express moral (or social) disapproval of cheating. The punishers do not want to speak to the economic calculations of cheaters. They want to teach them a moral lesson. As always with signaling, this only works as intended if cheaters also perceive it as a moral lesson. This need not be the case, however. A government might introduce a fine to discourage antisocial behavior as a signal that the government morally condemns the behavior. Or a government might for the same moral reason implement a regulation, as in the case of the banning of smoking in bars and restaurants.[16] But agents might perceive this differently. They might perceive this as a cheap way of 'big government' to raise tax revenues so as to afford 'big spending', for example. Depending on their perceptions, agents might respond differently.

6   No shortage of possible mechanisms; what are the policy implications?

By bringing in several sorts of motivation, several sorts of incentives, several sorts of interaction effects and signaling, things become quite complicated and messy. It also opens up several pathways and mechanisms via which monetary rewards can crowd out or crowd in non-economic motivation, as Bowles and Polanía-Reyes' (2011) useful overview points out. Bowles and Polanía-Reyes partition extant explanations of 'crowding out' in the literature into three categories. Explanations that crucially involve inferences by agents about the motives of the persons administering the monetary rewards constitute the first category. If agents believe that the introduction of monetary rewards by some policy maker betrays distrust of agents by the policy maker, for example, then agents might respond adversely. The second category consists of explanations stressing that monetary incentives provide cues for agents about what behavior is appropriate. Introducing a fine might suggest to agents that moral engagement is no longer expected and that henceforth economically motivated behavior is appropriate, for example. Finally, explanations in the third category emphasize that the introduction of monetary incentives 'over-justifies' the targeted activity and compromises the agents' sense of autonomy and self-determination.

As Bowles and Polanía-Reyes (2011) admit, it is not always straightforward in what category to put some given explanation. I think there is no doubt that the discussion by Levitt and Dubner (2005) of the introduction of the fine in the Israeli day-care centers, which closely follows Gneezy and Rustichini (2000), belongs to the second category. As we saw above, Levitt and Dubner argue that after the fine was introduced, moral 'incentives' were substituted by economic 'incentives'. The discharging of moral content of late coming, as I called it, seems to be identical to the moral disengagement that explanations in the second category typically refer to. Yet Bowles and Polanía-Reyes (2011) put Gneezy and Rustichini (2000) in the third category. As for another example, Bowles and Polanía-Reyes put Ariely et al. (2009), which as we saw is an empirical confirmation of Bénabou and Tirole (2006), in the first category. As Bénabou and Tirole (2006) refer to overjustification, I think it fits the third category better. But in the model by Bénabou and Tirole (2006) it is not the agents' sense of autonomy that is assumed to be compromised by the introduction of a monetary reward, but the agents' social motivation to behave prosocially. Indeed, none of the three categories seem to fit Bénabou and Tirole (2006) well, since Bowles and Polanía-Reyes (2011) do not make room for social motivation as a separate motivation alongside economic and moral motivation (see Vromen 2012a for further discussion). Thus, there might even be more mechanisms underlying 'crowding-out' than Bowles and Polanía-Reyes (2011) make room for.

It is sometimes not clear whether explanations really differ with respect to the mechanism they identify, or that they are merely different labels attached to the same mechanism. Bowles and Polanía-Reyes suggest that Gneezy and Rustichini (2000) and Heyman and Ariely (2004) belong to a different category. They put Gneezy and Rustichini (2000) in the third category and Heyman and Ariely (2004) in the second category. Hence, they are presented as different mechanisms, whereas I would argue that they are roughly the same. In both explanations, an introduction of a fine is seen as a shift in the choice context: after the fine is introduced, parents come to see continued tutelage of their children after closing time as a commercial service that one has to pay for.[17]

It is not just that different economists put forward different explanations for 'crowding-out', quite different explanations are sometimes put forward by the same economists. Bénabou and Tirole and Ariely are cases in point. The studies by Bénabou and Tirole (2003, 2006) seem to be different explanations of the same phenomenon, and so are Heyman and Ariely (2004) and Ariely et al. (2009). This raises the issue how these economists see the relation between their explanations. Given that Bénabou and Tirole (2011) try to synthesize the studies by Bénabou and Tirole (2003, 2006) in one encompassing model, they seem to believe that the two mechanisms can work simultaneously. The simultaneous working of the two mechanisms indeed seems to be a genuine possibility. Things seem to be different with the two mechanisms proposed by Ariely in Heyman and Ariely (2004) and in Ariely et al. (2009). Given that Ariely is one of the authors in both papers, it seems Ariely is content with just observing that several possible mechanisms are identified that might explain 'crowding out'. Ariely does not say whether he believes that the mechanisms can work simultaneously or that either the one or the other mechanism works in concrete situations. It seems that the mechanism identified in Heyman and Ariely (2004) is not likely to co-occur with the mechanism in Ariely et al. (2009). It seems that the two explanations exclude each other. After the fine is introduced either parents believe it is appropriate to see the tutelage provided by the day-care center as a standard commercial service, or they believe that picking up their children no longer clearly signals to others that they are good, conscientious parents. At any rate, no attempt is made to specify the conditions under which the one or the other mechanism is likely to work.

By way of an *interim* conclusion, I think it is fair to say that a lot is still poorly understood. We do not know whether 'crowding out' is a robust phenomenon that exists also outside the laboratory experiments. Or at least this is still a contested issue among economists. Insofar as it is regarded a phenomenon calling for an explanation, the explanations offered are many and various. There is not yet a shared understanding among economists of when monetary incentives and non-economic motivation are separable, when they are complements and when they are substitutes. There is also no shortage of mechanisms specified by economists that give different answers to the question when and why monetary incentives and non-economic motivation are substitutes. It seems we need to have the correct answer to this question if we are to devise optimal incentive schemes to solve problems in concrete particular situations. If so, current economic theory gives little theoretical guidance to devising optimal incentive schemes in concrete particular situations.

Bowles and Polanía-Reyes (2011) concede that the difficulties facing what they call a *sophisticated social planner*, who wants to take into account that monetary incentives and non-economic motives can be complements and substitutes, might be formidable. Their overview shows that it is already difficult to determine *ex post* what mechanism produced some observed 'crowding out' phenomenon. They rightly argue that determining *ex ante* in some given situation whether monetary incentives and non-economic motives will be substitutes, and if so which mechanism is causally responsible for them, is much more difficult. Yet they maintain that we can draw some general conclusions from their overview about what incentive schemes are optimal.

One general conclusion they draw is that greater use of monetary incentives might be recommendable, even if they partially substitute non-economic motivation to behave prosocially. This is analogous to the doctor who discovers that his treatment is less effective than he thought, Bowles and Polanía-Reyes (2011) argue. Instead of prescribing weaker doses, the doctor might be well advised to opt for stronger ones. This seems incontrovertible. But recall Levitt and Dubner's insightful discussion of increasing the fine in the day-care center (2005). High fines might engender a lot of ill will in parents, they argue. Parents, not just the ones who initially sometimes picked up their children too late, might search for other solutions and take their children from the day-care. As a result, higher fines might have adverse effects for late coming and for the day-care center. Furthermore, high monetary stakes might also incite more cheating. In the case of picking up your children, it is difficult to imagine how cheaters could get away with their cheating without being caught. But in other cases, that is very easy to imagine.

A more ambitious conclusion Bowles and Polanía-Reyes (2011) draw is that introducing fines should be accompanied by an explicit justification by the policy maker. One of the problems with the day-care center fine, they argue, was that no attempt was made to explain to the parents why the fine was introduced. If parents had been told that the fine signaled a moral message or social disapproval of the latecomers' lack of public mindedness, the fine probably would have been more effective. I am not so sure. Parents might rightly feel that it is not due to a lack of public mindedness on their side that they sometimes pick up their children late. If so, they are likely to see the justification given as a sign that they are distrusted by the day-care center's management. The consequence might well be more rather than less late coming. Note that this would be what Bowles and Polanía-Reyes call a category one mechanism. Moreover, there are other ways of expressing social disapproval that do not raise the suspicion with parents that the day-care center introduced the fine just for the money. Here it would be the intention (or motivation) of the day-care center's management that would be distrusted by the parents. Note that this is similar to the mechanism described in Bénabou and Tirole (2006), but this time the intentions of the policy maker rather than those of the agents are distrusted. The latter suspicion might be salient especially when the policy maker is the government. The more the government tries to appeal to social and moral motivation of citizens when introducing or increasing monetary incentives, the more citizens might get the suspicion that this is just a sneaky way to raise tax revenues. The more general underlying problem here is that signaling only has the intended result if receivers believe the signal is trustworthy. The latter need not always be the case, of course. How receivers see the signal (and what it signals) is a matter of perception and interpretation. And perceptions and interpretations do not seem to be things that can be easily predicted, controlled and manipulated.

I think we can conclude that Bowles and Polanía-Reyes' (2011) helpful overview of the present state of the art does not warrant the general policy conclusions that Bowles and Polanía-Reyes want to draw from it. Even if we were to give economists a perfectly free hand to concoct optimal incentive schemes to solve all kinds of problems, current economics is not of much help. Current economics offers a multitude of different possibilities, some more contested than others. In devising an optimal incentive scheme for some particular situation we need to know which, if any, of these possibilities obtains. As it stands, current economic theory is unable to tell us which possibility obtains.

7 Conclusion

Let us take stock. We can conclude that Levitt and Dubner's (2005, 2009) account of incentives and how people respond to them quite accurately reflects the present state of the art in the academic economics literature. Incentives are seen by all economists as important determinants of behavior. To the typical (micro-)economist, effective and efficient policy-making is largely if not wholly a matter of devising optimal incentive schemes. Most economists distinguish incentives more sharply from the motivations they attend to than Levitt and Dubner and Kaplow and Shavell (2007). It has become customary to assume that in their behavior agents are led not only by economic motivation, but also by non-economic motivation. Room is made for moral motivation and sometimes also for social motivation as separate arguments in the utility function. A socially motivated agent cares about his own social image and attends to social approval and disapproval as external rewards and punishments. Social motivation only comes into play if agents believe their behavior can be watched by others. A morally motivated agent is not led by expectations of external rewards. Moral motivation is assumed to also lead to prosocial behavior if agents do not expect to reap external rewards from doing so. Even though external rewards are thus assumed to play no role in moral motivation, there might be non-intrusive ways to strengthen the moral motivation of agents from the outside, as the notion of moral suasion indicates. Whether these are effective ways to promote prosocial behavior is contested. Many economists seem to believe that the potency of moral motivation is relatively weak.

Current economic theory provides little guidance in devising optimal incentive schemes for some particular problem. Here again, it seems we can conclude that Levitt and Dubner (2005, 2009) give a fair impression of the limits of current economic theory. A growing number of economists seem to agree with Levitt and Dubner that different sorts of incentives can both be complements, as in the case of reducing smoking, and substitutes, as in the case of the day-care center fine. For policy purposes, if we want to devise an optimal incentive scheme in some particular situation, we need to know not only what are the relevant costs and benefits for the agents involved, but also whether the incentives that can be manipulated by a policy maker are complements or substitutes. Levitt and Dubner do not tell us when, under what conditions, incentives are complements or substitutes. They do not get beyond the observation that incentives have this 'strange nature' of being complements in one situation and substitutes in another. They note that devising an optimal incentive scheme amounts to striking the right balance, yet they do not tell how this right balance is to be found. It seems current economic theory is not able yet to do better.[18] Recognizing other sorts of motivations than strictly economic ones and other sorts of incentives than monetary ones, as is increasingly done in present-day economic models, can be seen as a major step forward. But it also introduces the possibility of all kinds of 'strange' and complex interaction effects. Economists have only started to explore these complex effects. There is no shortage of mechanisms proposed that can possibly account for interaction effects, but a profound shared understanding of interaction effects still seems to be far off.

The complexity is amplified by acknowledging that incentives can be seen by agents as messages or signals of various sorts. This brings in issues of interpretation and perception, both on the side of agents and policy makers, things that seem notoriously difficult to pin down and predict. All this complicates devising optimal incentive schemes considerably. Is the introduction of a new tax on wasteful behavior seen by agents as a signal that there is nothing morally wrong with exhibiting the behavior, as long as one pays for it? Or is it seen as an expression of moral disapproval of wasteful behavior by the policy maker? Or as evidence that the policy maker distrusts agents? Or that the policy maker is in need of money? Or as morally reprehensible theft? Or perhaps as some or all of them? It is clear that the behavioral consequences of the tax might depend on how agents perceive the tax. There seems to be a growing awareness among economists that such perceptions are one of the many variables determining behavior. That 'context matters' a great deal is increasingly recognized. Levitt and Dubner also show an awareness of this when they argue that:

> Human behavior is influenced by a dazzlingly complex set of incentives, social norms, framing references, and the lessons gleaned from past experience – in a word, context. We act as we do because, given the choices and incentives at play in the particular circumstances, it seems most productive to act that way. This is also known as rational behavior, which is what economics is all about. (2009, p. 122)

Levitt and Dubner might be right that it is possible to treat the dazzlingly complex ways in which behavior responds to 'context' as rational behavior, especially if one is given a free hand to play with what are the relevant costs and benefits for the agents involved. But this is an *ex post* exercise. In devising an optimal incentive scheme, we need to know the relevant costs and benefits and all the rest *ex ante*. For that purpose, the dazzling complexity might simply be too much to handle – even for an economist.

Acknowledgements

Thanks to N. Emrah Aydinonat and a referee for their comments on an earlier draft. The usual caveat applies.

Notes

1. My selection of the economic literature discussed is inevitably incomplete, of course. I cannot even claim that my selection presents a representative sample of the extant literature. But as will become clear below, this does not pose a problem for what I argue, namely that there is not yet a profound shared understanding in economics of 'the strange nature' of incentives.

2. What Levitt and Dubner (2005) and other economists say about concepts such as 'social incentives' and 'moral incentives' leaves room for slightly different interpretations than the one I put forward. Indeed, generally speaking the writings of economists do not seem to excel in terms of conceptual clarity and precision. I claim no more than that my interpretations are charitable and are consistent with the available textual evidence.

3. In Vromen (2009), I suggest to reserve 'incentive' for something external to agents. As we shall see below, this seems to be in line with how most economists conceive of incentives.

4. Note that people might feel good about themselves when they help others because they have complied with their own moral norms, that is *not* because they have complied with prevailing social norms. Thus a finer grained distinction might (and for some purposes perhaps should) be made between 'because it makes you look good' and 'because it makes you feel good'.

5. The distinction between sympathy and commitment discussed by Sen (1977) comes to mind here. Impure altruism would be driven by sympathy, whereas pure altruism would be driven by commitment.

6. Note that one way to read Levitt and Dubner's discussion of the Israeli day-care center is that late coming was *dis*charged of its moral content when the fine for late coming was introduced.

7. Kaplow and Shavell (2007) tell a similar story about associating acts with positive external effects with proportional intensity of feelings of virtue.

8. I would not analyze the relation between trying to promote a favorable social image and trying to avoid doing things one would be ashamed about here, as this is not necessary for my argument.

9. At least they would not immediately lead to the predicted behavioral responses. Arguing along the lines of Becker (1962), it could be maintained that they would eventually lead to the predicted changes nonetheless, because of their effects for the agents' opportunity sets.

10. Experimental findings as the ones reported in Dana, Daylian and Dawes (2006) and Dana, Weber and Kuang (2007), in which subjects are given the opportunity to conceal what they choose for others, seem to point in this direction.

11. Elster (2007) holds a similar view on the difference between social and moral norms.

12. In Vromen (2012a), I call the former effect 'non-standard price effects' and the latter, as one of the possible explanations of this effect, the 'crowding-out hypothesis'.

13. This runs counter to Falk and Kosfeld (2006), e.g., who argue that control by employers is perceived as a sign of distrust by employees, leading to less rather than more effort on their part.

14. This also raises the issue of whether social image should be a separate argument in the utility function next to 'greed' if social image is valued only instrumentally as a means to increase wealth. Further discussion of this issue has to wait for another occasion.

15. If moral motivation evolved biologically, as Bowles and Gintis (2011) argue, this might explain the sort of price-responsiveness of moral motivation Bowles and Gintis allude to (although this would strictly speaking amount to mistaking functionality for instrumentality; see Vromen (2012b) for further discussion).

16. This seems to be similar to 'expressivism' in the legal literature, which holds that laws should not be seen as just incentives: with their laws, legislators express what they take to be the values and norms of society. See Stout (2011) and Bénabou and Tirole (2011) for interesting discussions of expressivism.

17. Norms-based accounts, such as the ones favored by Bicchieri (2006) and Guala and Mittone (2009), also seem to assert something similar.

18. Ariely (2010) seems to agree.

References

Andreoni, J. (1989), 'Giving with Impure Altruism: Applications to Charity and Ricardian Equivalence', *Journal of Political Economy*, 97(6), 1447–1458.

Andreoni, J. (1990), 'Impure Altruism and Donations to Public Goods: A Theory of Warm-Glow Giving', *Economic Journal*, 100(401), 464–477.

Andreoni, J., and Bernheim, B.D. (2009), 'Social Image and the 50–50 Norm: A Theoretical and Experimental Analysis of Audience Effects', *Econometrica*, 77(5), 1607–1636.

Ariely, D. (2010), *The Upside of Irrationality: The Unexpected Benefits of Defying Logic at Work and at Home*, London: Harper.

Ariely, D., Bracha, A., and Meier, S. (2009), 'Doing Good or Doing Well? Image Motivation and Monetary Incentives in Behaving Prosocially', *American Economic Review*, 99(1), 544–555.

Becker G.S. (1962), 'Irrational Behavior and Economic Theory', *Journal of Political Economy*, 70(1), 1–13.

Becker G.S. (ed.) (1996), 'Spouses and Beggars: Love and Sympathy', in *Accounting for Tastes*, Cambridge, MA: Harvard University Press, pp. 231–237.

Bénabou, R., and Tirole, J. (2003), 'Intrinsic and Extrinsic Motivation', *Review of Economic Studies*, 70(3), 489–520.

Bénabou, R., and Tirole, J. (2006), 'Incentives and Prosocial Behavior', *American Economic Review*, 96(5), 1652–1678.

Bénabou, R., and Tirole, J. (2011), 'Laws and Norms', NBER Working Papers 17579, National Bureau of Economic Research.

Bicchieri, C. (2006), *The Grammar of Society: The Nature and Dynamics of Social Norms*, Cambridge: Cambridge University Press.

Bolton, G., and Ockenfels, A. (2000), 'ERC: A Theory of Equity, Reciprocity, and Competition', *American Economic Review*, 90(1), 166–193.

Bowles, S., and Gintis, H. (2011), *A Cooperative Species: Human Reciprocity and Its Evolution*, Princeton, NJ: Princeton University Press.

Bowles, S., and Polanía-Reyes, S. (2011), 'Economic Incentives and Social Preferences: Substitutes or Complements?', Quaderni del dipartimento di economia politica e statistica 617, University of Siena.

Dal Bó, E., and Dal Bó, P. (2011), 'Workers, Warriors, and Criminals: Social Conflict in General Equilibrium', *Journal of the European Economic Association*, 9(4), 646–677.

Dana, J., Daylian, M.C., and Dawes, R.M. (2006), 'What You Don't Know Won't Hurt Me: Costly (But Quiet) Exit in Dictator Games', *Organizational Behavior and Human Decision Processes*, 100(2), 193–201.

Dana, J., Weber, R.A., and Kuang, J.X. (2007), 'Exploiting the Moral Wiggle Room: Experiments Demonstrating an Illusory Preference for Fairness', *Economic Theory*, 33(1), 67–80.

Deci, E.L. (1971), 'Effects of Externally Mediated Rewards on Intrinsic Motivation', *Journal of Personality and Social Psychology*, 18(1), 105–115.

Deci, E.L. (1975), *Intrinsic Motivation*, New York: Plenum Publishing.

DiNardo, J. (2007), 'Interesting Questions in Freakonomics', *Journal of Economic Literature*, 45(4), 973–1000.

Elster, J. (2007), *Explaining Social Behavior: More Nuts and Bolts for the Social Science*, Cambridge: Cambridge University Press.

Falk, A., and Kosfeld, M. (2006), 'The Hidden Costs of Control', *American Economic Review*, 96(5), 1611–1630.

Fehr, E., and Schmidt, K. (1999), 'A Theory of Fairness, Competition, and Cooperation', *Quarterly Journal of Economics*, 114(3), 817–868.

Frey, B.S., and Jegen, R. (2001), 'Motivation Crowding Theory', *Journal of Economic Surveys*, 15(5), 598–611.

Gneezy, U., and Rustichini, A. (2000), 'A Fine is a Price', *The Journal of Legal Studies*, 29(1), 1–17.

Goodin, R.E. (1980), 'Making Moral Incentives Pay', *Policy Sciences*, 12(2), 131–145.

Guala, F., and Mittone, L. (2009), 'Paradigmatic Experiments: The Dictator Game', *Journal of Socio-Economics*, 39(5), 578–584.

Harford, T. (2008), *The Logic of Life: The Rational Economics of an Irrational World*, New York: Random House.

Heyman, J., and Ariely, D. (2004), 'Effort for Payment: A Tale of Two Markets', *Psychological Science*, 15(11), 787–793.

Kaplow, L., and Shavell, S. (2007), 'Moral Rules, the Moral Sentiments, and Behavior: Toward a Theory of an Optimal Moral System', *Journal of Political Economy*, 115(3), 494–514.

Landry, C.E., Lange, A., List, J.A., Price, M.K., and Rupp, N.G. (2011), 'Is There a "Hidden Cost of Control" in Naturally-Occurring Markets? Evidence From a Natural Field Experiment', NBER Working Papers 17472, National Bureau of Economic Research.

Landsburg, S.E. (2007), *More Sex is Safer Sex: The Unconventional Wisdom of Economics*, New York: Free Press.

Lepper, M.R., Greene, D., and Nisbett, R.E. (1973), 'Undermining Children's Intrinsic Interest With Extrinsic Rewards: A Test of the Overjustification Hypothesis', *Journal of Personality and Social Psychology*, 28(1), 129–137.

Levitt, S.D., and Dubner, S.J. (2005), *Freakonomics: A Rogue Economist Explores the Hidden Side of Everything*, New York: William Morrow.

Levitt, S.D., and Dubner, S.J. (2009), *SuperFreakonomics: Global Cooling, Patriotic Prostitutes, and Why Suicide Bombers Should Buy Life Insurance*, New York: William Morrow.

Levitt, S.D., and List, J.A. (2007), 'What do Laboratory Experiments Measuring Social Preferences Reveal About the Real World?', *Journal of Economic Perspectives*, 21(2), 153–174.

Masclet, D., Noussair, C., Tucker, S., and Villeval, M. (2003), 'Monetary and Nonmonetary Punishment in the Voluntary Contributions Mechanism', *American Economic Review*, 93(1), 366–380.

Romans, J.T. (1966), 'Moral Suasion as an Instrument of Economic Policy', *American Economic Review*, 56(5), 1220–1226.

Sen, A.K. (1977), 'Rational Fools: A Critique of the Behavioural Foundations of Economic Theory', *Philosophy and Public Affairs*, 6(4), 317–344.

Stout, L.A. (2011), *Cultivating Conscience: How Good Laws Make Good People*, Princeton, NJ: Princeton University Press.

Vromen, J.J. (2009), 'The Booming Economics-Made-Fun Genre: More Than Having Fun, But Less Than Economics Imperialism', *Erasmus Journal for Philosophy and Economics*, 2(1), 70–99.

Vromen, J.J. (2012a), 'Theoretical Isolation and the Dynamics of Dispute: Going Beyond Mäki's De- and Re-Isolation', in *Economics for Real: Uskali Mäki and the Place of Truth in Economics*, eds. A. Lehtinen, J. Kuorikoski and P. Ylikoski, London: Routledge, pp. 112–134.

Vromen, J.J. (2012b), 'Human Cooperation and Reciprocity', in *Evolution and Rationality: Decisions, Cooperation and Strategic Behavior*, eds. Okasha Samir, Ken Binmore, Cambridge: Cambridge University Press, pp. 158–184.

On the philosophy of the new kiosk economics of everything

Uskali Mäki

Academy of Finland Centre of Excellence in the Philosophy of the Social Sciences, Department of Political and Economic Studies, University of Helsinki

The article suggests a list of principles that guide this new genre of popular writing in and on economics: the new kiosk economics of everything. These well-selling books seek to show how the simple ideas of economics are able to reveal hidden mechanisms that unify a surprising variety of everyday phenomena and by doing so entertain their readers and improve the public image of economics. It is also argued that there is a special limited sense in which this qualifies as scientific imperialism.

1 Introduction

Economics is a public science in the broad sense that it is connected to the concerns and comprehensions of the general public. These connections were far more direct in the past than they are today. Academic economics has become a technical subject inaccessible to anyone not specifically educated to grasp it. Given these facts, it is unsurprising that a genre of economics writing has emerged to serve the function of mediating between academic inquiry and common-sense understanding regarding economic matters.

As I see it, the recent flow of this popular literature comes in two waves. Reflecting the atmosphere of disciplinary complacency from the 1990s onwards, the first wave of these books is largely self-congratulatory in praising the capabilities and achievements of economics, portraying it as everybody's universal social science (titles include *Hidden Order: The Economics of Everyday Life; Freakonomics: A Rogue Economist Explores the Hidden Side of Everything; The Logic of Life: Uncovering the New Economics of Everything; Discover Your Inner Economist; The Economic Naturalist: Why Economics Explains Almost Everything; Everlasting Light Bulbs: How Economics Illuminates the World; The Undercover Economist; More Sex Is Safer Sex: The Unconventional Wisdom of Economics*, etc.). Many of these books appeared on the eve of the financial crisis of 2008–2009.

The second recent wave of popular books, largely prompted by the crisis, has a predominantly unflattering and even derogatory orientation. These books are mostly critical of economics, diagnosing its failures and suggesting remedies (titles include *Economyths: Ten Ways that Economics Gets It Wrong; Zombie Economics: How Dead Ideas Still Walk among Us; Economics for the Rest of Us: Debunking the Science That Makes Life Dismal; Dismal Science: How Thinking Like an Economist Undermines Community; The Skeptical Economist: Revealing the Ethics Inside Economics; Animal*

Spirits: How Human Psychology Drives the Economy and Why It Matters for Global Capitalism; How Markets Fail: The Logic of Economic Calamities, etc.).

These waves are not completely distinct, nor are the messages they convey always purely laudatory or critical. In what follows, the focus is on the former wave in its purest forms. I take this genre of popular economics writing to be the layman's version of economics imperialism, presenting economics as offering a simple but powerful theoretical arsenal that is capable of explaining amazingly vast ranges of phenomena in our social and personal lives – phenomena that one had not traditionally thought of as economic at all – and explaining them in terms of 'hidden mechanisms'. It turns out that this genre of popular writing shares much in common with its academic counterpart.

In the following, a brief examination of the 'philosophical foundations' of the new kiosk economics is presented. I will identify some of its guiding principles and briefly examine its relationships with the issue of economics imperialism.

2   Guiding principles

We are dealing with a phenomenon that is somewhat complex. This manifests itself in the diversity of labels used of the genre. These include 'Economics made fun' and 'Pop economics' (see Vromen 2009) as well as my own 'The new kiosk economics (of everything)'. Each of these and other such labels capture just aspects of the whole package, the elements of which support and depend on one another. A more informative way of characterizing the genre is using a list of principles that guide the reasoning in PopEcon books. Here is a suggestion:

(1) There are rival frameworks, so choose the right one to make a difference.
(2) Reveal hidden mechanisms beneath deceiving common-sense appearances by means of models.
(3) Maximize unification of apparently diverse phenomena.
(4) Entertain audiences by relying on the familiarity of topics and explanatory surprise (sensu 2 & 3).
(5) Provide disciplinary and professional self-defence and self-promotion.

Each of these principles highlights an aspect of the genre. Together they characterize the philosophy of the new kiosk economics – a philosophy that actually guides the new kiosk economics, not one for assessing the credentials of kiosk economics. In this paper, I will ignore some of the interesting differences between particular contributions (such as those between more theoretically driven approaches and let's-start-from-the-numbers approaches). I will focus on the explanatory uses of theories and models and ignore their use for institutional design, which is prevalent in the kiosk literature.

(1) The importance of (the right) framework

This principle is expressed in phrases like 'how economists think' and 'how economists see the world' and sometimes 'how mainstream economists think' (Landsburg 1993, pp. viii, ix). They suggest that there is a special framework of concepts and explanatory policies through which educated economists look at the world. Kiosk economics informs its readers about this framework through specific applications.

The *weaker* part of this idea is that economists see the world differently from the way ordinary folks see it, the latter being based on the familiar common-sense framework. But there is a *stronger* component of the principle. It is the conviction that the economists' framework is superior; indeed, it is the right framework (or at least more correct than any other available framework). Books in kiosk economics not only aim to familiarize their readers with the economic way of seeing the world, but also to impress them and thus persuade them to learn to see the world in that way. The folk views or common-sense conceptions do not get the facts right, so had better be replaced by those that do, namely those developed in terms of the economists' framework.

The weaker idea of there being different frameworks acknowledges the *relativity* of perception and cognition to frameworks: the world looks different when viewed through the lenses of different frameworks. This does not amount to *relativism* that would allow the different views to be equally correct. On the very contrary, relativity becomes combined with a *realism* that considers one framework to be superior in getting the facts right.

The weaker idea suggests, for example, that '[l]earning economics is like learning to speak a new language' (Frank 2007, p. xii). This principle is behind the notion of the 'economic naturalist' suggesting that just as by learning some biology one can perceive more patterns in nature, by learning the economic framework 'you can see things you didn't notice before' (Frank 2007, p. 7). This idea is also captured by a sentence of praise for *The Undercover Economist*: 'After reading this book a trip to the supermarket is an entirely different experience'. The framework makes a difference for what you see.

The stronger version of the principle is instantiated in the first passage of another book in the genre: 'Common sense tells you that promiscuity spreads AIDS, population growth threatens prosperity, and misers make bad neighbors: I wrote this book to assault your common sense ... remember that common sense also tells you the earth is flat' (Landsburg 2007, pp. xi–xii). The assault phrased in the framework of the science of economics is presented to provide 'unconventional wisdom' that goes beyond the common-sense framework. This is straight *scientific realism*: science has the best chances of telling the true story about how things are in the world. The common sense often misleads.

In the spirit of *optimistic epistemological realism*, the fun-seeking *Freakonomics* is driven by the serious belief that 'the modern world, despite a surfeit of obfuscation, complication, and downright deceit, is not impenetrable, is not unknowable, and – if the right questions are asked – is even more intriguing than we think. All it takes is a new way of looking' (Levitt and Dubner 2005, p. xii). Here is yet another way of putting the epistemological optimism based on the right framework: 'There are rich textures and patterns in everyday experience that become visible to the practised eye of the economic naturalist' (Frank 2007, p. 217).

(2) Hidden mechanisms to be isolated

The second principle provides more contents to the first principle. It has three components: there are mechanisms in the world, giving rise to phenomena; those mechanisms are 'hidden' (from ordinary folk views); and it takes simple models to gain epistemic access to those deeper mechanisms. (In fact, kiosk economics – unlike academic economics – seems to use the vocabulary of 'process' and 'pattern' and 'logic' and 'trend' more frequently than that of 'mechanism', but I will bracket this issue here. Nor will I consider the limitations of statistical analysis favoured by freakonomics for causal inference.)

So if one wants to 'know how the world really works' (Levitt and Dubner 2005, p. xi) and, as part of this, to explain and understand some phenomenon, the thing to do is to describe the mechanism or process that produces it (or that might produce it). Since the mechanism is 'hidden', this requires (using familiar metaphors) getting beneath the surface manifestations to underlying forces and mechanisms and processes so as to '[d]iscover the secrets behind many everyday enigmas' (Frank 2007, back cover). Economists persistently pursue just this: 'Economists are always looking for the hidden logic of life, the way it is shaped by countless unseen rational decisions' (Harford 2008, p. ix). In contrast to the shallow conventional wisdom, the 'economist's way of thinking suggests a deeper view' (Harford 2008, p. x).

The rhetoric of revelation is common in the literature: 'When economists see the world [through their superior framework], they see hidden social patterns, patterns that become evident only when one focuses on the essential underlying processes' (Harford 2006, p. 15). The common-sense perspective is unable to penetrate the complexities of the social world, while economics has the capacity to remedy this shortcoming: 'the complications of everyday life often hide the larger trends behind the scenes ... The economist's job is to shine a spotlight on the underlying process' (Harford 2006, p. 11).

So how does the economist 'shine a spotlight on the underlying process?' Anyone knowing any economics knows how: by building simple models. This practice is also part of 'how economists think' and so unsurprisingly a theme in kiosk economics.

Kiosk economists take models to be imagined surrogate systems – just as the recent philosophy of science literature on models mostly considers them. The world is complex and its secrets are hidden; it is 'full of mysteries', so economists 'practice by trying to solve similar mysteries in fictional worlds that we invent and call models' (Landsburg 1993, p. viii). Models are invented; they are imagined simple worlds that can be manipulated and examined for their behaviour. They are volitional constructions that have just the properties that are attributed to them by the economist.

Even though models are simple fictional worlds, they can be used for representing the complex real world. Models are intended as surrogate objects that have as their targets some real-world objects, so they provide means for achieving epistemic access to reality. Just as academic economists, kiosk economists claim that even though models simplify, they contain much 'truth' about 'how the world really works' (Harford 2006, pp. 10–11). This combines semantic realism about truth with optimistic epistemological realism about finding it.

However, much truth is not the whole truth. Models isolate, and good models isolate the causally and otherwise important parts of the world. Other parts are not included, even though ' ... in the real world, there are other elements [besides those captured by the model] to consider ... ' (Harford 2006, p. 11). Models can provide information about the complex real world *even though* models are simple – and also *in virtue of* being simple. Therefore, the modeller must avoid making his or her images of the world too complex. 'The truth is that it's simply not possible to understand anything complicated without focusing on certain elements to reduce that complexity ... we gain from that focus ... an understanding of the "system" – the economic system ... ' (Harford 2006, p. 15). This is an argument popular also in academic economics.

Just as x-rays, economic theories and models isolate what is believed to be important from what is not so believed, and because of this, economists aspire to gain a new deeper way of seeing the world. Or at least so do kiosk economists think: 'In the hands of economists, "rational choice theory" produces an x-ray image of human life. Like the x-ray, rational choice theory does not show everything ... But it shows you something important, and something that you could not see before' (Harford 2008, p. xii). This links the first and second principles together: simple models constructed within the right framework expand the horizons of perception so as to access the important deep truths about the world.

The economist typically begins with a model world in which only one isolated factor is in operation. 'If the goal is to understand why particular constituencies want to outlaw silicon breast implants, we might begin by thinking a world where men choose their marriage partners on the basis of breast size' (Landsburg 1993, p. viii). The economist then checks what happens in the model that isolates just such a single factor, and thereafter perhaps adds some further factors, and again checks what happens in that modified fictional world that is fully under the modeller's control.

Kiosk economics insists that economists do not examine models for their own sake, but use them for gaining access to real-world targets: models are surrogate systems that provide bridges to real systems. There are many ways of conceiving of this ambition, as well as many ways of justifying the strategy. Here is one: 'We think about models not because they are realistic, but because thinking about models is a good warm-up exercise for thinking about the world we live in. The goal, always, is to understand our own world' (Landsburg 1993, p. viii). On the basis of this view, simple models provide test grounds for 'warm-up exercises' of cognitive skills that eventually will be used for understanding the real world.

Many of the other standard arguments for unrealistic models familiar to academic economics can also be found in kiosk economics. Presenting models as useful benchmarks is one of them. So while models with perfect markets are not 'realistic', they provide 'a clear benchmark ... economists find it much easier to start from them and work out what is going wrong, rather than start from scratch and work out what is going right' (Harford 2006, pp. 79–80).

The negligibility argument (Musgrave 1981; Mäki 2000) is also used, for example, in defending the rationality assumption: '... people are sufficiently rational often enough ...' (Harford 2008, p. 7). This is to say that deviations from the idealizations of rationality are negligible so that they are 'sufficiently' close to the truth, or are true 'often enough'. A nice analogy for expressing this idea is to suggest that rational choice theory is akin to 'perfectly spherical-earth theory' (the falsehood of which is negligible for many purposes), rather than to 'flat earth theory' (that is hopelessly far from the truth for most purposes) (Harford 2008, p. 12).

Kiosk economists seldom spell out the complete list of assumptions behind their reasonings, but they may sometimes start doing it, such as after designing rules for waiting lines, admitting that 'there are a lot of assumptions here' such as people being informed and all in the line being equally needy for what they are after. These are then supported with a negligibility argument: 'Those assumptions can all be tolerably well approximated in the queues for telephone customer service' (Landsburg 2007, p. 127).

(3) Unification of apparently diverse phenomena

This is a core principle in the new kiosk economics. The subtitle of *The Economic Naturalist* explains what this principle is: *Why Economics Explains Almost Everything*. Another representative title is *The Logic of Life: Uncovering the New Economics of Everything*. The subtitle of *Freakonomics* explains how this principle is connected to the previous one: *A Rogue Economist Explores the Hidden Side of Everything*.

This is the principle of explanatory unification. It is the principle of explaining as much as possible by as little as possible. Before a unificatory accomplishment, a variety of classes of phenomena appear to have nothing or little in common; they appear to be diverse, disconnected, and different. Each such class therefore seems to require a different theory to become explained. Unification is achieved once those kinds of phenomena are explained in terms of the same theoretical ideas. They no more appear diverse but are rather shown to be of the same kind. This requires answering questions such as 'What do school teachers and sumo wrestlers have in common?' (title of chapter 1 of *Freakonomics*). What previously appeared to be separate things are shown to have something important in common: recycling and dating, parenting and rush-hour commuting, drugs and democracy, high heels and school uniforms, crime and divorce, racism and suicide bombing, revolutions and justice systems, sex and prostitution, seat belts and heart attacks, football and rectangular milk cartons. These and many other things are unified by showing what they share in common.

The pursuit of explanatory unification is part of 'thinking like economists', which means, among other things, using 'one major economic model to deepen our understanding of a variety of situations' (Harford 2006, p. 29). Explanatory unification is an efficiency principle, as it were: explain much by little. It combines the minimal parsimony and simplicity of the shared *explanantia* with the maximal scope of a variety of *explananda*.

Kiosk economists are typically explicit in citing the simple unifying principle that they claim to rely on throughout the case applications so that 'the basic principles remain the same' (Harford 2006, p. 11). Frank cites opportunity cost and the cost–benefit principle as the simple ideas that are able to explain much (Frank 2007, p. 11). Landsburg simplifies his simple *explanans* so as to maximize its elasticity: 'Most of economics can be summarized in four words: "People respond to incentives". The rest is commentary' (Landsburg 1993, p. 3). This is also announced to be the ultimate unifying explainer in *Freakonomics*. In the beginning of the later *SuperFreakonomics*, Levitt and Dubner report that there were complaints about their previous book not having a 'unifying theme' and that they did not clearly see it themselves – but that they now see there was one: 'in truth, the book *did* have a unifying theme, even if it wasn't obvious at the time, even to us. If pressed, you could boil it down to four words: *People respond to incentives*' (Levitt and Dubner 2009, pp. xi–xii).

In subscribing to the principle of explanatory unification, kiosk economics joins academic economics as well as much of the rest of science. Indeed, this is one of the widely shared desiderata of good scientific theory. Disagreements may arise regarding whether a given theory actually achieves unification and what unification exactly is taken to require. As to the latter issue, one may be content with thinking of unification in terms of sentences and their relationships, making it nothing more than an inferential accomplishment, one of deriving a variety of *explanandum* sentences using the same parsimonious set of *explanans* sentences or explanatory schemata over and over again (derivational unification); or one may insist that the explanation has to represent ontic unity in the world by showing how various phenomena are caused or constituted similarly, for example, by finding the same underlying forces behind them (ontological unification). (See Mäki 2001; Mäki and Marchionni 2009.) It seems that the new kiosk economics of everything largely subscribes to the goal of ontological unification.

The ideal of ontological unification is in line with scientific realism. In the process of explanatory unification, one moves from apparent diversity to real unity, from the common-sense conception of diverse phenomena to a scientific representation of them as manifestations or aspects of the same thing. This is another exemplification of the alleged capacity of economics to proceed from misleading appearances (of diversity) to underlying reality (of unity).

(4) Sources and functions of entertainment

The new kiosk economics is also economics for fun. No doubt the authors of these books seem to derive a lot of fun from writing and publishing, but our focus is on their readers.

The present principle brings the audiences of kiosk economics to the picture. This genre of writing is supposed to entertain its readers. How does it manage to do it, what are the sources of entertainment? We can start answering this question partly by appealing to the principles discussed above. Note that kiosk economics and academic economics largely share principles 2 and 3. In addition, kiosk economics uses them in a way conducive to entertainment.

To be able to entertain its audiences, kiosk economics must connect to their spheres of experience. Given that these audiences to a large part are not educated economists, these spheres must be familiar domains of everyday life, such as love, your next meeting, and your dentist (cited in the subtitle of Cowen 2007). The issues are familiar, and so are the basic ingredients involved. The reasoning deals with common-sense components and proceeds through rather simple structures. Full deductive chains are not spelt out, so many of the implicit background assumptions and steps in reasoning are not made explicit. Typically, technical jargon and mathematical exposition are avoided to increase accessibility. The familiarity of issues attracts readers, and the familiarity of ingredients and vocabularies as well as the simplicity of reasoning ensure that they are not scared off.

We might say that the familiarity of the topics analysed and the ease and accessibility of the reasoning are one source of entertainment in themselves (see Vromen 2009, pp. 72–73). But it is also the case that these qualities – familiarity and accessibility – are among the preconditions of further sorts of entertainment. We might call the latter *explanatory entertainment*.

In attracting the potential readers' attention, kiosk economics sets out to arouse curiosity by promising, in the titles of the books, to convey unconventional wisdom on hidden secrets. And the contents of the books work hard to deliver what has been promised. The economic wisdom is construed by contrasting it with shallow common-sense understanding and presented as a powerful way of uncovering the concealed depths of the way the world really works (see Vromen 2009, p. 73).

The contrast with folk views is key to the explanatory entertainingness of kiosk economics. In confronting ordinary views, the new kiosk economics works through challenge, surprise, paradox and counter-intuitive excitement. The above two principles of explanation play important roles here – one about depth and the other about breadth. As to *depth*, explaining phenomena in terms of hidden patterns and processes thrills the reader by showing him or her the way beyond the deceiving appearances and by revealing counter-intuitive secrets to him or her. As to *breadth*, explanatory unification takes the reader with surprise in that a simple set of ideas is shown to explain astonishingly many sorts of phenomena generated by similar underlying mechanisms. Deliberately phrased paradoxes like *More Sex Is Safer Sex* will be found exciting and appetizing. Resolving such a paradox exhibits both kinds of explanatory capacity, in terms of depth and breadth alike.

So, at least part of the fun derives from epistemic achievement – hence 'explanatory entertainment'. The capacity of kiosk economics to entertain depends on the alleged explanatory performance of providing surprising accounts of surprisingly many kinds of familiar phenomena: 'surprises are fun' (Landsburg 2007, p. xii). What had appeared to be a boring subject with dull theories emerges as a source of amusement and adventure: 'But rational choice theory is not merely useful – it's also fun. The new economics of everything – sex and crime, racism and office politics – offers us perspectives that are unexpected, counterintuitive, and refreshingly disrespectful of the conventional wisdom' (Harford 2008, pp. 7–8). Challenging conventional wisdom by producing counter-intuitive surprises is effective both for attracting readers and for enlightening them:

'I prefer to write about things that are both true and *surprising* ... I dare hope there are readers who are actually interested in learning something' (Landsburg 2007, p. 22).

Note that this body of popular literature does not just popularize some of the contents of academic economics so as to inform the non-expert public about recent achievements of frontline academic inquiry in an accessible fashion. Importantly, it also sets out to do two other things: to share some novel and unusual applications and to correct what it takes to be misconceived common-sense beliefs about the economy.

So we can say that the new kiosk economics offers *entertainment by enlightenment* – generating enjoyments by unexpected explanatory accomplishments. At the same time, it also offers *enlightenment by entertainment* – attracting readers to correct their world views by providing intellectually enjoyable experiences. Such experiences can be reported by statements such as 'Reading this book is like spending an ordinary day wearing X-ray goggles' (praise for Harford 2006 by David Bodanis).

Principle 1 suggests that the framework makes a difference, and that the non-economists of us are stuck to the ordinary common-sense frameworks that often mislead. Then how are those of us able to learn to see the world in the way economists see it? Perhaps this can be explained by the idea of our 'inner economist' and the role of kiosk economics in helping us to 'discover' it (Cowen 2007). Maybe the idea of the inner economist could be put as follows: there is an inner economist in us, but it is latent and dormant, not in an active state. So it needs to be wakened up and activated. Just as there are hidden structures of the social world that need to be revealed in terms of economics, there is a hidden 'inner economist' in us that needs to be awakened to see the hidden side of things in the right way. It is a task of kiosk economics to help discover and mobilise the inner economists in the readers. Entertaining them assists in the accomplishment of the task.

(5) Self-defence and self-promotion

The new kiosk economics sets out to remedy the image of economics at least in two respects. First, by presenting some of the simple basic principles of economics in action, and by doing it in a familiar context using only minimal technical vocabulary, kiosk economics aspires to demolish the reputation of economics as *dull, boring and incomprehensible*. Second, by offering exhibits of impressive explanatory virtuosity, kiosk economics has the function of annihilating the image of economics as an *irrelevant or otherwise failing* scientific discipline.

There are books such as Coyle (2007) that explicitly set out to defend economics against its presumably bad public image but that do not clearly exhibit all the other typical characteristics of the genre of the new kiosk economics of everything. While the new kiosk economics is keen on manifesting the powers of rather basic tools of economic theory, Coyle's message is that recent developments in economics are making it increasingly relevant (and humanly sensitive) in relation to contemporary social issues.

On the one hand, many of the books in the new kiosk economics are explicit about wanting to defend economics against what they see as a mistaken public image. They often trace the problem to public relations failures, including bad educational strategies. On the other hand, these books manifest pride and confidence about the intellectual powers of basic economics in dealing with real-world issues. Expressing their confidence, authors seek to *impress* their readers, calling for admiration for the brilliance of simple reasoning that challenges conventional understanding. There is no tension between the two: *impressing (readers) contributes to defending (economics)*. Entertaining helps a lot, but would alone be insufficient for a disciplinary defence.

The new kiosk economics is greatly helped by the spirit of our times, the spirit of entertainment that keeps intruding into ever new spheres of human life. Kiosk economics – economics for fun – is inspired and supported by the increasingly sensation-seeking and entertainment-laden media in the new pop culture society in which new generations of people experience the world through entertainment. Informing and educating by way of entertainment – *infotainment* and *edutainment* – are manifestations of this cultural development. The trend of *tabloidisation* provides the cultural context for buying your economics from the kiosk. 'Prepare to be dazzled!' says the ad for *Freakonomics* in tune with this trend.

We are invited to read these books almost as we are lured to buy a class of best-selling novels and movies: 'economics is a tool for solving mysteries, and solving mysteries is fun' (Landsburg 1993, p. viii). We might say that *the expansionist economics of the kiosk genre is riding on the expansionism of entertainment in contemporary culture*. Without the latter's support, it might be far less successful, or might not exist at all.

It would be unwise rhetoric to pretend omnipotence and errorless performance. So it is important to remind the readers that the 'economists' way of thinking about the world isn't guaranteed to produce the right answer' (Harford 2006, p. 9), and that models can fail and mislead too: 'The simplifications of economic models have been known to lead economists astray' (Harford 2006, p. 15). Perhaps because the excellence of economics exhibited in kiosk economics books mainly lies in explanatory accomplishments (and partly in institutional design), occasional concessions can be made about its less glaring predictive performance: 'Economists are typically wrong about the future ...' (Harford 2008, p. 233). Making these acknowledgements helps accommodate suspicion while delivering the dominant message of success.

3   The new kiosk economics as scientific imperialism?

'Economics imperialism' designates a metaphoric and rather vague concept that has been used for describing new kiosk economics (e.g. Fine and Milonakis 2009 argue that economics imperialism 'reaches its extreme' in freakonomics) – and this use can be questioned (as does Vromen 2009). I will briefly discuss what possibilities there might be for justifying the use of the term. As I see it, kiosk economics might be considered imperialistic in two directions: towards academic disciplines other than economics and towards the common sense. Insofar as I can tell, the latter has not been discussed previously.

3.1   Imperialism towards other academic disciplines?

Consider first the issue of imperialism as an interdisciplinary relationship. We are now talking about economics being an imperialistically expansionist discipline towards other academic disciplines, such as sociology, law and political science. Might the new kiosk economics of *everything* qualify as economics imperialism in this sense?

The immediate objection is that kiosk economics is not an academic discipline, so it cannot participate in interdisciplinary imperialism. Not to let our inquiry stop here, we can appeal to two observations. First, much of the writing in kiosk economics reflects what is happening in academic economics, summarizing and popularizing arguments published in academic economics journals. Second, the accessible and entertaining writing in kiosk economics may pave the way for further imperialistic achievements in the academic sphere (e.g. by providing an encouraging model for economics students, and for offering other social scientists an easy access to less technical versions of expansionist applications). In other words, the influences can run in both directions between the two.

Gary Becker is often portrayed as an economics imperialist who applies 'the economics approach' to phenomena that traditionally had not been regarded as economic – such as discrimination, marriage and crime. Becker himself has accepted this label. Now we may ask, in response to a claim by the authors of *SuperFreakonomics*: if ' … what Becker was doing was actually freakonomics – marrying the economic approach to a rogue, freakish curiosity … ' (Levitt and Dubner 2009, p. 13), then aren't we entitled to conclude that what freakonomists are doing is actually economics imperialism – and can't we extend this to the rest of kiosk economics?

Jack Vromen (2009) does not think that we are entitled to draw the conclusion. He argues that economics-made-fun is not imperialistic because, among other things, economics does not invade, conquer, appropriate or exploit other disciplines. Economists, individually or collectively, do not have a deliberate plan to enter those disciplines so as to impose their own approach on non-economists, or otherwise to rule and dominate them.

As I see it, the issue largely boils down to what we take 'economics imperialism' to mean. If indeed we characterize it in the way Vromen does, we can largely – but perhaps not entirely – agree with his conclusions. But we might want to be careful about the concept by distinguishing between various aspects and kinds of economics imperialism and then take another look at the issues (see, e.g. Mäki 2009; Mäki and Marchionni 2011).

There is one important distinction between domain-only and disciplinary imperialism. In the *domain-only* version, the imperializing discipline sets out to explain phenomena that used to 'belong' to the domain studied by some other non-economics discipline. This is supposed to promote explanatory unification of various kinds of phenomena by showing that they can be similarly explained, but there is no intrusion into other disciplines. In contrast, *disciplinary* imperialism is a matter of entering the institutional lives of other disciplines and attempting to change their practices and cultures. Vromen's claim can be translated as saying that there is no disciplinary imperialism going on. However, this is consistent with the rather obvious claim that a lot of domain-only imperialism is being exercised by kiosk economics.

Another important distinction lies between economists and non-economists implementing imperialistic moves in either of the above two senses. Vromen resists using the label because *economists* are not busy with forcing or imposing their ideas and approaches on non-economists. But – in line with more literal uses of the term in non-academic real-world contexts – there is a subtle metaphoric use of the term 'imperialism' that accommodates the possibility of imperialism being implemented by *non-economists* who adopt and apply economic ideas in their home domains. A non-economist being inspired by a book in kiosk economics might not be entirely inconceivable.

Finally, it is important to see that an intellectual imperialism – perhaps just of a domain-only variety – may have consequences for the relative statuses and resources enjoyed by participant disciplines. These effects do not have to be deliberate or direct. Our perspective will be too narrow if merely restricted to whether economists have an interest in influencing what happens in other disciplines. We need to look at complex units such as discipline-in-an-academic-system-in-society and economics and other disciplines as their elements. There are conceivable scenarios in which kiosk economics helps to make economics more attractive among students, and in consequence of growing student enrolments, there will be a reallocation of resources between disciplinary departments.

This scenario might be fortified by the exposure of university administrators to the culturally expanding popularity of the language of economics and to the claims of kiosk economics to explain widely and rigorously virtually anything that sociology might try to explain, so presumably turning sociology redundant.

3.2   *Imperialism towards the common sense?*

Consider then the confrontation between kiosk economics and folk views. Kiosk economists are explicit about their wish to challenge the intuitions behind common-sense views and of replacing these with a scientific understanding of how the world really works. They think that the conceptual and cognitive horizons of folk views are too limited to yield an in-depth understanding. Might this qualify as scientific imperialism?

Indeed, in one of its many meanings, 'scientific imperialism' refers to a trend of 'scientification' in the course of which science imperializes increasing portions of human life, leaving decreasing portions of them to the culturally sustained subjective meanings and intuitions of the common sense and the patterns of everyday experience. So we have scientific physics challenging folk physics and similarly folk biology and folk psychology being questioned by the respective scientific disciplines. In each case, the challenge and suggested replacement is based on the conviction that the superficial folk views get facts wrong and that the respective science will do better. The same motivation grounds the project of undermining the canons of *folk economics* and replacing them with scientific economics (Mäki 1996; Rubin 2003). This project subscribes to an important version of scientific realism: science is the best way of finding out what is real.

The challenge by kiosk economics of folk views can be considered an example of scientific imperialism in this sense. This presupposes meeting the objection that we noted above, namely that kiosk economics is not a scientific discipline. The argument I used for refuting the objection remains the same. Kiosk economics is continuous with academic economics, with the influences and benefits between the two flowing in both directions. Kiosk economics is a spokesperson of scientific economics and its representative towards lay audiences. It is both a messenger and an advocate.

It is noteworthy that in its relations towards folk views, kiosk economics seems more openly and aggressively imperialistic than academic economics. The challenge and assault (with a roguish smile) are explicit; indeed, they are built in the very idea of kiosk economics.

4   Conclusion

I have sought to take a few steps towards characterizing the philosophy of the new kiosk economics by identifying some of its guiding principles, such as the announced pursuit of deep and counter-intuitive understanding by unifying a disparate class of phenomena in terms of similar mechanisms and processes; using these achievements for entertaining its audiences with exciting disclosures of the secrets behind familiar phenomena; and using all this for defending and promoting economics at large. I also pointed out ways in which the new kiosk economics could be considered an instance of scientific imperialism. On the rather low degree of detail of these suggestions, all of this is consistent with a minimal scientific realism.

Yet none of this implies that the new kiosk economics has got the facts right about everything, or even anything. But its principles are such that it might. The adverse fault-finding stream of popular writing about economics serves as a reminder of the possibility of imperfection. Whatever the case is with this issue, the fun survives.

Acknowledgements

The paper was prepared within TINT – Academy of Finland Centre of Excellence in the Philosophy of the Social Sciences, sponsored by the Academy of Finland and the University of Helsinki.

References

Cowen, T. (2007), *Discover Your Inner Economist: Use Incentives to Fall in Love, Survive Your Next Meeting, and Motivate Your Dentist*, New York: Dutton.

Coyle, D. (2007), *The Soulful Science: What Economists Really Do and Why It Matters*, Princeton, NJ: Princeton University Press.

Fine, B., and Milonakis, D. (2009), *From Economics Imperialism to Freakonomics*, London: Routledge.

Frank, R.H. (2007), *The Economic Naturalist: Why Economics Explains Almost Everything*, New York: Basic Books.

Harford, T. (2006), *The Undercover Economist*, London: Little, Brown.

——— (2008), *The Logic of Life: Uncovering the New Economics of Everything*, London: Little, Brown.

Landsburg, S. (1993), *The Armchair Economist: Economics and Everyday Life*, New York: Free Press.

——— (2007), *More Sex Is Safer Sex: The Unconventional Wisdom of Economics*, New York: Free Press.

Levitt, S.D., and Dubner, S.J. (2005), *Freakonomics: A Rogue Economist Explores the Hidden Side of Everything*, New York: HarperCollins.

——— (2009), *SuperFreakonomics: Global Cooling, Patriotic Prostitutes, and Why Suicide Bombers Should Buy Life Insurance*, London: Allen Lane.

Mäki, U., et al. (1996), 'Scientific Realism and Some Peculiarities of Economics', in *Realism and Anti-Realism in the Philosophy of Science*. Boston Studies in the Philosophy of Science. ed. R.S. Cohen, Vol. 169, Dordrecht: Kluwer, pp. 425–445.

——— (2000), 'Kinds of Assumptions and Their Truth: Shaking an Untwisted F-Twist', *Kyklos*, 53, 303–322.

——— (2001), 'Explanatory Unification: Double and Doubtful', *Philosophy of the Social Sciences*, 31, 488–506.

——— (2009), 'Economics Imperialism: Concept and Constraints', *Philosophy of the Social Sciences*, 39(3), 351–380.

Mäki, U., and Marchionni, C. (2009), 'On the Structure of Explanatory Unification: The Case of Geographical Economics', *Studies in History and Philosophy of Science*, 40, 185–195.

——— (2011), 'Is Geographical Economics Imperializing Economic Geography?', *Journal of Economic Geography*, 11, 645–665.

Musgrave, A. (1981), '"Unrealistic Assumptions" in Economic Theory: The F-Twist Untwisted', *Kyklos*, 34, 377–387.

Rubin, P.H. (2003), 'Folk Economics', *Eastern Economic Journal*, 70, 157–171.

Vromen, J.J. (2009), 'The Booming Economics-Made-Fun Genre: More Than Having Fun, but Less Than Economics Imperialism', *Erasmus Journal for Philosophy and Economics*, 2(1), 70–99.

Economics is a serious and difficult subject

Roger E. Backhouse[a,b]

[a]Department of Economics, University of Birmingham, Birmingham, UK; [b]Erasmus Institute of Philosophy and Economics, Erasmus University, Rotterdam, The Netherlands

This paper argues that by focusing on simple problems that can be resolved by the use of simple economic logic, usually involving the assumption that agents are rational, the economics-as-fun literature inevitably distracts from more difficult problems that are harder to solve and which may need to be tackled in different ways and may create a bias towards solutions that rely on the market.

1 Introduction

'Economics as fun' is a label that has been applied to a very diverse literature (Vromen 2009; Fleury 2010). It covers work that is very diverse in its objectives and there is scope for debate over whether it should be seen as a single genre. However, a general feature is that it shows the power of a certain type of reasoning. It presents paradoxical facts as well as facts that might seem to bear little relation to economics and uses economic logic to show that these facts are not so strange after all. Very often the search for intriguing phenomena leads outside economics, the drama coming from the application of economic analysis to social problems that the reader might have presumed would not be amenable to such methods. The search for striking examples regularly takes writers into problems that are inherently trivial, such as patterns in baby-naming or a company's dress code. The literature can be criticised for focusing on such trivia, but the argument made here is that the literature trivialises economics in a different and possibly far more important sense: it selects only those topics that are amenable to simple explanations, thereby giving a distorted picture of economics and running further risk of making economic explanations tautological by suggesting that whatever people do is what they wished to do (Stigler 1984, p. 302; Medema 2011). Such trivialisation is quite apart from any trivialisation that may result from the topics selected for discussion. Suggesting that economics is simple may reduce people's openness to more difficult ways of thinking – that are less fun – about economic phenomena that produce less clear-cut conclusions. To say this is not to argue, with many heterodox economists, that economics as currently practised is so flawed that it needs to be abandoned in favour of a new paradigm that is as yet completely unproven. Economics can boast of successes, but these have to be placed in the context of its limitations. Economics is, to modify a point made by Robinson (1932), both a serious and a difficult subject.

The strategy in this article is first to document my claim about the economics as fun literature, something that can be done very briefly. I then relate this to instances of economics being used to solve serious problems, pointing out examples of both success and failure and, more important, suggesting that though economic theory can be very powerful under the right circumstances, it has limitations that the economics-made-fun literature plays down. The economics as fun literature is then reviewed in the light of these limitations, drawing attention to its methodological limitations.

2 Economics-made-fun

The variety found in the economics-made-fun literature can be shown through three examples, John Kay's *Everlasting Light bulbs* (2004), Tim Harford's *The Logic of Life* (2008), and Steven Levitt and Stephen Dubner's *Freakonomics* (2005) , each of which represents a different approach. For the present purpose I will take it that *Freakonomics* is unquestionably within the genre, that *The Logic of Life* is also, and that *Everlasting Light bulbs* is marginal, coming close to a book such as Thaler and Sunstein's *Nudge* (2008) which I have decided not to include (the reason its aim is to make a case for approaching economic policy in a particular way).

Whether or not others were there first, the archetype of the economics-made-fun literature is probably *Freakonomics: A Rogue Economist Explores the Hidden Side of Everything* (Levitt and Dubner 2005). The phrase 'rogue economist' suggests unconventional, counter-cultural activity and exploring the 'hidden side of everything' is a common theme (found in both the books by Harford and Kay). 'The conventional wisdom is often wrong', Levitt and Dubner argue, the reason being that it is not conventional to apply economic reasoning sufficiently rigorously and systematically to problems that are not ostensibly economic. Some chapter titles used in these books sound paradoxical – 'What do schoolteachers and sumo wrestlers have in common?' or 'How is the Ku Klux Klan like a group of real-estate agents?' Others pick out homely problems that the reader might think would defy economic analysis, such as why drug dealers live with their mothers, or parenting practices. These examples are, of course, used to show the power of economic reasoning and the consistency of explanations across a wide range of social phenomena, but they also serve to contribute to the 'counter-cultural' persona that the authors wish to create – more conventional examples simply would not work.

An important facet of Levitt and Dubner's discoveries is their data analysis. In some cases it is finding previously unknown data sources, such as the data on school teachers cheating so as to improve their students' performances in standardised tests. In others it is finding previously unnoticed correlations, such as that between the rise in the number of abortions and the subsequent fall in crime. But data analysis is only part of the story, for what makes the evidence significant is that they explain what is going on. In some cases, such as the link between abortion and crime, logic is enough (if fewer people are born into socio-economic groups out of which criminals are most likely to emerge, there will be fewer criminals), but in most cases explanation takes the form of showing why this behaviour is rational for the individuals concerned. Rationality may involve seeking one's own economic advantage, or it may involve moral ends, such as feelings of guilt about being late in collecting one's children from the child minder, or altruism in giving blood. Either way, the stories never violate the rule that incentives are what matters.

Another clear example of the genre is *More Sex is Safer Sex* (Landsburg 2007). The essay from which the book's title is taken, and ones such as 'Be fruitful and multiply', 'What I like about Scrooge' and 'Who's the fairest of them all?' are clearly designed to be fun. Much rests on data analysis, such as the evidence that people perceived as being more attractive get better job offers and higher salaries. The explanations run in terms of incentives, notably (though the word is not used), externalities: if the consequences of an action are felt by someone else, decisions will not generally be socially optimal. Landsburg illustrates this with the example of people in a street each trying to blow fallen leaves out of their garden into their neighbours: it would be better if no one did this, though it happens because no one takes account of the harm done to their neighbour by blowing leaves from one garden into another. This arises in problem after problem and is frequently the factor that takes the argument beyond what is merely statistical. The first chapter, for example, is based primarily on an argument about the speed with which HIV will spread in a population where abstinence by HIV negative people implies that those who do have sexual encounters are more likely to do so with people who are HIV positive. It is only arguments about incentives that turn it into an economic case.

The book does contain discussions of big social issues, with chapter on reforming politics and the criminal justice system, reducing crime, pollution, time wasted queuing and grade inflation, and solving the shortage of kidneys for transplant. However, in all of these cases, the emphasis is on showing that seemingly outrageous solutions would be beneficial. Thus he argues that if a juror finds someone not guilty, they should be required to have the defendant as a house guest, demonstrating their confidence in the person's good character; and he argues that less time would be spent in queues if people joining queues went to the front rather than to the back (knowing that they might never get to the front, people would opt to leave, or never join, long queues).

Harford's book, as its title implies, is driven by the explicit objective of showing the power of economic logic where that logic is not surprisingly that of rational choice. He starts (2008, p. x), in typical economics-made-fun style, with a homely example, of why the street furniture in Hackney is so much more run down than in neighbouring Stoke Newington. Dismissing commonly offered explanations such as greater affluence and higher taxes in Stoke Newington, or the greater political involvement and influence of its middle-class residents, he concludes that the difference can be explained as the outcome of rational choice. Hackney has a much more transient population which, entirely rationally, has less commitment to the area and is therefore less willing to make long-term investments in the neighbourhood.

The book continues through some equally 'homely' examples: betting at Las Vegas and the questions of whether divorce is underrated or bosses are overpaid. In the process he introduces ideas of strategy (where one person's optimal action depends on what the others will do, which in turn depends on their view of what he will do) and incentives. The book becomes much more serious in Chapter 6, 'in the neighbourhood' where he turns to problems of crime and discrimination. These arguably bridge the gap Fleury discerns between the social concerns exhibited that dominated the 1960s generation and the personal concerns had become prevalent by the 2000s. Social issues are being viewed seriously, though in a way that presumes people are driven by events close to home rather than by concern for society in general.

The remaining chapters offer rational explanations of racism (again), the phenomenon of dramatically different prices in different places and revolutions. He explains why people do not have any rational incentive to vote (if having Al Gore elected raised one's welfare by $3000, and the only reason for voting was to get him elected, the expected payoff would be no more than 1%, explaining why many people stay at home). But this does not undermine the rational choice model, for Harford concludes that people vote because it makes them feel good. The rational choice model is reconciled with the data but it becomes tautological: because people vote even though they have no material incentive to do so, it must be the case that it makes them feel good. In contrast, sugar producers do have an incentive to lobby for subsidies, so that even if such legislation costs the public $1.9 billion but benefits a small group of voters (those involved in the sugar industry) $1 billion, it is rational for it to be maintained. Though it costs the public a lot, the cost to any individual is too low for it to be worth their while to fight the legislation.

Harford does not claim that rationality explains everything – though we are not presented with examples where it fails – but that it explains a lot. Incentives even explain the course of economic growth over a million years of human history.[1]

In contrast, Kay's book is different in its emphasis. The book is full of incidents, whether true or fictitious, from the author's own life, much of the text being written in the first person. The book contains numerous examples that suggest it should be placed in the economics-made-fun genre: seniority rules in business (and in Oxford's Senior Common Room), the problem of using respirators on people with beards (or even stubble), dress codes, restaurant prices, where economists go on holiday and gift-giving at Christmas. Yet the dominant theme in the book is with much more serious issues, as befits a book that originated in columns in the *Financial Times*. These include the significance of quality changes for the measurement of inflation, regulation, trade policy and the structure of industry. Homely examples are almost always used to make a point that is much more general. For example, the discussion of beards and respirators is making a general point about different types of regulation; prices in his favourite restaurant make a point about measuring inflation; meeting a friend from London whilst on holiday in Kashmir, makes a point about networks; the prices faced by tourists taking holidays abroad illustrate purchasing power parity; and so on.

Much more clearly than Harford, Kay is making a case for the virtues of the market, his target being what he calls do-it-yourself economics. His message is that many commonly held economic ideas are wrong and that the world should be guided by economists. More than that, he is arguing the case for markets and incentives. Communism failed, he argues, not because people were irrational but because the incentives were wrong: in the command economies of Eastern Europe, people had no incentive to behave in ways that improved the welfare of society, as by raising productivity, but in capitalist countries they did. It may be that this implication arises simply from silence about cases where government intervention would improve social welfare, or for the use of the tax system to redistribute income, but the book comes across as a sustained argument for free markets. Economics, in his presentation, provides the rationale for largely 'free market' economic policies.

In arguing that his book is a marginal example of the genre, it is helpful to make a comparison with an earlier book making the case for free markets, *Free to Choose*, by Milton and Friedman. (Friedman and Friedman 1980) Friedman and Friedman may go further than Kay in propounding the virtues of free markets,[2] and may place a greater emphasis on freedom, but much of its central message is the same: people respond to incentives and prosperity provided that incentives are appropriate. It is also true that, as in much economics, simple examples are used to make general points. Friedman and Friedman start with the example of making a pencil, a process involving activities from felling trees to mining graphite and designing the packaging, to illustrate division of labour in a modern economy. However, not only are homely examples much thinner on the ground, but also the book is structured around big themes: the power of the market and the tyranny of controls, welfare provision, income redistribution, education, consumer and worker protection and inflation. The reader is left in no doubt that this is a serious book making a clear argument about the role of markets, conforming more closely to the notion of relevance that prevailed, as Fleury (2010) explains, in the 1960s rather than the notion of relevance (relating to peoples immediate circumstances) that came to prevail after the millennium. Despite the similarity of its message to that of Harford, Key and Levitt (though not to some others contributing to the genre), *Free to Choose* has a message that is too traditional to qualify as economics-made-fun in the way that the others do.

3   When does economics work?

The message of the economics-made-fun literature tells emphatically that economics works. Economics is defined by its method, which is the systematic exploration of the consequences of the idea that people respond to incentives. They may be motivated by concern for others or by moral considerations (to make this consistent with the argument that people responding to incentives, the satisfaction derived from behaving morally or altruistically is taken into account) but the emphasis is on self-interest. The market system fails when incentives an individual faces do not reflect all the consequences of his or her actions. It may require imagination to get beneath the surface and to find the hidden rationality, or to find surprising evidence, but in essence it makes economics appear, in essence, easy.

Before examining this argument it is worth exploring what the limitations of this type of reasoning are. One problem is that this literature attaches great importance to logic: the argument is considered settled when a logical argument about incentives makes sense of the evidence that has been found. The problem with this approach is that though the explanation is convincing once the 'inner logic' has been revealed, our intuitions may be incorrect, for there may be further layers of the problem that have not been considered. It is appropriate to ask not merely whether the resulting theories make sense of data known to the theorist, but whether they result in the solution of real problems. This means that it is helpful to consider a different type of example: case where economic reasoning has been used to guide policy. In addition, if we are to explore the limits of economists' reasoning, it is necessary to consider possible failures as well as successes.[3]

An excellent example of a policy success that confirms the importance of getting incentives right is the introduction, in the United States, of trading in permits for sulphur dioxide emissions by electricity generators. Regulation was failing to reduce the level of emissions, for it was not possible to design a policy that accommodated uneven spread of emissions (which reflect prevailing winds), and which provided the right incentives to adopt new, cleaner technologies. There was also the problem that electricity companies were continually lobbying for exemptions on the grounds that they were unfairly hit by the regulations. Instituting tradable permits provided appropriate incentives and, moreover, did not provide claims for exemption because if companies were in difficulty, they had merely to buy more permits.

An important characteristic of this example[4] is that it is comparatively self-contained (there is a limited number of electricity generators), that is the policy objective was clear, and those involved in the scheme were professionals concerned with their own profits. The same features were true of another instance where a market was created, apparently successfully – the auctioning of the radio spectrum for third generation telephony. Here the British and American governments designed auctions that raised billions of pounds and dollars (some other countries raised comparable amounts but in some countries auctions were much less successful). The problem was self-contained, involving professional players who could learn and understand the rules. However, in this case, the objectives were less clear. *Ex post*, success was judged by the enormous revenues raised, but when plans were originally laid governments had set a broader range of objectives, from encouraging innovation to encouraging competition and keeping the costs of telephone usage low. Because the outcome of the auction was to place the winning bidders under considerable financial pressure, it may have contributed to restructuring the industry and, in the opinion of some, to slowing down innovation. The point is not that the spectrum auctions failed so much as that it is hard to be certain whether or not they did succeed in all the objectives that were initially specified.

An even stronger example of eventual failure is financial innovation. The financial services industry has never, at least in recent times, been free of regulation, but starting in the 1970s, regulations were removed allowing financial institutions to innovate. From the mid-1970s, financial derivatives proliferated under a regulatory regime that was much lighter than what had gone before. The fortunes made by investors in hedge funds and other institutions investing in these markets would seem to confirm the view underlying much of the literature discussed above that if people are allowed to pursue their own interests, the result will be beneficial. Of course, as we now know, the problem was that incentives were not right, and managers had incentives to take decisions that dramatically increased the risks that major institutions would fail, making the financial system far more fragile than before the changes.

All of these examples are significant but they remain isolated examples of markets in action. They are cases where the problems involved have sufficiently clear boundaries that the economist can form a fairly complete picture of how the market works and hence the incentives that will operate. However, economists also advise on much more complex issues, where this is not possible. One example is the so-called emerging markets: the countries of Eastern Europe that had to undergo a transition from socialism to capitalism. Here, whole societies were involved and, as a consequence the problems faced by policy-makers were far more complex. Not only is an economy comprising millions of markets too complicated for it to be possible for the economist to consider in detail all the effects of a policy change, but the objectives of policy (and hence the criteria by which success it so be judged) are also hard to specify in anything but very general terms. There are too many conflicting interests that need to be resolved. More important, the economic cannot be separated from the political and the social.

Experience in the countries that made the transition from socialism to capitalism was very mixed. In the largest country involved (leaving aside China on the grounds that its system still retains much state control), Russia, it was a disaster. The absolutely decisive evidence for this is that, in the space of a few years, life expectancy fell by a decade. The newly created market economy failed to provide the incentives needed to ensure that large sections of the population were in a position to find employment and access the goods and services they needed. Whether or not the policy of rapid liberalisation and privatisation pursued by Yeltsin and Gaidar was politically inevitable in a country where the government was rapidly losing control, the result was chaos. The legal system was weak and it was difficult either to restrain monopoly or to force firms to honour contractual agreements. Enterprises were stripped of their assets and much wealth was moved abroad, resulting in massive gains for a minority and hardship for the majority. In part this was because some people understood what was going on, and how to take advantage of it, whereas others did not, but it also reflected very unequal opportunities.

Another important economic issue that involves entire societies is 'globalisation' – the package of measures involving free trade, market liberalisation and the removal of regulations that separate national markets from each other. These measures are supported on grounds very similar to those used in the economics-made-fun literature. Easterley, writing about economic development, has said:

> People do what they get paid to do; what they don't get paid to do, they don't do .... People respond to incentives; all the rest is commentary .... If we do the hard work of ensuring that the trinity of First World aid donors, Third World governments, and ordinary Third World citizens have the right incentives, development will happen. If they don't, it won't. (Easterley 2002, p. xii)

In so far as they recognise that incentives may be non-monetary, Harford or Levitt might dissent from the baldness of the claim that people have to be 'paid' to do anything, but leaving aside such details, it is precisely this idea that underlies the 'hidden' side of everything.

Yet, for all the claims of supporters of free trade, privatisation and deregulation, it is far from clear that globalisation has been universally beneficial. The number of people living in poverty according to the World Bank is a statistic with such a large margin of error that it is impossible to be certain about whether it has risen or fallen (even without taking into account any effects of the 2008 financial crisis). Moreover, if there has been a fall, it will be dominated by the reduction in poverty in China, a country that has liberalised very selectively and which retains a large measure of state control. Poverty in the rest of the Third World is less likely to have improved and in some countries, notably in parts of sub-Saharan Africa, it has probably risen.

4   The consequences of making economics fun

The first consequence of making economics fun is that focusing on incentives tends, irrespective of whether it is the authors' intention, to create a bias in favour of 'free market' or what are sometimes called 'neoliberal' conclusions (in the same way that reasoning in terms of 'society' might create biases the other way). The reason would appear to be that the most abstract models are ones that suggest markets work – rational behaviour implies that agents will take optimal decisions given the prices they confront, and if markets are competitive, prices will reflect scarcities in the economy as a whole. There are, of course, exceptions to this in that, as Landsburg makes particularly clear, there are spillover effects if one person's action affects someone else. Economists have developed elaborate theories of monopoly, bilateral bargaining, public goods and externalities that explain why markets may fail. However, these are generally considered to be complications that need to be argued case by case. The economics-made-fun literature plays such complications down because making economics fun requires that arguments should be simple so that economics can be shown to be powerful. Take away the simplicity and the fun becomes less: readers to not want headaches.

It is also arguable that even if incentives are always important, forcing all explanations into the 'rational choice plus incentives' approach would focus on those incentives that are simple to understand. For example, the notion that if something becomes more expensive people will buy less of it is easy to understand; more difficult is the notion, developed by Stiglitz and others, that under conditions of asymmetric information a rise in price may have perverse effects. Thus a bank, unable to tell whether a borrower is likely to repay a loan, may conclude that willingness to accept a high interest rate may indicate potential borrowers more likely to default. If a problem is sufficiently complicated that the structure of incentives is not fully understood, forcing everything into the rational choice plus incentives framework may be systematically misleading.

Take the case of Landsburg. He emphasises spillovers and these play an essential role in his argument. Yet his conclusions about fixing politics, justice and 'everything else' generally involve the creation of finely tuned incentive structures. This is illustrated by his method of separating hard workers from 'goof-offs' in school: 'Starting in sixth grade, some classes get free encyclopedias, the others get free cigarettes – and you get to choose your class. That should sort everyone out pretty well' (Landsburg 2007, p. 118). This may not be intended as a serious proposal but it illustrates a way of arguing that would appear to result in a bias against regulations that are clearly not optimal but which might be justified on 'second best' grounds.

Thus although the economics-made-fun literature is undoubtedly right to see incentives as important, focusing solely on them may cause economists to miss the larger picture. This is illustrated by the problems faced by Russia. Kay (discussed in Section 2) makes the point that the problem with the Soviet model was not that people did not respond to incentives, but that the incentives were wrong. This point is undoubtedly correct. However, markets are able to work only because of the existence of a complex set of institutions that allow them to work. Contracts are of little value if there is no mechanism through which they can be enforced, it requires a functioning legal system that will help in this regard. Competition can exist only if there are mechanisms in place that will prevent the creation of monopolies. Even if institutions can be provided by private firms, this may not be a quick process. Farmers, for example, can sell their produce to consumers living a thousand miles away only if there are merchants who can buy and distribute their produce, but such merchants, equipped with the necessary infrastructure, do not appear overnight. The problem in Russia was that privatisation was so rapid that when the socialist institutional infrastructure was removed, there was sometimes nothing to take its place. The point here is not that making economics fun neglects institutions (even something as trivial as a dress code could be seen as an institution) but that making things easy to understand may lead to oversimplification.

The point here is that in the Russian context, focus on incentives led to a focus on markets, without paying attention to ensuring, in each market, that institutions were in place to enable economic activity to continue. When this did not happen, many people faced hardship. The problem arises because incentives are effective at the margin, whereas the collapse of an economic system involves changes that, by any standard, go beyond marginal adjustments.

The discomfort felt by some contributors to the economics-made-fun literature at solutions that do not involve rationality, competition and incentives are nicely illustrated by Landsburg.[5] He describes himself as an 'ideological free marketeer' (Landsburg 2007, p. 232) and admits that the idea that regulation may raise social welfare 'makes him squirm'. However, despite this, he accepts that society may be better off if insurance is compulsory and that society should defend some 'core values' such as dignity and freedom irrespective of cost-benefit calculations (2007, p. 237). He recoils from censorship even when his cost-benefit analysis recommends it (2007, p. 247). Yet this honest statement of his position very clearly makes the point that he, like most of the economics-made-fun authors, would appear to be biased towards free market solutions.

There are at least two weaknesses with this approach. Even though authors may start with data analysis, the economics-made-fun literature is able to show the power of economics by showing that phenomena can be explained using elementary logic about the incentives facing rational individuals. The problem is that the framework may be sufficiently elastic that any observed behaviour can be rationalised as consistent with rational choice. If behaviour appears inconsistent with pecuniary costs and benefits rational choice can, and sometimes is, saved by appealing to unobservable non-pecuniary rewards – to the benefits someone gets, for example, from knowing they have done the right thing. Rational choice is in a sense unfalsifiable.

A second weakness is that the literature, even when it introduces spillovers, is based on an overly simple view of the way markets operate. For example, in describing the benefits of compulsory motor insurance, Landsburg describes the benefit as lower insurance premia, not as ensuring that victims receive the compensation they are due, which will not happen if this would push an uninsured driver into bankruptcy. Perhaps the reason is that admission of the possibility of bankruptcy has the potential to undermine many of the arguments about costs and benefits on which the book depends. As Stiglitz (see, for example, Stiglitz 2002) has repeatedly argued, information asymmetries and bankruptcy have the potential to undermine conventional intuitions about how markets work. To admit that would be to question the intuitions on which the persuasiveness of most of the literature's case studies relies.

Fascination with incentives also focuses attention on efficiency at the expense of distribution. Presumably the explanation is that their methods to not provide any basis for forming judgements about this. Yet in the policy realm, it is probably true to say that because every policy change that benefits someone makes at least someone worse off, it is always necessary to include the costs or benefits of redistributing wealth along with the costs and benefits deriving from allocating resources more efficiently. Further more if, as Wilkinson and Pickett (2009) have argued, equal societies are happier than more unequal societies, it may be that by neglecting income distribution, contributors to the economics-made-fun literature are in fact neglecting the most important contribution to social welfare.

A case can be made that it is legitimate, even essential, for economic problems to be simplified. Simplification is a feature of all popular writing with the result that even books by eminent biologists or astrophysicists may contain statements that would be considered oversimplifications were they repeated in an academic article. In popular biology, evolutionary arguments may well be used in a way that is as elastic as is economist's use of the rational choice model. It is also necessary to simplify for the purposes of teaching.[6] However, it remains the case that focusing on one dimension of economic problems necessarily distorts them; and the economics-made-fun literature, for the most part focuses on simple cases involving rational agents making choices under very simple incentive structures. Because students are looking for rational-choice explanations, that is what they will find, making them less open to more complicated explanations.[7] Of course, to neglect such incentives, as is done by some heterodox economists and some other social scientists, is no better (maybe they unfairly weight the scales against markets),[8] but that does not invalidate the claims made here.

More serious is the charge that the economics-made-fun literature can and does show some of the limitations of market incentives. For example, Levitt and Dubner (2005) consider the example of a creche that tried to get parents to collect their children on time by changing them for lateness. The result was that more parents were late because being able to paying for additional time reduced the moral pressure to be on time, and once the moral sanction was removed, the fee was too small an incentive to make collection on time worthwhile. In similar vein Cowen (2008) explains that if a parent offers to pay their child to wash dishes, the result may be that the child rationally chooses not to do so. In both cases, an example typical of the economics-made-fun literature shows that non-market incentives may be important. However, it remains the case that these examples are significantly rarer than those that show how market incentives work, and in some cases, apparently irrational behaviour is shown to be rational by looking more closely at the way people are reasoning. However, the most important point is that they encourage the view that economic problems, once understood, are essentially simple.

5 Conclusions

Economics is made fun through finding paradoxical results that can easily be explained using economic reasoning. This can, without any doubt, tackle serious problems through showing how improving incentives can produce better outcomes. There are real-world policy changes, such as the case of sulphur dioxide emissions trading scheme in the United States, that illustrate this. However, the contention of this article is that by forcing all problems into this framework, making economics fun over-simplifies the subject and systematically biases it towards free-market solutions to economic problems. Intuitions about supply-and-demand, on which many examples rely, may be systematically misleading in a world where information is unequally distributed and where bankruptcy is possible. The assumption of rationality, whilst undoubtedly very powerful and applicable in many circumstances, may not always be the appropriate way to view behaviour given that people may be motivated by considerations that are unobservable and may change in response to the environment in which agents find themselves. As the case of the Russian transition to capitalism shows, the simplicity of the rational-choice, perfect-competition model may divert attention from the institutional infrastructure needed if markets are to work in the efficient way that the model assumes. And the approach fosters the belief that externalities and spillover effects are exceptions rather than the rule.

In short, economics is a difficult subject. It is made out to be the key that solves all problems only by selecting comparatively simple problems, or problems where the economist can find a paradoxically simple explanation, and by regarding success as finding an intuitively appealing, apparently logical explanation. If policy examples, such as the reduction of poverty (whether in industrial countries or in the Third World), economic development, or even the design of effective macroeconomic policy were considered, it would be necessary to confront much messy, recalcitrant detail and it would become clear that economic logic of the type found in the economics-made-fun literature, though it may be an important part of the answer, is unlikely to be the key to solving everything. Economic logic is powerful, but it has limits that the economics-made-fun literature does not concede sufficiently often. It seems very likely that more important economic problems, such as how to reduce world poverty, how to improve macroeconomic performance, or how to solve environmental problems are more complicated than the economics-made-fun literature can handle, require a very different approach to the subject.

Acknowledgements

I am grateful to Jean-Baptiste Fleury, Philippe Fontaine, Steven Medema, Jack Vromen and an anonymous referee for valuable comments on an early draft of this article. Whilst they may have saved me from some errors, they bear no responsibility for any that remain.

Notes

1. In its coverage this is reminiscent of Seabright (2010).
2. However, it should be noted that Friedman and Friedman are less critical of government intervention than many present day free market economists. For example, they concede that

many new deal work creation programmes served a useful function at a time of acute distress (Friedman and Friedman 1980, p. 121).

3. The remainder of this section draws on the case studies in Chapters 2–5 of Backhouse (2010).
4. For other examples, see McMillan (2002).
5. This is not true of all contributors to the genre. Ariely (2009) achieves dramatic effect by arguing that people are irrational.
6. Fleury has pointed out that Robert Frank's work in this genre is focused on teaching.
7. I owe the point about confirmation bias to Vromen.
8. This is deliberately noncommittal not to suggest that heterodox economists or other social scientists are free from bias but simply because the concern of this article is economics.

References

Ariely, D. (2009), *Predictably Irrational: The Hidden Forces that Shape our Decisions*. London: Harper Collins.

Backhouse, R.E. (2010), *The Puzzle of Modern Economics*, Cambridge: Cambridge University Press.

Cowen, T. (2008), *Discover your Inner Economist: Use Incentives to Fall in Love, Survive your next Meeting, and Motivate your Dentist*, London: Plume.

Easterley, W. (2002), *The Elusive Quest for Growth: Economists' Adventures and Misadventures in the Tropics*, Cambridge, MA: MIT Press.

Fleury, J-B. (2010), 'The Evolving Notion of Relevance: An Historical Perspective to the "Economics Made Fun" Movement', unpublished paper, Rotterdam.

Friedman, M., and Friedman, R. (1980), *Free to Choose: A Personal Statement*, Harmondsworth: Penguin Books.

Harford, T. (2008), *The Logic of Life: Uncovering the New Economics of Everything*, London: Little, Brown.

Kay, J.A. (2004), *Everlasting Light Bulbs: How Economics Illuminates the World*, London: Erasmus Press.

Landsburg, S.E. (2007), *More Sex is Safer Sex: The Unconventional Wisdom of Economics*, New York: Free Press.

Levitt, S.D., and Dubner, S.J. (2005), *Freakonomics: A Rogue Economist Explores the Hidden Side of Everything*, London: Penguin Books.

McMillan, J. (2002), *Reinventing the Bazaar: A Natural History of Markets*, New York, NY: W.W. Norton.

Medema, S.G. (2011), 'A Case of Mistaken Identity: George Stigler, "The Problem of Social Cost," and the Coase Theorem', *European Journal of Law and Economics*, 31(1), 11–38.

Robinson, J.V. (1932), *Economics is a Serious Subject: The Apologia of an Economist to the Mathematician, the Scientist and the Plain Man*, Cambridge: W. Heffer & Sons.

Seabright, P. (2010), *The Company of Strangers: A Natural History of Economic Life*, Princeton, NJ: Princeton University Press.

Stigler, G.J. (1984), 'Economics: The Imperial Science?', *Scandinavian Journal of Economics*, 86, 301–313.

Stiglitz, J.E. (2002), *Globalization and its Discontents*, London: Allen Lane.

Thaler, R.H., and Sunstein, C.R. (2008), *Nudge: Improving Decisions about Health, Wealth and Happiness*, London: Penguin.

Vromen, J.J. (2009), 'The Booming Economics-Made-Fun Genre: More than Having Fun, but Less than Economics Imperialism', *Erasmus Journal of Philosophy and Economics*, 2(1), 70–99.

Wilkinson, R., and Pickett, K. (2009), *The Spirit Level: Why More Equal Societies Almost Always do Better*, London: Allen Lane.

The two images of economics: why the fun disappears when difficult questions are at stake?

N. Emrah Aydinonat

Department of Economics, Faculty of Economics and Administrative Sciences, Bahcesehir University, Istanbul, Turkey

The image of economics got somewhat puzzling after the crisis of 2008. Many economists now doubt that economics is able to provide answers to some of its core questions. The crisis was not so fun for economics. However, this not so fun image of economics is not the only image in the eyes of the general public. When one looks at economics-made-fun (EMF) books (e.g. *Freakonomics*, *The Undercover Economist*, etc.), economics seems to be an explanatory science which is able to provide interesting, unconventional, entertaining and enlightening explanations for almost every aspect of our lives. Isn't there a great contradiction between these two images of economics? Not necessarily. The present paper explicates why. Nevertheless, the paper also shows that EMF books run the risk of creating a false sense of understanding and explains how one should read the basic insights provided by EMF books to remove this risk. The paper contrasts the EMF version of the explanation of the effects of mandatory seat belt laws with actual research concerning the subject to illustrate its arguments.

Introduction

The image of economics got somewhat puzzling after the economic crisis of 2008. Many economists now doubt that economics is able to provide answers to some of its core questions. After the crisis, many articles and books by well-known and respected economists stated that economists' focus on self-interest and economizing action is misguided. Some announced that there was no invisible hand; others emphasized animal spirits instead of *Homo Economicus*. When one looks at debates concerning the crisis, it appears that economics is also in a crisis: it cannot provide explanations for its core problems, it cannot predict economic outcomes, etc. This is the first image of economics.

The crisis was not so fun for economics. However, this not so fun image of economics is not the only image in the eyes of the general public. The so-called economics-made-fun (EMF) books (such as the *Freakonomics* and *The Undercover Economist*) say something else: doing economics is fun and economics could provide interesting, unconventional, entertaining and enlightening answers to questions concerning almost every aspect of our lives. So when one looks at EMF books, economics is an explanatory science and it is able to explain diverse phenomena practically with the incentives matter principle. This is the second image of economics.

The emerging picture is somewhat confusing: One the one hand, economics is presented as a way of thinking that is successful in explaining everyday phenomena, but on the other hand it seems to fail in addressing and explaining the most pressing economic matters. Could a science that cannot answer its core questions explain the logic of life? Isn't there a great contradiction between these two images of economics?

This paper aims to provide a better understanding of the relationship between these two apparently contrasting images of economics. It also provides a methodological and philosophical analysis of the use of 'incentives matter principle' in EMF books. Philosophers are well known for ending up defending a slightly improved version of the common sense after a rather lengthy and boring analysis of their subject. For this reason it may be worthwhile to present the commonsense view that I will end up defending, in the beginning of this paper. Here is what Scott Adams (2008), the creator of Dilbert, says about economics:

> If an economist tries to tell you where the stock market will be in a year, you can safely ignore that. But if he tells you a gas tax holiday is an unambiguously bad idea, that's worth listening to, especially if economists on both sides of the aisle agree. If you think it is okay to ignore economists because they are so often wrong, you're looking at the wrong questions. Economists are generally wrong with complicated models but right about concepts.

So, isn't there a great contradiction between the aforementioned images of economics? Not necessarily. The beloved Scott Adams may be right in arguing that 'economists are generally wrong with complicated models but right about concepts'. The present paper argues that the two images of economics are not as contradictory as they seem. Economists are generally right about certain individual tendencies such as economizing action, but when it comes to more complex phenomena such as economic crises, their conjectures concerning these tendencies may not be enough for providing satisfactory explanations and/or predictions. EMF books generally focus on micro-principles. Macroeconomics commonly tackles more complex phenomena. Economists are generally right about some micro-principles, but this does not necessarily translate into good explanations of macro-social phenomena. However, the real dichotomy is not between micro- and macro-explanations, the *apparent* contradiction is caused by the conception that economists fail to explain and predict complex phenomena, although that they seem to get the simple principles, such as 'incentives matter', right. There is no contradiction between being right about the fact that incentives matter and failing to provide successful explanations of complex (commonly, macro-social) phenomena. This is the first argument of this paper.

The second argument concerns the risks of focusing on simple principles, such as the 'incentives matter' principle, that plays a key role in most EMF books. Most economic phenomena are complex. For this reason, simple principles or tendencies often fail to provide satisfactory explanations. By way of focusing on simple principles, EMF books run the risk of creating a false sense of understanding. Because some of the arguments in EMF books make it to economics textbooks, it is important to understand the extent to which such simple principles are explanatory and the way in which they may contribute to our understanding of complex economic phenomena. Basic explanatory principles that are used by EMF books are based on highly abstract economic models. Such models only provide a partial understanding of the phenomenon at stake. They show how certain tendencies, such as economizing, *may* contribute to explanations of economic phenomena. They serve to our understanding by expanding the menu of possible causes that we may use in our explanations of particular economic phenomena. In fact, satisfactory explanations of particular economic phenomena often require using more than one model, and thus more than one explanatory tendency. Commonly, many explanatory factors are needed. For this reason, much of the fun in economics disappears when complex phenomena are at stake. This is the second argument of this paper. A case in point is the explanation of the effects of seat belt regulations. EMF books argue that because seat belts decrease the risks and costs of driving, rational individuals will respond to a mandatory seat belt law by way of changing their driving habits. The result will be more reckless driving and more accidents. However, as will be shown, the explanation of the effects of seat belt use requires a more complex set of explanatory factors and the individual tendency to take more risks cannot provide a satisfactory explanation.

The plan of the paper is as follows. The second section briefly presents the two apparently contradictory images of economics. The third section discusses the prominent role of the incentives matter principle in EMF books and argues that the incentives matter principle could only provide us with partial explanations. The fourth section presents the seat belt example. The fifth section explicates why the incentives matter principle fails to explain the effects of seat belt use. The sixth section explains the extent to which the seat belt use model is useful and presents a better way to understand the contributions of EMF books in this context. The last section concludes the paper.

Two images of economics

In the last decade there were at least two important events that shaped the public conception of economics as a science. The first was the economic crisis of 2008 and its aftermath, and the second is the publication of Levitt and Dubner's best-selling *Freakonomics* (2005). After the crisis, economists started questioning and debating the explanatory and predictive value of their models. Well-known and respected economists expressed their worries about the current state of economics. A few excerpts from Nobel Prize winner Paul Krugman's *The New York Times* column will suffice to convince the reader that the image of economics changed after the crisis:

> It's hard to believe now, but not long ago economists were congratulating themselves over the success of their field. Those successes – or so they believed – were both theoretical and practical, leading to a golden era for the profession. [...] Last year, everything came apart. Few economists saw our current crisis coming, but this predictive failure was the least of the field's problems. More important was the profession's blindness to the very possibility of catastrophic failures in a market economy. [...] The economics profession went astray because economists, as a group, mistook beauty, clad in impressive-looking mathematics, for truth. [...] The central cause of the profession's failure was the desire for an all-encompassing, intellectually elegant approach that also gave economists a chance to show off their mathematical prowess. Unfortunately, this romanticized and sanitized vision of the economy led most economists to ignore all the things that can go wrong. They turned a blind eye to the limitations of human rationality that often lead to bubbles and busts; to the problems of institutions that run amok; to the imperfections of markets – especially financial markets – that can cause the economy's operating system to undergo sudden, unpredictable crashes; and to the dangers created when regulators don't believe in regulation. (Krugman 2009)

Not surprisingly, his column created a lively discussion on the blogsphere (see e.g. DeLong 2009; Mankiw 2009). Although he had his critics, he was not alone. Some of his fellow economists and heterodox economists were making similar points. For example, Colander et al. (2009) published a working paper entitled 'The Financial Crisis and the Systemic Failure of Academic Economics'. Not to mention the fact that on 18 July *The Economist*'s cover story was entitled 'What went wrong with economics?' (*The Economist* 2009a,b,c). Moreover, two respected economists, George Akerlof and Robert Shiller (2009), published book-length arguments that supported Krugman's emphasis on the 'importance of irrational and often unpredictable behavior'. While the invisible hand and rationality were losing grounds, *Animal Spirits* were on the rise.

The point is that after the crisis the image of economics changed in a rather negative fashion. As Akerlof and Shiller (2009) argue, economists' basic principles such as rationality and invisible hand were not able to answer most of their core and pressing questions, such as those concerning economic depressions, unemployment, poverty, and the volatility of financial prices and corporate investment.

> None of these questions can be answered if people are viewed as having only economic motivations which they pursue rationally – that is, if the economy is seen as operating according to the invisible hand of Adam Smith. (Akerlof and Shiller 2009, p. 6)

However, the other and positive image of economics is based exactly on concepts such as rationality and the invisible hand. That *incentives matter* is the core principle of this image of economics. This second image is based on a series of economics books that became popular with the publication of *Freakonomics* (Levitt and Dubner 2005). In a nutshell, *Freakonomics* showed that doing economics is fun and that economists could explain almost everything in our daily lives. The economic success of *Freakonomics* gave rise to more books of its kind. Tim Harford's *The Undercover Economist* (2006) and *The Logic of Life* (2008), Tyler Cowen's *Discover Your Inner Economist* (2007), Robert Frank's *Economic Naturalist* (2007), Steven Landsburg's *More Sex is Safer Sex* (2007), Levitt and Dubner's *Superfreakonomics* (2009), and Klein and Bauman's *The Cartoon Introduction to Economics* (2010) were books that made economics comprehensible and fun. As Vromen (2009) explains, the *economics-made-fun-genre* is not new. Steven Landsburg's *The Armchair Economist* (1993) could be considered as the first example of this genre (for other examples, see Friedman 1996; Wheelan 2002; Smith 2003; Coyle 2004; Kay 2004). However, after the publication *Freakonomics*, this genre became more popular and some of these books became best sellers (see Vromen 2009 for a lengthy discussion of these books).

As opposed to the crisis image of economics, the EMF image of economics presents economics as a fun and successful explanatory science. Nevertheless, EMF books ask different questions, such as the following: What do schoolteachers and sumo wrestlers have in common? How is the Ku Klux Klan like a group of real-estate agents? Why do drug dealers still live with their moms? What makes a perfect parent? (Levitt and Dubner 2005). EMF books explain coffee pricing, oral sex trends, crime, cheating, racial differences in education, drunk driving, marriage, etc. On the one hand, we have economists who cannot answer our most pressing questions concerning economic crises and poverty; on the other hand, we have economists who can answer all sorts of interesting questions excluding the core questions.

Incentives matter

Isn't there a great contradiction between the aforementioned images of economics? Not necessarily. In fact, the two images are not as contradictory as they seem. Before going further, it is important to note that the apparent contradiction is not new. It became more visible after the crisis and the popularity of EMF books. If one looks at highly abstract microeconomic models and compares these with explanations of macroeconomic phenomena, one can see a similar tension. Commonly, microeconomic models and explanations seem to be much more successful than macroeconomic models and explanations. It is no wonder that stand-up economist Yoram Bauman mocks macroeconomists by describing macroeconomic principles with the following words: blah blah blah! (http://www.standupeconomist.com/). Nevertheless, the real dichotomy concerning explanatory power is not between microeconomics and macroeconomics. It is between models that are based on simple principles and models that aim to explain complex economic phenomena.

If you have read one EMF book, you probably know that incentives matter and that people respond to incentives. If you have read many, you are probably irrecoverably convinced that incentives matter and that one can use this principle to explain almost everything. Landsburg (1993) starts his book by explaining the power of incentives. In Levitt and Dubner (2005) you can see that the principle is used in explanations in almost every part of the book. Almost every other EMF book follows the same line of reasoning which is based on the incentives matter principle. In fact, that incentives matter is one of the core principles of economics. Greg Mankiw's (2012) popular textbook lists 'incentives matter' as the fourth principle of economics and puts a great emphasis on it.

Incentives matter principle is based on the idea that rational individuals evaluate the costs and benefits of the available options and respond to the changes in these cost and benefits. As stand-up economist Yoram Bauman suggests, the idea that people respond to incentives is almost tautological: There is nothing surprising in the fact that 'individuals are motivated by things that motivate them!' However, economists usually make quite restrictive assumptions when using this principle. First, they assume that individuals are rational; second, that they know the relevant cost of benefits; and third, that they are well informed about the changes in these costs and benefits. Given these assumptions and individuals' preferences, economic models explore the ways in which individuals would respond to changes in the relevant costs and benefits. Such models provide important insights concerning economic behaviour and its impact on aggregate variables, such as price levels. EMF books commonly make use of these insights to explain curious economic phenomena.[1] They also use these insights to explain interesting facts that fall outside the generally accepted domain of economics. In fact, EMF books are popular because they expand the domain of economics. The next section discusses a well-known exemplary explanation which uses the incentives matter principle to explain the impact of mandatory seat belt regulations on the number of car accidents and injuries caused by these accidents. But before that we need to look at the limitations of economic explanations which are based on simple principles.

To understand how EMF books are considered as providing explanatory insights, and why economists fail to explain and predict more complex phenomena such as economic crises, one needs to understand the explanatory characteristic of highly abstract economic models. The explanatory role of abstract models in economics is one of the main topics of philosophy of economics. However, it is hard to argue that there is a unified answer to the following question: How do highly abstract models explain, given that they use many unrealistic assumptions? A special issue of *Erkenntis* presents the recent state of the debate concerning abstract economic models and their explanatory power (Cartwright 2009; de Donato and Zamora-Bonilla 2009; Grüne-Yanoff 2009; Knuuttila 2009; Kuorikoski and Lehtinen 2009; Mäki 2009; Sugden 2009). Most of the authors (except Cartwright) in this special issue think that highly abstract economic models may be explanatory, but for different reasons. It is impossible to discuss the relevant literature here. Instead, I will briefly summarize my own view and explain how we should approach to highly abstract models in economics (for an extensive discussion, see Aydinonat 2007, 2008; Ylikoski and Aydinonat 2011).

By their definition abstract models make use of some restrictive assumptions concerning the phenomenon at stake. For this reason, they cannot fully explain their target phenomenon in its full complexity unless their assumptions hold. Moreover, usually such models do not aim to provide a full explanation, rather they aim to provide possible explanations of some of the chosen aspects of their target phenomenon. My favourite example here is Schelling's (1978) well-known checkerboard model of residential segregation (Aydinonat 2007).

It does not explain how and why ethnically segregated neighbourhoods emerge in particular cities, rather it explains how mildly discriminatory preferences *may* bring about segregation. It presents yet another possible cause of segregation in addition to its other well-known causes, such as racism (strong discriminatory preferences), welfare differences between ethnic groups, and organized discrimination. If one wishes to explain segregation in Chicago, Schelling's model alone cannot be helpful. To explain real-world segregation (as opposed to the segregation in Schelling's model world), one needs to take into account other explanatory factors, that is, mildly discriminatory preferences will not suffice. Abstract models, such as Schelling's, generally fall short in explaining particular, more complex economic phenomena. If one looks at how economists explain real-world phenomena, this becomes evident. For example, if one wishes to explain international trade patterns, one model, such as the Heckscher-Ohlin model, will not suffice, because the Heckscher-Ohlin model focuses on one of the possible causes of international trade; differences in factor endowments of countries. However, international trade has other causes such as differences in technology and tastes. Explaining real-world patterns of international trade requires taking these other causes into account. Because international trade patterns are determined by a complex set of factors, explaining them would not be as easy as identifying a possible cause of international trade. The point is that although developing abstract models of international trade and identifying its possible causes is not easy, explaining complex real-world phenomena is much more difficult.

What abstract economic models do is commonly to expand the *menu of possible causes*, or explanatory factors that one can use in explaining complex real-world phenomena (Ylikoski and Aydinonat 2011). For example, a Ricardian model of international trade, on the one hand, identifies differences in technology as one of the possible causes of international trade. Heckscher-Ohlin model, on the other hand, expands the menu of possible causes of international trade by identifying yet another possible cause of international trade. Other models of international trade expand this menu of possible causes even further by way of identifying other possible causes such as differences in tastes and increasing returns. Similarly, Schelling's model expands the menu of possible causes of residential segregation by way of introducing an additional explanatory factor (mildly discriminatory preferences) to the list of racism, welfare differences, etc.

In summary, abstract economic models help us understand economic phenomena because they identify those explanatory factors that may help us explain particular real-world phenomena. How is this related to the incentives matter principle? That individuals respond to changes in the relevant costs and benefits (i.e. that incentives matter) is one of the core tendencies that economists use in developing their economic models. However, in an abstract model world relevant costs and benefits are defined by the assumptions of the model. When one wishes to understand how real individuals (as opposed to the model-theoretic individuals) would respond to changes in the real world, one needs to identify costs and benefits that those real individuals consider as relevant. First, this commonly requires taking other models into account. Second, it is also necessary to identify which of the potential explanatory factors (provided by the cluster of relevant models) are actually explanatory, and to find out the relevant costs and benefits. This requires a through empirical investigation. This again implies that arguing that incentives matter is much easier than doing the actual explanatory work.

The success of EMF books is partly based on the fact that they show how looking at the way in which incentives change may provide a new light on the explanatory task at hand. They expand the menu of possible causes that their readers may use in explaining real-world phenomena. Some of the explanations in EMF books do not tackle very complex phenomena. For example, Harford's (2006, chap. 1) explanation of why coffee is more expensive at coffee shops, which are located in or near metro stations, is rather simple. Yet, it provides the reader with a fresh view about differences in coffee prices by way of identifying location as one of the possible causes of differences in coffee prices in different places. Such explanations use explanatory factors suggested by economic models without introducing much complexity into the model because the explanatory task at hand does not require this. When one contrasts such explanatory tasks with explanatory tasks that macroeconomists are faced with, it is easy to understand why, one the one hand, EMF books provide a rather pleasant picture of economics, and why economics of crisis, poverty and unemployment presents an unpleasant image. Many of the macroeconomic issues to be explained are so complex that it is difficult to see how potential explanatory factors, which are suggested by abstract economic models, interact in producing the phenomenon at hand.

In fact, if we compare different explanations in EMF books we can see a similar tension. Even in EMF books, the amount of controversy concerning the explanation increases, as the explanatory task gets more complex. In fact, some of the explanations in EMF books rest on serious academic work which tries to explain quite complex phenomena. *Freakonomics*, for example, presents the findings of Steven Levitt's original research. Levitt is very careful in identifying the actual costs and benefits that individuals consider as relevant. Moreover, he very carefully explores the menu of available explanatory factors and cautiously eliminates them until he reaches at an explanation. For example, to explain the falling crime rates, Levitt and Dubner (2005, chap. 4) discuss almost all the potential explanatory factors at great lengths (see Donohue and Levitt 2001 for orginal research). After this lengthy analysis, they suggest abortion as 'one of the greatest crime-lowering factors in American history' (Levitt and Dubner 2005, p. 129). Even with such careful analysis, the explanation is not as easy to accept as it is to accept Harford's coffee price explanation. The reason simply is that crime rates are influenced by many factors most of which change during the time period that Levitt investigates. The explanatory task is very complex and this shows in the amount of controversy created by Donohue and Levitt's (2001) explanation of the falling crime rates (see e.g. Donohue and Levitt 2003; Hilsenrath 2005; Levitt 2005; *The Economist* 2005; Lott and Whitley 2007; Foote and Goetz 2008; Joyce 2009). In comparison, Levitt and Dubner's explanation of the incentives of cheating teachers and sumo wrestlers (Duggan and Levitt 2002; Jacob and Levitt 2003) is easier to accept, because the task at hand is limited to identifying the fact that teachers and sumo wrestlers cheat (data analysis) and exploring the possible causes of cheating.

The point is that as explanatory tasks get more complex, it becomes much more difficult to use the insights provided by abstract economic models in providing a satisfactory explanation. There is no contradiction between the two images of economics. It is just that EMF books usually deal with simpler tasks than contemporary macroeconomists. And as we have seen in the abortion and crime case, even EMF books may lose their fun image and provide a dismal picture.

It is important to note that even though EMF books usually deal with less complex explanatory tasks, they still run the risk of oversimplification and creating an illusion of understanding. The reason for this is that EMF books often hide the complexities of the task at hand to produce more readable and fun texts. The next section will examine the case of mandatory seat belt regulations to make this point. The examination of the EMF version of the seat belt case in comparison to the actual economic research that it is based on will also fortify the arguments I made up to this point.

Seat belt case as presented in EMF books and textbooks

As I have mentioned earlier, Steven Landsburg's *The Armchair Economist* (1993) starts with a chapter on the power of incentives. In the beginning of the chapter, he discusses the impact of mandatory seat belt regulations. His argument is as follows. The introduction of mandatory safety regulations changes the incentives of the drivers. Since seat belts reduce the risk of injury (reduced costs), and because rational drivers respond to incentives, they will drive less carefully or engage in more reckless driving. This result is based on a simple cost–benefit analysis. For example, if there are benefits to be gained from faster driving (e.g. reducing commute time), then drivers who wear seat belts will drive faster than those who do not wear seat belts. Incentives matter! Landsburg concludes that the result of the seat belt regulation will be more accidents. The question is whether more accidents mean more deaths? Landsburg argues that the total effect of auto safety regulations cannot be answered by pure logic because there are two opposing forces at work. While safety regulations reduce fatalities, less careful and more reckless drivers will increase the number of fatalities. One should look at the actual numbers to find out the net effect. To answer the question, Landsburg uses Samuel Peltzman's (1975) well-known (and controversial, as we will see in a moment) research. He concludes that the 'two effects were of approximately equal size and therefore cancelled each other out' (Landsburg 1993, p. 4). However, he argues, one could see the effect of the change in incentives by looking at the change in pedestrian deaths. If this number had increased, then there was more careless and reckless driving. In fact, Peltzman reports that the number had increased!

This is typical of EMF books. They give their readers interesting and surprising results based on real research. However, EMF authors sometimes forget to mention the details and difficulties of the actual research. Landsburg's discussion of mandatory seat belt regulations is a good example of this. Landsburg oversimplifies Peltzman's research and ignores the controversies around it. Moreover, he seems to underestimate the complexity of the subject and the explanatory task at hand. You may think that this kind of oversimplification is harmless because EMF books' target is layman. This is not true. Students of economics read these books. Moreover, EMF accounts of actual research could also be found in textbooks. For example, Mankiw's (2012) *Principles of Economics* introduces the incentives matter principle in a similar fashion with the seat belt example. Here is what Mankiw says:

> Consider how a seat belt law alters a driver's cost–benefit calculation. Seat belts make accidents less costly because they reduce the likelihood of injury or death. In other words, seat belts reduce the benefits of slow and careful driving. People respond to seat belts as they would to an improvement in road conditions – by driving faster and less carefully. The result of a seat belt law, therefore, is a larger number of accidents. The decline in safe driving has a clear, adverse impact on pedestrians, who are more likely to find themselves in an accident but (unlike the drivers) don't have the benefit of added protection. (2012, p. 7)

Similar lines of reasoning could be found in other books. For example, using Peterson, Hoffer, and Millner's (1995) results, Hirshleifer, Glazer, and Hirshleifer argue that:

> Airbags reduce, on average, the severity of auto injuries and the risk of death from motor accidents. But given that additional safety margin, it might well be rational for motorists to drive more aggressively! (2005, p. 10)[2]

Safer cars, reckless drivers?

Let us look at Peltzman's original research. First thing to note is that Peltzman's (1975) research on the effects of automobile safety regulation is 50 pages and includes a complex set of assumptions, models, data and approximations. It is very interesting but not fun to read at all! Peltzman's argument concerning the change in the incentives of drivers is based on a mathematical model. The model makes a set of assumptions. First, 'the effects on nondrivers are ignored'. Second, it is assumed that 'drivers receive no direct utility from either safety or risky driving' (1975, p. 721). Third, Peltzman assumes that drivers are wealth maximizers:

> Wealth is enhanced by devoting less time to driving a given mileage, and more to work. The cost of this increased speed, passing of other cars, taking of shortcuts, etc., is an increased probability of accident. (1975, p. 721)

Fourth, 'the effects of legal restraints and costs (traffic fines) on the driver's decision are ignored' (1975, p. 721).

Now remember Landsburg's presentation of Peltzman's findings. He fails to mention that all these assumptions are made. However, these assumptions are of crucial importance. If, for example, the effects on non-drivers are not ignored, then drivers would consider harming pedestrians as a part of the costs of reckless driving and therefore may not drive faster after the introduction of mandatory seat belt laws. In fact, if you think about it, many drivers would consider harming pedestrians or the passengers as a real risk. Thus, Landsburg's presentation may in fact be wrong in concluding that wearing seat belts makes one a less careful and faster driver. The second assumption suggests that drivers receive no direct utility from safer driving. This may not be true. Third and fourth assumptions suggest that drivers will make necessary calculations concerning their wealth while driving (i.e. they will calculate the probability of making an accident and benefits of faster driving), but they will ignore traffic fines and other legal results (including, prison) of reckless driving. This again is an unrealistic assumption. Many drivers would consider receiving a ticket or going into prison after causing fatalities or great damages as an important cost. The point is that the argument that seat belt regulations cause less careful and faster driving is not as straightforward as it seems in Landsburg's presentation.

Now let us look at results of Peltzman's empirical analysis of the aggregate impact of auto safety regulations. The aggregate effect on the number of deaths due to car accidents is ambiguous because seat belt regulations increase safety (i.e. reduce the number of deaths) and also cause careless and reckless driving (i.e. increase in the number of deaths). To find out the net effect of regulations, Peltzman analyses available data.

Peltzman's (1975) model for unregulated accident rates is as follows:

$R=f(P,Y,T,A,S,K,u)$

Here, R and P represent the accident rate (per mile) and costs (injury and property damage), respectively. Y is income, T is a linear trend, A is alcoholic intoxication and S is driving speed. K represents young drivers, and u represents random factors. According to this model, accident rate decreases as the costs of accidents increase, and increases as alcoholic intoxication, driving speed and number of young drivers increase. The effect of income is ambiguous (1975, p. 688).

As you may expect, finding appropriate data to test this model is not easy. Data concerning accident rates, costs, income and driving speed are less problematic, yet they require some adjustments. I would like to focus here on alcoholic intoxication and the number of young drivers, because they are crucial for our purposes of understanding whether seat belt regulations influence incentives in the way Landsburg and Makiw suggest.

A, alcoholic intoxication: Peltzman (1975, p. 691) uses the consumption of alcohol per person as an approximation of alcoholic intoxication. It is of course true that number of accidents may increase as the amount of alcohol consumption increases. However, it is doubtful whether one can induce that seat belt regulation causes more drunk driving if the alcohol consumption per person increases after the introduction of a mandatory auto safety regulation.

K, young drivers. Peltzman (1975, p. 692) measures the number of young drivers by the 'ratio of the 15–25-year-old population to those older'. This is of course an approximation. One may safely assume that as the number of 15–25-year olds increases in the population, the number of young drivers will increase. However, the question is the following: If the number of 15–25-year olds increases after the introduction of a mandatory safety regulation, could we conclude that the regulation caused an increase in the number of young drivers? Of course, not necessarily!

Now the tricky part! How does Peltzman measure the effect of the mandatory safety regulations? Here is how: Peltzman (1975, p. 688) 'presents estimates of the determinants of accident rates in the period before' regulation and 'uses these estimates to project, for the subsequent period, the rates that could have been expected without this regulation'. He then compares these 'expected rates with actual rates' to infer 'the effects of regulation'. He finds out that the accident rates are declining in the years before the regulation and assumes that if the regulation had not been introduced, the number of accidents would be decreasing in the same rate in the coming years. Then he looks at the actual numbers of accidents after the regulation and investigates whether the number of accidents fell more than they would in the absence of an auto safety regulation. In doing this he assumes that nothing other than the introduction of safety regulation has changed. In other words, all other factors are assumed to be constant before and after the regulation. Of course, this is a rather strong assumption to make.

As Landsburg mentions, Peltzman provides 'some evidence' (his exact phrasing) that the number of non-occupant deaths has increased after the regulation (Peltzman 1975, p. 699). The result is that even if safety regulations saved some lives, it saved drivers' lives, and the number of saved lives is lower than the number suggested by regulators. Peltzman concludes that:

> The safest inference from the time series, though, is that there has been a *shift in the burden of accident risk toward nonoccupants*, which is consistent with optimal driver response to an exogenous reduction of the expected loss from an accident. (1975, p. 700, emphasis added)

Nevertheless, none of this shows that seat belts or other safety regulations influence driver risk taking. This was an assumption of Peltzman's simple model. To see whether safety regulation in fact changed the behaviour of drivers, we have to answer the following questions. Did drivers increase their driving speed (more reckless driving) after the regulation? Did the introduction of the regulation increase the number of drunk drivers (less careful driving)? Did the increased safety of cars also increase the number of young drivers?

If you recall, Landsburg and Mankiw confidently argued that seat belt regulation would increase driving speed and cause less careful driving. However, they did not mention the amount of young drivers who are commonly assumed to be less careful drivers. Let us have a look at results of Peltzman's empirical analysis to see the answers to aforementioned questions.

Did drivers increase their driving speed? Peltzman argues that 'we must reject the hypothesis of a regulation-induced increase in vehicle speed' (1975, p. 703). Thus, there is no evidence that the drivers responded to the increased safety in their cars by increasing their driving speeds.

Did the introduction of the regulation increase the number of drunk drivers? Peltzman's data suggests that number of drunk drivers may have increased after the regulation. However, it is hard to conclude that this was caused by the auto safety regulation:

> Interpretation of these data as reflecting an increase in the demand for risky driving is, however, subject to an important qualification. The onset of safety regulation coincides with an increased spread of 'implied consent' laws, which make it easier for police to obtain evidence of driver intoxication. At the same time it is worth noting that annual growth of alcohol consumption has roughly doubled since 1965, so it risks exaggeration to attribute all of the reported increase in drunk driving to legal changes. (Peltzman 1975, p. 705)

This leaves us with one option. If the increased safety of cars has influenced some drivers, it may have influenced young drivers in that more parents may have thought that it is now safer to let their 15-year olds to drive. Thus, we should ask: *Did the increased safety of cars also increase the number of young drivers?* Peltzman argues that 'while driver participation (as measured by the ratio of drivers to nondrivers) among those over 25 increased at roughly the same rate in the two periods [i.e., before and after the regulation], participation among the young accelerated after 1965 [i.e., after the regulation]', and he concludes that 'this may help explain the substantially increased pedestrian risk' (1975, p. 704).

In summary, it is hard to argue that seat belt regulations caused drivers to drive faster or drunk. However, it could be that safety regulations may have increased the number of younger drivers – this also is doubtful. Thus, Peltzman's results are dramatically different than Landsburg and Mankiw's representations of them. Yet, we have only looked at Peltzman's time series analysis. More doubt can be cast upon the confident 'results' presented by Landsburg and Mankiw, if one looks at the cross-sectional data. Peltzman states that 'the time-series and cross-section data disagree on both the overall importance of alcoholism and its relative impact on pedestrians and drivers' (1975, p. 710). Moreover, he argues that 'the most glaring contradiction between the time-series and cross-section data' concerns findings about youth. 'There is virtually no evidence' in cross-sectional data regarding 'the substantial age differentials in the death rate that show up in crude data and the time-series regressions, nor is there much evidence of a differential impact on pedestrians' (1975, p. 710). Moreover, there is no evidence in cross-sectional data that there is a shift from occupant to pedestrian deaths (1975, p. 714). Peltzman concludes that we should approach cross-sectional data concerning age with scepticism (1975, p. 712). Of course, one may also conclude that there is enough reason to be sceptical concerning the whole set of results!

Peltzman concludes the paper in the following way: either 'safety regulation has decreased the risk of death from an accident by more than an unregulated market would have, but drivers have offset this by taking greater accident risk', or 'the only response of drivers to safety regulation has been to have more severe accidents, while continuing to have fewer accidents'. Either interpretation suggests that 'the results of this paper contrast sharply with the apparent intent of safety regulation' (1975, p. 717).

In summary, Peltzman's suggests that positive impact of the safety regulation is offset by the change in drivers' behaviour (*offsetting behaviour argument*). However, there is enough reason to be sceptical about Peltzman's whole analysis, given that his model is based on unrealistic assumptions concerning driver behaviour, and that the data do not consistently illustrate the required results with enough confidence. In fact, many of the further tests of Peltzman's results reject Peltzman's offsetting behaviour argument, at least there is enough evidence for being sceptical about this argument (see e.g. Robertson 1977a,b; Joskow 1981; Nelson 1981; Crandall and Graham 1984; Graham 1984; Christopher 1985; Lund and O'Neill 1986; Traynor 1993; Peterson et al. 1995; Dee 1998;

Roh, Bessler, and Gilbert 1999; Cohen and Einav 2003; Harless and Hoffer 2003; Cropper and Kopits 2005; Winston, Maheshri, and Mannering 2006; Eluru and Bhat 2007; Carpenter and Stehr 2008).

The seat belt case demonstrates that EMF books run the risk of oversimplification and for this reason may create a false sense of understanding. Landsburg neither discusses the complexities of Peltzman's research, nor mentions the controversy concerning the offsetting argument. We have seen that the evidence presented by Peltzman is not as convincing as Landsburg presents and that later research casts doubt on his thesis. This is not to argue that incentives do not matter. In fact, incentives matter. However, incentives change in response to many things. If increased car safety were the only change in drivers' lives (as assumed by Peltzman), then they could have responded by more reckless driving. However, probably many things have changed in their lives. For example, safety regulation and its advertisement probably made drivers more aware of the risks of careless and reckless driving. Most probably accepted norms concerning driving behaviour also changed. The increased number of cars, motorbikes, bicycles and pedestrians and thus the increased complexity of driving probably had considerable impact on accident rates and pedestrian deaths. Moreover, although Peltzman ignores the effects of changing traffic rules, speed limits, number of traffic signs, red lights, etc., all of these may have influenced the benefits and costs of reckless and careless driving. Not to mention all other changes in drivers' life (life styles, work hours, etc.). It is in fact not surprising that the simple incentives matter principle presented in a *ceteris paribus* clause does not provide us with a satisfactory explanation of the impact of auto safety regulations.

Why Peltzman's research is important and how to understand its contribution

All the above is not meant to degrade the importance of Peltzman's research. In fact, it is quite important. As suggested in the third section, abstract models in economics are important because they expand the menu of possible causes. Peltzman's model is no exception. It alerts researchers and policy makers to a potential way in which individuals may respond to regulations. If one wishes to understand the impact of regulations, one should better check whether there is any offsetting behaviour. In many cases, it may turn out to be non-explanatory. However, there is nothing in the above analysis that proved the non-existence of offsetting behaviour. It has been shown that there are good reasons to be sceptical concerning the explanatory power of offsetting behaviour for the particular case (the case of US auto safety regulation of 1965) that Peltzman investigates. In fact, there may be cases where the Peltzman's assumptions are closer to truth and where we may use offsetting behaviour as an explanatory factor.

For example, evidence from safety regulations in NASCAR racing shows that while the increased safety of cars reduce the risks of accidents in NASCAR, drivers offset this because they respond to the increased safety by increasing their driving speed or by taking more risks (Russell and Todd 2007; Sobel and Nesbit 2007; Pope and Tollison 2010). It is easy to see why Peltzman's model explains the impact of NASCAR safety regulations better than the impact of auto safety regulations in the USA. First, in the NASCAR case, all other things are almost constant, thus the *ceteris paribus* assumption is closer to truth. Moreover, NASCAR drivers, who are better informed about the costs and benefits of their driving style, have enough reasons to calculate the costs and benefits of faster and reckless driving. They are motivated by the race prize, and thus it is worth to take more risks if the cars are safer. The NASCAR example shows that Peltzman's model could in fact be explanatory.[3]

Note that the NASCAR case confronts us with the same apparent contradiction that the two image of economics present. How could Peltzman fail in explaining the impact of US safety regulations and at the same time explain the impact of safety regulations in NASCAR. As I have suggested earlier, the reason is that explaining the impact of safety regulations in NASCAR is a comparatively easier task than explaining the impact of US regulations, because the latter case requires one to take more explanatory factors into account. The contradiction is apparent as in the case of two images of economics presented by EMF books and after the crisis debates.

Peltzman's research is important also because it shows that better data and more research is required if we wish to understand the results of such regulations, and because Peltzman himself opens up the way for better data analysis by a detailed examination of the available data and exposition of the types of data that are required for this kind of analysis. In fact, the literature that has sprung from his research shows this (despite the fact that generally his results are not supported). Later research produced better models, more data and new methods of identification. All thanks to Peltzman's suggestion that offsetting behaviour may be yet another factor that may influence the aggregate impact of auto safety regulations.

Unfortunately, the type of oversimplification, exemplified by Landsburg's fun version of the seat belt case, creates a false sense of understanding. Moreover, it also prevents us from seeing the several ways in which economic models that are based on the incentives matter principle could provide us with a better understanding, and from seeing the several ways in which models and empirical analyses in economics may be useful despite the fact that they fail to explain the particular case in hand.

Concluding remarks

How can economists fail to answer their most pressing questions concerning economic crises, unemployment, poverty, etc., and also claim that they can explain many facts of our daily lives? The present paper argued and explained that this is possible, and that the contradiction between the two images of economics that emerged from the EMF books and the debates of the 2008 crisis is illusory. It argued that 'economists are generally wrong with complicated models but right about concepts', as Scott Adams suggests. Moreover, it also argued that EMF books sometimes present oversimplified accounts of actual economics research, and this not only creates a false sense of understanding, but also prevents their readers from understanding how economic models work and explain. In fact, the two images of economics seem contradictory when looked from the perspective of EMF books, not from the perspective of actual economic methodology. Explaining complex macro-social phenomena is one of the key challenges of economists and they use an army of models and empirical tools to overcome this challenge. Using the simple insights provided by EMF books for complex explanatory tasks is not as easy as it first seems.

The aim of this paper was to discuss the apparent contradiction presented by the two recent images of economics. The issues and arguments put forward in this paper may be useful also for discussing in other important topics. An obvious topic is the use of abstract economic models in anti-regulation arguments. Given that most EMF books have this anti-regulation flavour, the reader may be wondering why I did not discuss this subject. The reason simply is that using models for or against certain economic policy options is a subject that is too complex to be dealt with in a paper which aims at presenting a concise discussion of other issues. I hope to address this subject in my forthcoming work.

Acknowledgements

I thank Jack Vromen, John Davis and Wade Hands for their helpful comments and suggestions.

Notes

1. However, note that the precise meaning of the 'incentives matter' principle is not always clear in EMF books. See Vromen (this issue) for an extended discussion of the ambiguities involved in using and interpreting the incentives matter principle. Vromen also discusses the kind of incentives (monetary, moral, social, etc.) that economists seem to use in their explanations and the difficulties that stem from the fact that different kinds of incentives are rarely appropriately identified. For the purposes of the present paper, we may safely assume that for some given theoretical model, the 'incentives matter' principle is clear. In the context of the present paper, the problem of identifying incentives arise when one wishes to use economic models in order to explain real-world complex phenomena – as will be seen in my discussion of the seat belt example.
2. To be fair, Hirshleifer et al. (2005) is much more careful than Landsburg in presenting this argument.
3. The NASCAR case could be considered as a controlled field experiment where Peltzman's basic insights are tested.

References

Adams, S. (2008), 'What Good are Economists?', *Dilbert by Scott Adams*, 22 August. http://www.dilbert.com/blog/entry/what_good_are_economists/ (accessed January 2012).

Akerlof, G.A., and Shiller, R.J. (2009), *Animal Spirits: How Human Psychology Drives the Economy, and Why It Matters for Global Capitalism*, Princeton, NJ: Princeton University Press, pp. xiv, 230.

Aydinonat, N.E. (2007), 'Models, Conjectures and Exploration: An Analysis of Schelling's Checkerboard Model of Residential Segregation', *Journal of Economic Methodology*, 14(4), 429–454.

――― (2008), *The Invisible Hand in Economics: How Economists Explain Unintended Social Consequences*. (INEM Advances in Economic Methodology). London: Routledge.

Carpenter, C.S., and Stehr, M. (2008), 'The Effects of Mandatory Seatbelt Laws on Seatbelt Use, Motor Vehicle Fatalities, and Crash-Related Injuries Among Youths', *Journal of Health Economics*, 27(3), 642–662.

Cartwright, N. (2009), 'If No Capacities Then No Credible Worlds', *Erkenntnis*, 70(1), 45–58.

Christopher, G. (1985), 'A Note on Peltzman's Theory of Offsetting Consumer Behavior', *Economics Letters*, 19, 183–187.

Cohen, A., and Einav, L. (2003), 'The Effects of Mandatory Seat Belt Laws on Driving Behavior and Traffic Fatalities', *Review of Economics and Statistics*, 85(4), 828–843.

Colander, D., Föllmer, H., Haas, A., Michael, G., Katarina, J., Alan, K., Thomas, L., and Brigitte, S. (2009), 'The Financial Crisis and the Systemic Failure of Academic Economics', Kiel Working Paper 1489, Kiel Institue for the World Economy.

Cowen, T. (2007), *Discover Your Inner Economist: Use Incentives to Fall in Love, Survive Your Next Meeting, and Motivate Your Dentist*, New York: Dutton, pp. vi, 245.

Coyle, D. (2004), *Sex, Drugs, & Economics: An Unconventional Introduction to Economics*, Australia/New York: Thomson Texere, pp. xv, 263.

Crandall, R.W., and Graham, J.D. (1984), 'Automobile Safety Regulation and Offsetting Behavior: Some New Empirical Estimates', *The American Economic Review*, 74(2), 328–331.

Cropper, M., and Kopits, E. (2005), 'Why Have Traffic Fatalities Declined in Industrialized Countries ? Implications for Pedestrians and Vehicle Occupants', Implications for Pedestrians and Vehicle Occupants, World Bank Policy Research Working Paper 3678.

de Donato, X., and Zamora-Bonilla, J. (2009), 'Credibility, Idealisation, and Model Building: An Inferential Approach', *Erkenntnis*, 70(1), 101–118.

Dee, T.S. (1998), 'Reconsidering the Effects of Seat Belt Laws and Their Enforcement Status', *Accident Analysis and Prevention*, 30(1), 1–10.

DeLong, B. (2009), 'The Economist's Take on the Sate of Macroeconomics Once More'. http://delong.typepad.com/sdj/2009/07/the-economists-take-on-the-state-of-macroeconomics-once-more.html> (accessed 28 January 2012).

Donohue, J.J., and Levitt, S.D. (2001), 'The Impact of Legalized Abortion on Crime*', *Quarterly Journal of Economics*, 116(2), 379–420.

——— (2003), 'Further Evidence that Legalized Abortion Lowered Crime: A Reply to Joyce', National Bureau of Economic Research Working Paper Series 9532.

Duggan, M., and Levitt, S.D. (2002), 'Winning Isn't Everything: Corruption in Sumo Wrestling', *American Economic Review*, 92(5), 1594–1605.

The Economist (2005), 'Oops-Onomics: Did Steven Levitt, author of "Freakonomics", Get His Most Notorious Paper Wrong?', *The Economist*, 1 December. http://www.economist.com/node/5246700/ (accessed 22 January 2012).

——— (2009a), 'Financial Economics: Efficiency and Beyond', *The Economist*, 18 July, http://www.economist.com/node/14030296 (accessed 28 January 2012).

——— (2009b), 'The State of Economics: The Other-Worldly Philosophers', *The Economist*, 18 July, http://www.economist.com/node/14030288 (accessed 28 January 2012).

——— (2009c), 'What Went Wrong with Economics: And How the Discipline Should Change to Avoid the Mistakes of the Past', *The Economist*, 18 July. http://www.economist.com/node/14031376 (accessed 28 January 2012).

Eluru, N., and Bhat, C.R. (2007), 'A Joint Econometric Analysis of Seat Belt Use and Crash-Related Injury Severity', *Accident Analysis & Prevention*, 39(5), 1037–1049.

Foote, C.L., and Goetz, C.F. (2008), 'The Impact of Legalized Abortion on Crime: Comment', *The Quarterly Journal of Economics*, 123(1), 407–423.

Frank, R.H. (2007), *The Economic Naturalist: In Search of Explanations for Everyday Enigmas*, New York: Basic Books, pp. xiii, 226.

Friedman, D.D. (1996), *Hidden Order: The Economics of Everyday Life* (1st ed.), New York: HarperBusiness, pp. xi, 340.

Graham, J.D. (1984), 'Technology, Behavior, and Safety: An Empirical Study of Automobile Occupant-Protection Regulation', *Policy Sciences*, 17(2), 141–151.

Grüne-Yanoff, T. (2009), 'Learning from Minimal Models', *Erkenntnis*, 70(1), 81–99.

Harford, T. (2006), *The Undercover Economist: Exposing Why the Rich are Rich, the Poor are Poor – and Why You Can Never Buy a Decent Used Car!*, Oxford/New York: Oxford University Press, pp. x, 276.

——— (2008), *The Logic of Life: The Rational Economics of an Irrational World* (1st ed.), New York: Random House, pp. xiv, 255.

Harless, D.W., and Hoffer, G.E. (2003), 'Testing for Offsetting Behavior and Adverse Recruitment Among Drivers of Airbag-Equipped Vehicles', *Journal of Risk and Insurance*, 70(4), 629–650.

Hilsenrath, J.E. (2005), '"Freakonomics" Abortion Research is Faulted by a Pair of Economists', *The Wall Street Journal*, 28 November. http://online.wsj.com/public/article/SB113314261192407815-7O0CuSR0RArhWpc9pxaKd_paZU0_20051228.html (accessed 22 January 2008).

Hirshleifer, J., Glazer, A., and Hirshleifer, D. (2005), *Price Theory and Applications: Decisions, Markets, and Information*, Cambridge: Cambridge University Press.

Jacob, B.A., and Levitt, S.D. (2003), 'Rotten Apples: An Investigation of the Prevalence and Predictors of Teacher Cheating', *The Quarterly Journal of Economics*, 118(3), 843–877.

Joskow, P.L. (1981), 'Comments on Peltzman', *Journal of Law & Economics*, 24(3), 449–455.

Joyce, T. (2009), 'A Simple Test of Abortion and Crime', *Review of Economics and Statistics*, 91(1), 112–123.

Kay, J. (2004), *Everlasting Light Bulbs: How Economics Illuminates the World*, London: Erasmus Press.

Klein, G., and Bauman, Y. (2010), *The Cartoon Introduction to Economics* (1st ed.), New York: Hill and Wang, pp. v.

Knuuttila, T. (2009), 'Isolating Representations vs', *Credible Constructions. Erkenntnis*, 70(1), 59–80.

Krugman, P. (2009), 'How Did Economists Get It So Wrong?', http://www.nytimes.com/2009/09/06/magazine/06Economic-t.html (accessed 29 January).

Kuorikoski, J., and Lehtinen, A. (2009), 'Incredible Worlds, Credible Results', *Erkenntnis*, 70(1), 119–131.

Landsburg, S.E. (1993), *The Armchair Economist: Economics and Everyday Life*, New York: Free Press, pp. ix, 241.

––––––– (2007), *More Sex is Safer Sex: The Unconventional Wisdom of Economics*, New York: Free Press, pp. xii, 275.

Levitt, S.D. (2005), 'Abortion and Crime: Who Should You Believe?', http://www.freakonomics.com/2005/05/15/abortion-and-crime-who-should-you-believe/ (accessed 22 January 2008).

Levitt, S.D., and Dubner, S.J. (2005), *Freakonomics: A Rogue Economist Explores the Hidden Side of Everything* (1st ed.), New York: William Morrow, pp. xii, 242.

––––––– (2009), *Superfreakonomics: Global Cooling, Patriotic Prostitutes, and Why Suicide Bombers Should Buy Life Insurance* (1st ed.), New York: William Morrow, pp. xvii, 270.

Lott, J.R., and Whitley, J. (2007), 'Abortion and Crime: Unwanted Children and Out-of-Wedlock Births', *Economic Inquiry*, 45(2), 304–324.

Lund, A.K., and O'Neill, B. (1986), 'Perceived Risks and Driving Behavior', *Accident Analysis & Prevention*, 18(5), 367–370.

Mäki, U. (2009), 'MISSing the world', *Erkenntnis*, 70(1), 29–43.

Mankiw, N.G. (2009), 'The Arbiter of Ignorance', http://gregmankiw.blogspot.com/2009/06/arbiter-of-ignorance.html (accessed 28 January 2012).

––––––– (2012), *Principles of Economics* (6th ed.), Mason, OH: South-Western Cengage Learning.

Nelson, P. (1981), 'Comments on Peltzman', *Journal of Law & Economics*, 24(3), 457–459.

Peltzman, S. (1975), 'The Effects of Automobile Safety Regulation', *Journal of Political Economy*, 83(4), 677–725.

Peterson, S., Hoffer, G., and Millner, E. (1995), 'Are Drivers of Air-Bag-Equipped Cars More Aggressive? A Test of the Offsetting Behavior Hypothesis', *Journal of Law and Economics*, 38(2), 251–264.

Pope, A., and Tollison, R. (2010), '"Rubbin" is Racin': Evidence of the Peltzman Effect from NASCAR', *Public Choice*, 142(3), 507–513.

Robertson, L.S. (1977a), 'A Critical Analysis of Peltzman's "The Effects of Automobile Safety Regulation"', *Journal of Economic Issues (Association for Evolutionary Economics)*, 11(3), 587–588.

––––––– (1977b), 'Rejoinder to Peltzman', *Journal of Economic Issues*, 11(3), 679–683.

Roh, J., Bessler, D.A., and Gilbert, R.F. (1999), 'Traffic Fatalities, Peltzman's Model, and Directed Graphs', *Accident Analysis & Prevention*, 31(1–2), 55–61.

Russell, S.S., and Todd, M.N. (2007), 'Automobile Safety Regulation and the Incentive to Drive Recklessly: Evidence from NASCAR', *Southern Economic Journal*, 74(1), 71–84.

Schelling, T.C. (1978), *Micromotives and Macrobehavior*. (Fels lectures on Public Policy Analysis). (1st ed.), New York: Norton, pp. 252.

Smith, D. (2003), *Free Lunch: Easily Digestible Economics, Served on a Plate*, London: Profile Books, pp. 282.

Sobel, R.S., and Nesbit, T.M. (2007), 'Automobile Safety Regulation and the Incentive to Drive Recklessly: Evidence from NASCAR', *Southern Economic Journal*, 74(1), 71–84.

Sugden, R. (2009), 'Credible Worlds, Capacities and Mechanisms', *Erkenntnis*, 70(1), 3–27.

Traynor, T.L. (1993), 'The Peltzman Hypothesis Revisited: An Isolated Evaluation of Offsetting Driver Behavior', *Journal of Risk and Uncertainty*, 7(2), 237–247.

Vromen, J. (2009), 'The Booming Economics-Made-Fun Genre: More Than Having Fun, But Less Than Economics Imperialism', *Erasmus Journal for Philosophy and Economics*, 2(1), 70–99.

Wheelan, C.J. (2002), *Naked Economics: Undressing the Dismal Science* (1st ed.), New York: Norton, pp. xxii, 260.

Winston, C., Maheshri, V., and Mannering, F. (2006), 'An Exploration of the Offset Hypothesis Using Disaggregate Data: The Case of Airbags and Antilock Brakes', *Journal of Risk and Uncertainty*, 32(2), 83–99.

Ylikoski, P., and Aydinonat, N.E. (2011), 'Understanding with Theoretical Models', Paper presented at the 9th Conference of the International Network for Economic Methodology, 1–3 September 2011, Helsinki, Finland.

Inland empire: economics imperialism as an imperative of Chicago neoliberalism

Edward Nik-Khah[a,b] and Robert Van Horn[c]

[a]Center for the History of Political Economy, Duke University, Durham, NC, USA; [b]Department of Business and Economics, Roanoke College, Salem, VA, USA; [c]Department of Economics, University of Rhode Island, Kingston, RI, USA

Recent work such as Steven Levitt's *Freakonomics* has prompted economic methodologists to reevaluate the state of relations between economics and its neighboring disciplines. Although this emerging literature on 'economics imperialism' has its merits, the positions advanced within it have been remarkably divergent: some have argued that economics imperialism is a fiction; others that it is a fact attributable to the triumph of neoclassical economics; and yet others that the era of economics imperialism is over. We believe the confusion results in part from a lack of historical understanding about the nature and aims of economics imperialists. We seek to improve historical understanding by focusing on the activities of a cadre of economists at the epicenter of economics imperialism, the University of Chicago. These activities – led, in the first instance, by Aaron Director and, in the second, by George Stigler – stemmed from the effort to forge a new liberalism or a 'neoliberalism.' We then consider Steven Levitt's *Freakonomics* in light of the insights gained from our historical study. Our analysis leads us to question each of the three positions on economics imperialism held by economic methodologists.

1 Introduction

The topic of economics imperialism has recently caught fire within the field of economic methodology. One can point to several reasons for the emergence of a new discussion about economics imperialism: a rather triumphalist piece praising economics imperialism within the *Quarterly Journal of Economics* (Lazear 2000), the recent fascination of methodologists with new forms of disciplinary boundary crossing such as neuroeconomics and economic psychology, the establishment of Uskali Mäki's Trends and Tensions in Intellectual Integration [TINT] program and the fanfare surrounding new books by an economist claiming to have found the 'hidden side of everything' (Levitt and Dubner 2006, 2009).[1]

It is instructive lingering a bit on the reception of *Freakonomics* by methodologists, because it can provide perspective on the state of discussion concerning economics and its neighboring disciplines. To some methodologists, *Freakonomics* appeared as a bellwether for a new form of interdisciplinary economics. To others, it was unclear how

Freakonomics influenced the relationship between economics and contiguous disciplines. In the debate among methodologists about the significance of *Freakonomics*, Ben Fine and Dimitris Milonakis (2009, p. 9) launched the opening salvo. They argued that 'mainstream economics has readdressed the social, allowing it to appear more attractive to the other social sciences,' but warned that Levitt's *Freakonomics*, along with other recent developments, actually amounted to a new stage of economics imperialism, which, if not resisted, would result in economists lording over the other social sciences with methodological individualism, utility maximization, equilibrium and efficiency as their lodestars (p. 145). In objecting to Fine and Milonakis's characterization of Levitt (and other economists), Vromen (2009) argues that Levitt (along with other scholars he classifies as contributing to the 'economics-is-fun' genre) wants only to 'enlighten the general public about the hidden economic side of everyday phenomena' (p. 74) and to improve the public image of a discipline still viewed by many as the 'dismal science.' In addition to his speculation on the intent of Levitt and others, Vromen provides both a meditation on the terms 'invading,' 'conquering,' 'exploitation,' and 'appropriation,' and an observation on the state of present-day economics, which, without doing too much violence, might be summed up as: with the advent of 'neuroeconomics' (the field singled out by Vromen), 'economic psychology' and 'behavioral economics,' when 'concepts and insights developed in other social sciences have started to find their way into economics' (p. 96), don't discussions of economics imperialism seem a little passé? Modern day economics, according to Vromen, offers a language that facilitates communication between economics and other sciences: the beliefs that 'people respond to incentives' and that the 'cost-benefit principle' is useful in many different applications (p. 91) are flexible enough to accommodate and thereby to bring rival views about human behavior into conversation. Consequently, Vromen suggests abandoning the term 'economics imperialism.'

Contrasting Fine and Milonakis' understanding of the significance of *Freakonomics* with that of Vromen is instructive. Unlike Fine and Milonakis, Vromen has a problem with the common usage of the term 'economics imperialism' – even when applied by economists like Gary Becker. According to Vromen (p. 82), 'There is no clear evidence that [economics imperialism's] protagonists made sustained efforts to promote the spread of economic analyses into other social sciences'; Becker and other 'alleged economics imperialists' engaged only in gaining acceptance of the study of nontraditional topic *within* economics. For Vromen the resort to the language of economics imperialism serves mostly to distract attention from the significant problems that might beset these approaches.

Because Vromen is a well-respected authority on the interactions between the fields of biology and economics,[2] we are advised to take Vromen's observations on relations between the disciplines very seriously and heed Vromen's claim that the term 'economics imperialism' is misleading as well as unnecessary. But one inconvenient fact prevents us from retiring the term 'economics imperialism': economists have a long history of self-referentially using this term. Examples range from Gordon Tullock's decision to give his (1972) article (in which he calls for the 'invasion' and 'reorganization' of the other social sciences) the name 'Economic Imperialism' to Hirshleifer's (1985, p. 53) celebration of 'the imperialist expansion of economics into the traditional domains of sociology, political science, anthropology, law and social biology' to the participation of Tullock and Hirshleifer, along with Henry Manne and several others, in putting together *Economic Imperialism: The Economic Method Applied Outside the Field of Economics* (Radnitzky and Bernholz 1987). Moreover, George Stigler observed: 'So economics is an imperial science: it has been aggressive in addressing central problems in a considerable number of neighboring social disciplines and without any invitations' (1984, p. 311; see also Figure 1). Given these

Figure 1. Poster announcing George Stigler's lecture at Wabash College.[3]

numerous instances of economists using the term 'economics imperialism,' it is no surprise that Uskali Mäki (2009, p. 352) has observed '"imperialism" in the case of economics imperialism ... has been proudly adopted by the imperialists themselves with the purpose of celebrating it.'

So, who is right? Fine and Milonakis see economics imperialism as fact whereas Vromen sees it as fiction. While Vromen's argument for rejecting the term does at first appear persuasive, the fact remains that economists self-referentially use the term (and, as Mäki points out, do so *proudly*). While it is conceivable that these self-identified imperialists have not entirely thought through their usage (a position that is lent a bit of support by their use of 'economic imperialism' instead of 'economics imperialism' to describe their own work), or that they are showing a lack of respect for other disciplinary groups, it seems reasonable to explore whether there is something apart from sloppy thinking or a preference for the rigor of the 'economist's method' over, say, 'imprecision' (or, more neutrally, a reflexive preference for the familiar over and against the other) that motivates their calls for 'expeditionary forces,' 'invasion' and 'hegemony.' Put differently: what, precisely, has motivated so many well-respected economists to resort to bellicose language? Understanding this will help evaluate the appropriateness of the term 'economics imperialism,' thereby shedding light on the debate among methodologists over the existence and significance of economics imperialism.

While arriving at final judgments about economics imperialism also requires knowledge of the effects of the activities under question, it is important to note that methodologists have often referred to the presumed intentions of those undertaking these activities in supporting their judgments about them. There seems to be little agreement among methodologists about what motivated these economists. The range of portrayals by methodologists includes economists as seekers of 'virgin terrain,' prestige for the discipline, acceptance of unorthodox topics as acceptable areas of study by their colleagues, unification of method across the social sciences and enlightenment for the general public. We believe that the coexistence of such variegated accounts of imperialists' intentions stems from the fact that those assessing the motivations of economics imperialists exclusively rely on secondary sources and interviews and entirely ignore archival sources.

In pointing out the desirability of using historical evidence to better understand economics imperialism, we heed John Davis's (2012, pp. 209–212) call to 'apply history to philosophy.' Davis employs this method to advance an intermediate position between Vromen's and Fine and Milonakis's, leaving three distinct positions:

(1) Economics imperialism is a fiction. 'There is no clear evidence that [economics imperialism's] protagonists made sustained efforts to promote the spread of economic analyses into other social sciences'; Becker and other 'alleged economics imperialists' engaged only in gaining acceptance of the study of nontraditional topic *within* economics. (Vromen 2009, p. 82)

(2) Economics imperialism is a fact, at least since the advent of neoclassical economics. Neoclassical economics has always been naturally oriented by its 'historical logic' toward 'outward expansion'; *Freakonomics* is only the most recent stage in this century-long endeavor. (Fine and Milonakis 2009, pp. 6, 26)

(3) Economics imperialism is a fact, but it no longer predominates as a method of interacting with other disciplines. There have been 'many transformative effects that other disciplines have had on economics since the 1980s ... a whole new set of research programs within economics ... bear the imprint of these other disciplines.' (Davis 2012, p. 204)[4]

Davis supports Vromen's position that recent developments in economics have facilitated communication between economics and other disciplines, and denies Vromen's judgment that economists have never held imperial designs on other disciplines.[5] Moreover, Davis suggests that the interaction between economics and other disciplines in recent years should be described mainly as cross-fertilization, at least when considering the disciplines as a whole.

Our research complements Davis's work: whereas Davis heeds his own call for applying history to methodology by providing historical and methodological explications of recent developments in economics (e.g., behavioral economics, experimental economics, neuroeconomics), our paper uses archival sources to reconsider the intentions of a previous generation of scholars. As we will see, considering this earlier work has repercussions not only for whether one judges economics imperialism to be a fact or a fiction, but also for Davis's intermediate position.

Below we concentrate on the activities undertaken at the University of Chicago, the historical epicenter of economics imperialism. In Sections 2 and 3, we argue that understanding the intentions of Chicago imperialists must take into account that the imperialistic activities undertaken – led, in the first instance, by Aaron Director and, in the second, by George Stigler – stemmed from the effort to forge a new liberalism or a 'neoliberalism.'[6] In Section 4, we consider the 'Freakonomics' of Steven Levitt, in light of the insights developed from our historical study of Chicago imperialism. Our analysis leads us to question each of the three positions on economics imperialism held by economic methodologists.

2   The genesis of the Chicago imperial imperative

To appreciate the intentions of the Chicago imperialists, it is necessary to briefly consider the rise of Chicago neoliberalism, beginning with F.A. Hayek, a figure who is typically only tangentially associated with the rise of the postwar Chicago School. As the second author has argued elsewhere, Hayek not only laid essential institutional foundations for the development of the postwar Chicago School (Van Horn and Mirowski 2009), but he also influenced its initial intellectual trajectory in the late 1940s through his disciple Aaron Director (Van Horn in press). Understanding Hayek's influence on the rise of the Chicago School in the immediate post-WWII period and his relationship with Director at this time will allow us to comprehend how Director's work at Chicago from 1946 through the mid-1950s was at least in part motivated by his desire to countervail collectivism.

In 1945, Hayek went on a lecture tour in the United States to promote *The Road to Serfdom*.[7] After Hayek gave a lecture in Detroit, Loren Miller made arrangements for Harold Luhnow, the President of the well-endowed Volker Fund, to meet Hayek. An anti-New Deal conservative, Luhnow sought to support the rethinking of liberal politics in the United States. When they met, Luhnow asked Hayek to write a *Road to Serfdom* for an American audience and said that the Volker Fund would finance this endeavor. Hayek made a counteroffer: a study of the legal framework necessary for effective competition.

Hayek considered his counteroffer to be of the greatest importance. Hayek, who positioned himself as a passionate opponent of laissez-faire liberalism in *The Road to Serfdom*, championed the creation of an institutional framework, or what Hayek later called a 'competitive order,' so that effective competition would flourish. Hayek claimed that no one had ever conducted an in-depth study of the competitive order and attributed the failure of nineteenth century liberalism to the fact that liberals failed to go beyond the principle of laissez-faire liberalism and plan the legal foundations of competition. Hayek suggested that the task for the future would be to succeed where nineteenth century liberals failed: twentieth century liberals would need to thoroughly investigate and understand the competitive order.

Thus, when Hayek made his counteroffer to Luhnow, he hoped that the Volker Fund would provide the means to enable the building of a reinvigorated liberalism, that is, a 'neoliberalism.' Hayek and Luhnow reached the following agreement: a three-year, American-based study of the conditions necessary for an effective competitive system needed to be organized, and a product of this study, *The American Road to Serfdom*, would be used to influence American political opinion. Luhnow also agreed to Hayek's desire to outsource the study to a group of American economists.

When the efforts to organize the study got underway, Hayek eventually decided that the University of Chicago was the ideal location – this was partly due to the fact that Henry Simons, a friend and colleague of Hayek, would be able to help set up the project.[8] Besides Simons, Director – who was at this time working in Washington, DC – also helped organize the 'Hayek Project,' as Director and other principals involved in the study's organization called it.[9]

The fact that Director aided Hayek in organizing his project is not at all surprising. When Hayek came to the United States for his book tour, he had Director to thank for setting in motion the events that led to his popular *Road* tour and finding a publisher for *Road*. Moreover, Director helped publicize *Road* through his laudatory review in the *American Economic Review* (Director 1945). As his review makes clear, Director fully endorsed Hayek's vision in *Road*, including the need to study and promote the competitive order.[10]

Thanks to the persistent efforts of Hayek, the Hayek Project eventually came to fruition in the late summer of 1946.[11] Named after Director's outline, the Hayek Project became known as the 'Free Market Study' (FMS). In the spirit of *Road*, Director's outline listed a number of legal and policy areas to investigate in order to move toward a competitive order; these areas included antitrust law, corporate policy, tax policy and patent law.

Once the FMS got underway in the fall of 1946, its members – which included Milton Friedman (Economics Department) and Edward Levi (Law School) – convened regularly to debate on how to reconstitute liberalism and create a competitive order. The Study's members approached their task with a sense of urgency because of the perceived strength of collectivist forces.

For the second meeting of the FMS, Director wrote a proposal entitled: 'A Program of Factual Research into Questions Basic to the Formulation of a Liberal Economic Policy.' By empirically investigating the facts taken for granted by both liberals and collectivists, Director sought to develop a more robust liberal policy to counter collectivism and thereby reorient policy in the United States. Indeed, in a *New York Times* interview, Director indicated that one criterion for assessing the success of the FMS was its ability to exert political pressure to engender policy change.[12]

Director echoed his call for a reconstituted liberalism and a reconfigured policy approach in his 1947 Mont Pelerin Society (MPS) address.[13] Director delivered a talk on the topic '"Free" Enterprise or Competitive Order.' In the spirit of classical liberalism, his address broadly outlined the necessary steps to create a competitive order, including curtailing corporate power, preventing industrial monopoly, curbing labor power and mitigating income inequality. Director viewed these steps as essential to combat collectivist forces, especially pernicious collectivist ideas and policies. Notably, Director framed his plan for a competitive order as an attempt to reconstitute liberalism, which would then provide the crucial intellectual countervailing force to collectivism.[14]

When echoing the classical liberal tradition, Director gave voice to one of his teachers, Jacob Viner – a pillar of Chicago economics in the 1930s.[15] There were, however, crucial differences between Director and Viner. Viner did not view his academic work as compatible with political concerns.[16] He believed that academics should distance themselves from public debate and uphold the principle of academic objectivity. Viner refused to advocate a particular policy approach in public lectures or popular publications, to join intellectual movements that sought to advance long-run political objectives or to participate in organizations with a political agenda. Indeed, in 1947, Viner declined Hayek's invitation to join the MPS.[17] Therefore, when considering the imperialistic activities of Director below, it important to bear in mind that Director's organized efforts to reconstitute liberalism to countervail collectivism and thereby exert political pressure departed from the tradition of Chicago economics of the 1930s.

After the 1947 MPS meeting, the work of the FMS proceeded apace. The FMS undertook some empirical studies. One such study was Warren Nutter's evaluation of the extent of industrial monopoly in the United States (Nutter 1951). Nutter argued that there had been no significant increase in business monopoly since 1900. Director noted that Nutter's finding challenged the collectivist claim that efficiency of large-scale industry would inevitably give rise to more and more business monopoly, thereby resulting in less and less competition and necessitating socialist economic planning. Since collectivists hinged their argument on the premise that industrial monopoly had been significantly increasing and since, as Director pointed out, widespread belief in the inevitability thesis gave rise to collectivist policies (1951b, p. v), Nutter's investigation dealt a blow to collectivism.

Other developments of the FMS also sought to undermine collectivism. From 1950 to 1952, Director and other members of the FMS sharply departed from the classical liberal concern about the negative implications concentrations of business power.[18] In 1950, Director and Friedman maintained that industrial monopoly should no longer be seen as a relatively powerful, ubiquitous phenomenon in the United States, but rather as a relatively benign, un-pervasive force (Director 1950). As Director emphasized, the 'corrosive effects' of competition would always and eventually undermine industrial monopoly. In 1951, Director claimed that large corporations should no longer be considered a threat to competition because of their concentrated power, but should be considered another feature of a competitive market since corporations approximated the impersonal ideal of the market (Director 1951a). In short, the FMS came to maintain that concentrated markets tended to be efficient. Like Nutter's study, this conclusion countervailed the collectivist concern that the inevitable growth of industrial monopoly was overwhelming competitive forces and that therefore increased government control was necessary.

In sum, because of its determination to reconstitute liberalism to attack collectivism and because of its departure from the classical liberal opposition to concentrations of business power, the FMS served as an incubator for a new form of liberalism, 'Chicago neoliberalism.' In doing so, the work of the FMS set the stage for its sister project, the Antitrust Project, which began in 1952 as the FMS wound down. Director headed the Volker-funded Antitrust Project and Edward Levi (then Dean of the Chicago Law School) assisted with it. Other members included later luminaries of Chicago law and economics, such as Robert Bork and Ward Bowman. This Project, like the FMS, focused on the issue of industrial monopoly, but it also focused on select areas of antitrust law.[19]

Like the FMS, the Antitrust Project should also be viewed as an attempt to oppose collectivism. First, the Antitrust Project continued the mission of the FMS – that is, to create and advocate the competitive order. Second, during the time of the Antitrust Project, Director emphasized the importance of countering collectivism.[20] Third, the Chicago neoliberal conclusions of the FMS – particularly those concerning concentrations of business power – influenced the conclusions of the Antitrust Project.[21] For these three reasons, the Antitrust Project represented much more than simply the application of Chicago price theory to areas of antitrust law.

Once we acknowledge that the Antitrust Project sought to countervail collectivism, it is then possible to appreciate some of its imperialistic dimensions. Its members not only challenged the conventional wisdom of the legal profession, but they also organized conferences that exposed their views to noneconomists.

The Antitrust Project attacked the conventional wisdom of the legal profession in a number of ways – too many to summarize here and hence it is necessary to look at a sample. First, Bork claimed that vertical mergers did not enhance monopoly power. He therefore suggested that vertical mergers should always be legal. Consequently, Bork implied that one aspect of antitrust law precedent, requiring an investigation of the motives of a vertical merger in order to make a determination of its legality, was erroneous. Second, Ward Bowman maintained that the conventional legal wisdom – as represented by the *Report of the Attorney General's National Committee to Study the Antitrust Laws* (1954) – grossly exaggerated the effects of a tying arrangement.[22] The *Report* deemed the purpose of such arrangements to be monopolistic exploitation. In contrast, Bowman suggested that in most cases a tying contact was merely a means of effectively utilizing monopoly power that was already possessed, not a means of extending it.

Toward the end of the FMS and during the Antitrust Project, Director and Levi organized conferences. For example, in June 1953, they organized a ten-day, Volker-funded 'Antitrust Seminar' at which many of the Antitrust Project members presented. Those in attendance included law professors, partners of law firms and business leaders. Director and Levi also put together relatively smaller conferences. In 1951, Director, for example, presented the Chicago neoliberal position on corporations at 'The Conference on Corporation Law and Finance.' Like the 'Antitrust Seminar,' legal professionals, including lawyers from Chicago law firms, were in attendance.

Looking at these conferences in light of the rise of Chicago neoliberalism is instructive. During the early 1950s, Director viewed collectivism as a real and dangerous threat; like Hayek, he believed that pernicious government intervention would eventually lead to totalitarianism. Director saw arguments that portrayed the harmless actions of businesses as illegal to be deleterious because they supported government intervention that undermined the competitive order, leading to more collectivist policies. Consequently, the positions of the legal profession – be it the courts, government agencies or law professors – needed to be countervailed with scholarship that embodied a robust, reconstituted liberalism.[23]

It is also important to acknowledge that the Antitrust Project served to train and educate the next generation of Chicago neoliberals. Director, with the support of Levi and private funding, educated the first generation of Chicago neoliberal lawyers, including Ward Bowman and Robert Bork, who would be at the vanguard of the Chicago law and economics movement in the 1960s and 1970s. Not only did they publish in the spirit of Director's teaching, but since they acquired jobs in other law schools, they also obtained the financial resources that would have otherwise gone to a traditionally educated law professor. In the case of Bork and Bowman, they both found positions at the Yale Law

School. While at Yale, Bork and Bowmen played a crucial role in the Chicago law and economics movement in the 1960s and 1970s. Along with Richard Posner and other Chicago lawyer-economists, they helped Chicago law and economics become one of the dominant schools of jurisprudence in the 1980s.[24]

While the work of the Antitrust Project shares some superficial similarities to work on antitrust law completed at Chicago prior to 1946, there are key differences. First, the Antitrust Project was consciously organized. Before 1946, economists and law professors at Chicago had not undertaken the work on antitrust law as part of a project. Second, the Antitrust Project extensively trained noneconomists (as well as economists) in economic thinking and these noneconomists obtained positions in other law schools, where they conducted research in the spirit of the Antitrust Project. No such extensive training of noneconomists occurred prior to 1946 and, therefore, Chicago scholars exerted no direct influence on legal studies at other schools. Third, the desire to countervail collectivism provided a central motivating factor for the work on antitrust law at Chicago, leading to the publication of a number of journal articles, most of which were in law journals and many of which forcefully attacked the conventional wisdom of antitrust law. Prior to 1946 no such concentrated assault on the conventional wisdom of law by economists and law professors at Chicago occurred.

In light of the preceding history of the rise of Chicago neoliberalism in the 1950s, it is possible to appreciate a couple of heretofore-overlooked characteristics of Chicago imperialism. First, Chicago imperialists attempted to shape other disciplines – law in this case – as well as exert political pressures to influence policy. In doing so, Director substantially departed from the tradition of Chicago economics of the 1930s as represented by Viner. Second, it is inaccurate to solely understand the activities of the Antitrust Project in view of a single 'core' theory, such a Chicago price theory.[25] Director sought to counter the conventional legal wisdom when it supported the growth of collectivism. Third, the central rationale motivating imperialistic activities was not to improve the standing of the economics discipline, but to change attitudes of economists and noneconomists and ultimately influence state policy. Notably, it is only through an investigation of the archival record that this motivation comes into focus. Without examining the archival record, one could plausibly argue that Director simply applied price theory to the law to improve the standing of the economics discipline and that cross-fertilization without any intent of colonization occurred given Director's and Levi's collaboration.

3 Stigler and the governmental control over economic life

One might reasonably wonder whether an imperialistic relation with other disciplines was an attribute of Chicago neoliberalism, or just an approach specific to the single figure of Aaron Director and some of his acolytes. This section is designed in part to counter that suspicion by examining the approach of George Stigler. Although often regarded as a primary architect of the postwar Chicago School of Economics, Stigler also played a crucial institution building role at Chicago, a point argued by one of us elsewhere (Nik-Khah 2011a). Like Director, Stigler's work was in part motivated by a desire to counter collectivism.[26]

Upon his arrival at Chicago in 1958, Stigler was already viewed as a leading member of the Chicago School. He had been associated with the School through his friendships with Friedman, Allen Wallis and Director, and Chicago economists were quite familiar with his existing body of his work. Importantly, Stigler's stature at Chicago was bolstered by the Walgreen Foundation, which had been established by a grant from the drugstore magnate Charles Walgreen and was placed under Stigler's control by Wallis (now dean of Chicago's Graduate School of Business). Shortly thereafter, Stigler announced his intention to devote the Walgreen resources to a study of the "causes and effects of governmental control over economic life.'[27] He hired a full-time research assistant (Claire Friedland), established the famous Industrial Organization Workshop and funded research he deemed relevant to the study of governmental control. Stigler himself contributed studies of the regulation of electricity and securities and of the enforcement of antitrust laws (Stigler and Friedland 1962; Stigler 1964, 1966), and financed through Walgreen several others. Stigler motivated the 'governmental control' project by appealing to the need to counteract collectivism:

> ... the most fundamental issue posed by the increasing direction of economic life by the state [is] the preservation of the individual's liberty. ... If it can be shown that in important areas of economic life substantial and unnecessary invasions of personal freedom are already operative, the case for caution and restraint in invoking new political controls will acquire content and conviction. (1975, pp. 5–18)

Stigler used his Walgreen funds to recruit to Chicago a handful of leading economists (Gary Becker from Columbia University, Sam Peltzman from UCLA, Robert Lucas from Carnegie) and to finance short stays for other economists sympathetic to his efforts. Stigler's efforts set the tone at Chicago, not only through his published work, but also through his ability to shape the composition of the faculty and to finance their work on 'governmental control.'

By the early 1970s, Stigler had begun to envision a project that would engage in the 'close, objective study of the role of government in economic life.' In addition to the Walgreen Foundation, the key institution for developing and promulgating these studies would be the Center for the Study of the Economy and the State (CSES), which Stigler founded in 1977 with an initial roster that included Becker, Richard Posner, Peltzman, Peter Linneman and George Borjas (Stigler assumed the directorship). Since its founding the CSES has produced well over 200 papers.

One can find representative products of Stigler's project in the volume *Chicago Studies in Political Economy* (1988), which collected some of the most celebrated pieces from this self-described 'Chicago' approach to the study of politics. The scope is vast: topics range from the uses of primitive 'law' as an instrument for wealth maximization to an evaluation of the efficacy of mattress flammability standards, with digressions to consider such questions as the circumstances under which monarchy is more 'efficient' than democracy.

A handful of features of this volume are worth noting. First, the book was conceived as part of an imperialistic endeavor: 'The extension of economic analysis to include important areas of political phenomena is the subject matter of this book' (Stigler 1988, p. ix).[28] Second, this was a 'Chicago-style' book. Nearly every one of the contributors was employed at Chicago at the time of its publication, previously employed there, or trained there. And the contributions were united by a certain style: Stigler referred explicitly to these contributors as the 'Chicago students of regulation,' and distinguished their views from those of 'political scientists and economists at large' (pp. xv–xvi). The orientation of these studies was entirely consistent with the CSES mission, which calls for subjecting government institutions, policies and regulations affecting the private economy to a 'Chicago-style' analysis, defined by a 'deep appreciation of the role of private markets in improving human welfare' (Stigler Center 2009).

Yet, this was more specifically a 'Stiglerian' volume[29]: the research produced by Stigler's 'governmental control' project deviated from that of the previous generation of Chicago scholars. As Stigler noted elsewhere (1983, p. 529), providing economic explanations of politics marked a profound break with the approach of his teacher Frank Knight, who was deeply skeptical of discovering the principles governing political life. Not only did Stigler call for the exploration of a new subject matter, he also called for new methods to do so: 'it is reasonably certain that new theories and new methods will be required to unravel some of the major problems we have encountered [in understanding public regulation]' (1988, p. xvii). And as noted above, whereas Viner refused to participate in political discussions, Stigler's research was produced to counter collectivism. While published contributions are a bit short in programmatic statements, one can find such statements in unpublished documents. In a 1971 memo, Stigler laid out his rationale for researching governmental control:

> It would be absurd to say that this area is neglected, but most of the writings are either purely descriptive or highly propagandistic.... We legislate and administer primarily with the guidance of hope and blithely write off past failures and perversions of public control as the product of inferior men or inadequate resources. Yet it is probably true, to give just one example, that the democratic political process simply cannot cope with decisions which must be made quickly. Unless we can determine the capacities of the political process, political 'reforms' must often be futile or positively harmful.[30]

According to Stigler, the problem with existing studies of the government was that their lack of objectivity lent those studies an unrealistic view of the capacities of democracy, and thereby produced poor legislative and administrative decision-making. Stigler was especially contemptuous of the idea that problems in regulation stemmed from underfunding or corruption. He viewed these positions as motivated by the belief that regulation was sought for the public interest, whereas Stigler was intent on persuading that such problems were *endemic* to regulation. Stigler proposed 'close, objective' studies to replace these 'descriptive' and 'propagandistic' studies.

And who were the authors of these descriptive and propagandistic studies?

> 'Let us be candid: economists are beginning to apply their logic and analytical apparatus to the political process, and with luck will conquer much of political science!'; 'It is essentially and exclusively a scientific work, and is intended to work its effects upon the appropriate disciplines (economics and political science) than directly on public opinion. The work will often shatter the fond hopes of the scholarly professions.'

Stigler believed that political scientists, along with economists, were the main culprits. Stigler's project carried a rationale for imperialism similar to that of Director's project: Stigler believed that the theories of political scientists and economists needed to be countervailed with a reconstituted liberalism, and that one needed to advance on other disciplines to do so.

Viewing the project on governmental control as concerned primarily with countervailing collectivism helps one to appreciate the extent to which the different elements of the governmental control project cohered. Stigler's Research Institute memo called for two types of studies to impact political science and economics: '(1) Studies of the effects of past economic policies – to reduce unemployment, to stabilize prices, to control public utilities, to protect consumers and investors, etc. and (2) studies to develop and test hypotheses on the nature of the political process as it works in the economic scene.' Although only the second type of studies corresponds to the sort one often has in mind when thinking of economics imperialism – the development and application of an economic logic to address phenomena outside the traditional domain of economics – Stigler regarded the first set of studies as a crucial element of the same project. In a paper written at almost precisely the same time he was creating the CSES, Stigler clarified the relationship between the two:

> Until we understand why our society adopts its policies, we will be poorly equipped to give useful advice on how to change these policies.... Of course we shall not, and need not,

abandon all policy advising until we have unraveled all the mysteries of the political-regulatory process. The very measure of costs and benefits of a policy will influence opinion and policy. (1975, p. xi)

The nature of the 'influence' Stigler sought here differed from that resulting from employing economic theories of political institutions. Stigler's early studies tended to argue that regulation had no effect on economic performance. But he dispensed with this position, and instead encouraged the development of techniques for auditing and guiding, and thereby controlling, administrative bodies:

> An efficient enforcement system, therefore, requires intelligent guides to the regulators, telling them which things are good and also important, which good but unimportant, and which positively harmful. In too many cases, the system of values, or incentives, is now badly skewed. (Stigler 1973, pp. 13–14)

> The appraisal of the achievements of a regulatory body is not impossible: a whole series of such appraisals is gradually developing an arsenal of techniques for measurement. I may cite ... a large number of economic studies, many of which have appeared in the *Journal of Law and Economics*. It would at least be a minor improvement of our world if once a decade each major regulator was reviewed by a committee appointed by the appropriate scientific body, with funds and subpoena powers provided by the OMB. (p. 16)

Naturally, the *Chicago Studies* volume included a large helping of work in the *Journal of Law and Economics*. The most important upshot of this and related work was not in providing a specific set of results about the effectiveness of regulation, but in developing techniques of redirecting state policy. Regulation would no longer be portrayed as inevitably bad or inefficacious, but *improvable*.

To understand how this improvement would take place, it is helpful to peruse Stigler's favorite example, Sam Peltzman's critical examination of the FDA (Peltzman 1973).[31] His primary complaint about the FDA was that while it was supposed to have reduced the costs of producing information about drugs (by substituting FDA sanctioned information for drug company advertisements and doctors' experience with medicines), it had actually decreased the value of information available to consumers: FDA restrictions on pharmaceutical companies' claims would decrease the amount of information on non-sanctioned uses of drugs, while any reduction in marketing for a drug of a particular brand would reduce information about the drug type in general. Peltzman then connected the decrease in information to social welfare by attributing a decline in the demand for new drugs to the decrease in information, and therefore a decrease in the consumer surplus associated with consuming drugs. In this study the intended target was *clinical science*. Peltzman never actually engaged clinical science (a fact that was not lost on those clinical scientists who read Peltzman's piece); instead, Peltzman attempted to undermine the entire enterprise of using clinical science to guide regulation, and thereby to displace one set of goals (efficacy) with another set (consumer surplus, or in other cases, 'innovation') (Nik-Khah 2012). This tactic of introducing auditing techniques to displace the set of goals introduced by scientific studies was employed in addressing topics ranging from drug efficacy to mattress flammability to environmental harm.

Stigler's approach to regulation was a relatively straightforward consequence of his beliefs about how the public formed its views about markets. Like Director, Stigler believed that most people held incorrect views about markets and the government. Stigler believed that these anti-market views reflected a widespread instinctual revulsion to markets that was immune to reasoned reflection: 'I cannot believe that any amount of economic training would wholly eliminate the instinctive dislike for a system of organizing economic life through the search for profits' (1963, p. 95); 'the best econ[omics] in the US is not the one the public would elect.'[32] When it came to evaluating markets, Stigler saw little difference between academicians and the laity: he believed the instincts of political scientists, clinical scientists and (most) economists would lead them astray as well. Therefore, Stigler concluded, it was necessary to displace or somehow marginalize these rival academic views.

The history of Stigler's imperialistic program amplifies a number of points raised by the analysis of Director's project. First, as with Director's project, Stigler sought to influence the policy approach of the state by shaping other disciplines and displacing rival views. Second, Stigler's program to study 'governmental control' constituted a new and distinct approach, rather than mere application of a core Chicago approach to a new domain. It relied on conceptualizing politics and information as subject to the market, in direct contradiction to the views held by his teacher Frank Knight. Third, Stigler did not primarily intend to improve the status of economics in the public eye. He did not hold out a great deal of hope that economics would convince the public to change its mind about anything; nor did Stigler seek to improve knowledge about government, law and other noneconomic spheres of social life because they had become progressively more enmeshed with economic life, and therefore as a means to better understand the economic system.[33] Instead, Stigler sought to 'shatter the fond hopes' of scholars holding public interest theories of regulation, and to insulate regulatory bodies from the views of those he could not convince. Crucially, Stigler's motives for calling for an economics of politics and performance audits of government regulation would remain unapparent without considering archival evidence. Without examining the archival record, one could easily mistake Stigler's call for 'new theories and methods' in studying politics for a wish to benefit from open communication with political science and other disciplines.

4 Revisiting *Freakonomics*

One of the lessons driven home by study of the previous two cases is that it is necessary to look beyond the published word to come to an understanding of the motives of those at the Chicago School. Failing to consider a larger archive of information has resulted in misunderstanding about aims of Chicago imperialists. In turning our attention to Levitt, we would now like to argue that extant accounts on his work similarly misunderstand Levitt's project. Whereas Fine and Milonakis understand Levitt to be part of a sweeping, century-long project in economics, Vromen portrays Levitt as part of a novel 'economics-is-fun' genre. We believe a more promising route to understanding Levitt would be neither to locate him within a broad, sweeping century-long narrative about neoclassical economics, nor in a historically unprecedented genre, but instead within a specific part the postwar Chicago School.

We are not the first to portray Levitt as part of a new generation of Chicago School. Historians of the Chicago School often view Levitt as a crafter of a new generation of 'Chicago Price Theory': Ross Emmett (2008) identifies Levitt as part of the 'next generation of Chicago economists' and Steve Medema (2007, p. vii) portrays Levitt a part of the 'Chicago price theory tradition ... which includes besides Knight, Viner, and Friedman, ... Henry Simons, Aaron Director, George Stigler, Gary Becker, Ronald Coase, Richard Posner, [and] Kevin Murphy.' The same can be said of Van Overtveldt's journalistic account of the Chicago School, which states (2007, p. 148) that Levitt is 'working in the Beckerian tradition of economics.' Additionally, there are better reasons for viewing Levitt as a member of the Chicago School.

Levitt received his undergraduate training in economics at Harvard. After a stint as a management consultant at Corporate Decisions, Inc., he enrolled as an economics PhD student at MIT, eventually completing a PhD dissertation on political campaigns under James Poterba. Upon graduation he accepted an assistant professorship at the University of Chicago, a decision that provoked a profound intellectual transformation:

> Having learned my economics at Harvard and M.I.T., I took my first teaching job at Chicago with the very explicit idea that I would spend two or three years in Chicago to get to 'know the enemy.' After I figured out how they thought, I would escape back to more comfortable surroundings.

> Well two things happened that I didn't expect. First, it turned out that it wasn't so easy to learn to think like a Chicago economist. I've been trying to learn for more than a decade and I still have learned only the rudiments. Every day my colleagues teach me something I should know, but don't. Second, I decided that the Chicago approach to economics was the right one for me, even though I am not that good at it.[34]

Not only does Levitt distinguish Chicago from other approaches to economics, but he also identifies himself as an eager student of the Chicago tradition. Among the various colleagues at Chicago that Levitt credits for teaching him the Chicago approach, Becker stands out. Levitt views Becker as having had the greatest intellectual influence on him: calling Becker his 'role model' (Levitt and Dubner 2006, p. 206); finding Becker's articles to be 'controversial, unpopular, and almost certainly correct'; and extolling Becker: 'Becker is not only the Michael Jordan of economics, he is the Gordy Howe of economics as well.'[35] Levitt speaks of no one else with the reverence with which he discusses Becker: 'I look forward to the next ten years of learning at Gary Becker's knee.'[36] Therefore, Levitt not only considers himself to be working within the tradition of Chicago Price Theory, but he also associates himself with a specific version of that tradition.

Levitt's unabashed praise for Becker might be mistaken for mere empty flattery of a powerful colleague were it not for the fact that he has served as director of the Becker Center for Chicago Price Theory (the establishment of which historians of the Chicago School regard as marking the rejuvenation of Chicago Price Theory – see: Medema 2007; Hammond 2010). Since its June 2011 merger with the Milton Friedman Institute to form the Becker Friedman Institute, Levitt has continued to lead the initiative on Chicago Price Theory.[37] Levitt's directorship and leadership is significant because it links him to Chicago Price Theory in general, and to Becker's legacy for Chicago in particular:

> This Chicago-style approach, often known as 'Price Theory' because of the fundamental role that prices often play, has shed light not only on the most fundamental topics of traditional economics (e.g., consumption, saving, taxation, regulation), but also pioneered the use of economic tools in studying a wide range of other human behavior (e.g., crime and corruption, discrimination, marriage).[38]

The fact that Coase, Friedman (before his death) and George Shultz were members of the Becker Center's board of directors, and that Becker (along with Kevin Murphy) handed Levitt authority over an institution that 'builds upon the rich traditions of Chicago Price Theory,' strongly suggests that the previous generation of Chicago scholars have viewed Levitt as an advocate of Chicago Price Theory. Levitt's leadership involves a significant commitment to advancing Chicago Price Theory and utilizing the established institutional structures of his intellectual forbearers to do so: he administers conferences, professional fellowships, postdoctoral research fellowships, graduate scholarships, regular faculty positions, visiting positions, a 'summer camp' for price theory and brown bag workshops.

Particularly interesting is the Price Theory Scholars program, which aims at providing PhD students in their third or fourth year of study at other institutions the Chicago Price Theory perspective, and encourages them to share this perspective with their home institutions.[39]

Once we acknowledge that Levitt seeks to advance Chicago Price Theory, it is worthwhile to consider whether Levitt gives voice to Chicago ideology. One certainly does find Levitt pronouncing correctly some of Chicago's ideological *shibboleths*:

> 'If the recession lingers, as Chicago economists we'd have to start blaming the government for that'[40]; 'If there is demand for people who either want financial risk surrounding an event or want to hedge risk, why should the government get in the way?'[41]; 'The idea that tenure protects scholars who are doing politically unpopular work strikes me as ludicrous.... Tenure does an outstanding job of protecting scholars who do *no* work or *terrible* work, but is there anything in economics which is high quality but so controversial it would lead to a scholar being fired? Anyway, that is what markets are for. If one institution fires an academic primarily because they don't like his or her politics or approach, there will be other schools happy to make the hire.'[42]

Additionally, there are examples of Levitt explicitly embracing Becker's ideology. When discussing the US health care bill passed in 2010, Levitt deferred to Becker: 'For people who are interested in my views on health care ... my suggestion is to read Gary Becker's excellent post on the subject. His conclusions are remarkably similar to my own.'[43] He then amplified: 'Markets cannot function when the people who receive the benefits of a good or service are not the ones who are paying for it.'

Of course, one might object that examples selected from the blogosphere do not provide evidence of Levitt's esteem for Chicago Price Theory where it counts, in his published work. But one does find traces of it in *Freakonomics*, where Levitt's defining economics as 'primarily a set of tools, as opposed to a subject matter' (Levitt and Dubner 2006, p. 12) seems calculated to recall Becker's *Economic Approach to Human Behavior*. Moreover, his coauthor Stephen Dubner has called Levitt's work on real-estate agents a 'Chicago style paper ... a romp in price theory' (p. 208). By his second book, Levitt had taken to declaring (Levitt and Dubner 2009, p. 13), 'what Becker was doing was actually Freakonomics – marrying the economic approach to a rogue, freakish curiosity – but the word hadn't yet been invented.' By identifying his own work as applying 'the economic approach,' and crediting this approach to Becker, Levitt intended to place himself firmly within the Beckerian tradition.

Levitt revealingly interprets this Beckerian tradition. For example, in his second book, Levitt introduces Gary Becker's work on altruism, which Levitt describes as emphasizing the strategic element behind apparently altruistic behavior. Levitt then proceeds to acquaint the reader with (laboratory) experimental results (dictator and ultimatum games) that appeared to establish that altruism is a real phenomenon. Here Levitt's narrative gets going: Levitt draws on the work of the 'hated' experimental economist John List, who devotes himself to counteracting the work of other experimental economists by demonstrating that laboratory altruism was nothing but an artifact of experiment effects. Levitt, by singling out List's work in discussing altruism, reveals his views about the usefulness of other disciplines. While Levitt does mention the work of psychologists, sociologists and anthropologists in his discussion of altruism, it is only in the narrow context of their work on dictator and ultimatum games, and, crucially, *only as a prelude to showing their work was wrong*. Far from employing an expansive definition of incentives, Levitt wants to hew to a Beckerian definition, and is willing to throw out psychology, sociology and anthropology (and, arguably, experimental economics and behavioral economics) to do so.[44] More generally, this illustration suggests that Levitt's program in Chicago Price Theory promotes interactions between economics and other disciplines of the type likely to minimize the contributions of other disciplines.[45]

Our argument that one should view Levitt as operating with a Chicago tradition does not entail that one must deny that *something* has changed. To grasp the features specific to Levitt's program, consider the ideas that Levitt singles out as constituting his *Freakonomics* approach (Levitt and Dubner 2006, pp. 11–12):

- incentives are the cornerstone of modern life;
- experts – from criminologists to real-estate agents – use their informational advantage to serve their own agenda;
- the conventional wisdom is often wrong;
- dramatic events often have distant, even subtle, causes; and
- knowing what to measure and how to measure it makes a complicated world much less so.

At least two things are funny about this list. For example, while 'knowing what to measure' is important, Levitt never got around to presenting the reader with a well-developed general theory about how to arrive at this knowledge. Furthermore, while 'distant and subtle causes' might very well be important, the book never shared with the reader a general approach to sorting out the apparent from the real causes. The intended lesson would seem to be that the only way to find the 'hidden side of everything' is to find a clever expert.

Examining the activities of another important institution controlled by Levitt, 'The Greatest Good,' offers a valuable perspective on what Levitt believes a handful of clever experts finding the 'hidden side of everything' can accomplish.[46] The Greatest Good is not a research institute like the Becker Center, but a consulting firm. It boasts of 'the ability not just to analyze data but to do so differently and imaginatively – to look at data in ways others would not,' an ability employed in conducting 'hundreds of field experiments including dozens for corporate and philanthropic clients, covering aspects as varied as pricing, marketing, hiring, incentives, health care and wellness.' Levitt's profile reports that he has 'turned his attention to helping complex organizations make better decisions by better understanding and analyzing their data. [He] has advised Fortune 500 companies, non-profits, and international intelligence services tracking terrorists.' A 'Creative brief' on the Freakonomics Consulting Group (the former operating name of Greatest Good) demonstrates the strong connection between the activities of this firm and Levitt's own work:

> Dr. Levitt is creating a business-consulting company based on the same principles he uses for all his academic research.... Dr. Levitt and his team of economists will use data-driven analysis to show large companies how to make better decisions.... As a company, Freakonomics Consulting Group is small, smart, and iconoclastic. We're driven by the same principles that are laid out in the book, including: The conventional wisdom is frequently wrong; Dramatic effects often have distant, even subtle causes; Complicated problems can often be solved by simple solutions, as long as the right kind of thinking is applied.[47]

Significantly, this passage reveals how the ideas identified by Levitt as central to *Freakonomics* have naturally lent themselves to commercialization. One important element of Levitt's worldview is that difficult problems are susceptible to 'cheap and simple' fixes, a view revealed in his much-derided advocacy of a geoengineering solution for global warming (Levitt and Dubner 2009, pp. 177–203). The role of the expert is to offer these fixes at bargain rates.

While denying that economics has a natural and proper scope places Levitt within a tradition extending back through Becker to Stigler and Director (as does his avowal of the importance of the economists in constructing the conditions for markets to succeed), his stress on 'tools' suggests not merely a set of techniques, but also an expertise that can potentially be sold. Levitt's interest in building 'tools' in both senses of the term provides perspective on why when asked what important problems he wanted to work on, Levitt replied: 'Tax evasion. Money-laundering. I'd like to put together a set of tools that lets us catch terrorists' (Levitt and Dubner 2006, p. 210). In sum, Levitt's definition of economics as 'primarily a set of tools, as opposed to a subject matter' represents a perfect marriage between (Beckerian) Chicago Price Theory and commercialized science.

This union between Chicago Price Theory and commercialized science inevitably changes the public role for economists. Since it is important to the Greater Good business model that it provide its clients 'access to cutting-edge methods and techniques that are not yet in general application,' economic expertise must be held by the consultant alone, a fact which possibly explains why Levitt's themes remain undeveloped within *Freakonomics*.[48] Levitt's discussion of how he caught teachers cheating in the Chicago public school system provides the best example of such lack of development: *Freakonomics* (pp. 23–25) informs its reader that data from one of two classrooms indicates that one of the two teachers was cheating, confronts the reader with a dizzying array of numbers and letters, and then invites the reader to figure out which one was the cheater. Levitt then shares his solution to the problem: an algorithm (a 'tool') to catch teachers who had doctored the exam forms to improve their students' scores. Although Levitt does walk the reader through some of the reasoning he used to devise his algorithm, it never approaches a general theory about the role of incentives in education; instead, he embeds this story within a discussion of high-stakes testing, which serves as an example of how incentive design could go badly wrong.[49] The public role of the freakonomist is neither to enlighten the public by clarifying important issues, nor to improve the stature of economics, but instead to convince the public that it is unnecessary for humanity to make hard and painful choices because entrepreneurial experts are on the job.[50]

Moreover, not just *anyone* could be trusted to apply the economic approach, only one with the 'ability not just to analyze data but to do so differently and imaginatively – look at data in ways others would not.' Greatest Good's roster reveals who Levitt believed possessed this special ability. Many of Greatest Good's partners and affiliates hailed from Chicago Law and the Chicago Graduate School of Business; some were featured in *Freakonomics* and *Superfreakonomics*, like John List and Nathan Myhrvold (the advocate for a geoengineering 'global cooling' technology). Significantly, Greatest Good has listed as a founding partner the pioneer of the 'economic approach' himself: Gary Becker. Becker's partnership with Levitt lends further support to the proposition that Levitt's project represents a new stage in Chicago imperialism.

It is here, where expertise meets markets, that one can spot an important yet unappreciated tension in this new stage of Chicago imperialism. If one considers experts primarily as participants in the marketplace then one should expect experts to serve their own agendas; but how then should we view the claims of Levitt and his band of rogue freakonomists? Levitt's attempt to address the obvious antinomy – 'We tried to disabuse audiences of the notion that we are actually experts in anything' (Levitt and Dubner 2009, p. xvi) – might seem a bit disingenuous when read alongside the claims advanced on the Greatest Good website, but does hint at a presumption implicit to Levitt's project. For Levitt, the reason you should trust his freakonomists is because *the market has deemed them trustworthy*. Because people are willing to pay for his expertise (Levitt's work with

Chicago schools, intelligence services, even *Freakonomics* itself), the market has ratified Levitt's project ('that is what markets are for'). But if the market is so trustworthy, then the claim to be able to possess a unique form of access that would allow one to improve or enhance its working seems problematic; and if markets necessitate improving or enhancing by experts, then why should one trust them to judge the merit of experts? In short, Levitt urges us simultaneously to trust the judgment of markets and trust (some) economists to ameliorate troublesome markets, and these positions are in tension.[51] To the extent that one considers Levitt's project as representative of a new stage in Chicago imperialism, one reason to take interest in Levitt's work is that it allows us to view how a tension inherent to the project plays out.

5 Conclusion

While previous accounts of Chicago imperialism refer to the presumed intentions of imperialists, they misunderstand the intentions of these figures, and therefore the nature of Chicago imperialism. In particular, we have seen that Chicago imperialists did not develop their approaches merely for the purpose of improving the standing of the economics discipline or to find interesting new topics. They sought to respond to what they regarded as pernicious ideas in other disciplines and to change the policy approach of the state. To do so, Director and Stigler constructed a variety of approaches that diverged in important ways from the approaches of the two pillars of Chicago economics in the 1930s, Frank Knight and Jacob Viner. While we have focused only on the activities of Chicago imperialists, we can draw more general lessons for all the three positions on economics imperialism.

Our argument leads us to disagree with Position 1, that economics imperialism is a fiction: Director and Stigler (and arguably other economists as well) undertook sustained efforts to colonize law, political science and possibly other disciplines, *and said so*. Because there exists evidence that economists did seek to colonize other disciplines, arguments for rejecting using the term 'economics imperialism' on this basis are flawed.

It also leads us to raise serious questions about Position 2, that economics imperialism was part of the natural orientation of neoclassical economics, at least with respect to Chicago neoclassicals. At Chicago, imperialism was born of the belief that the classical liberalism of the previous generation of Chicago scholars was not up to the task of counteracting pernicious ideas in other disciplines. This previous generation tended to be skeptical of applying economic methods to noneconomic topics and of attempts to shape public policy. If economics imperialism was part of the natural orientation of neoclassical economics, one must explain why it took so long for this natural orientation to reveal itself, at least in the Chicago case.

Our research also raises questions about Position 3, because transformation of economics in response to encounters with other disciplines does not necessarily entail mutually beneficial communication between disciplines. Whereas one might argue that the revisions in Chicago price theory undertaken by Chicago imperialists provide evidence of successful communication between disciplines, a fuller accounting of all evidence, including the archival record, leads us to conclude that Chicago imperialism sought to displace the methods indigenous to target disciplines.

The activities of Chicago imperialists reveal the benefits of developing a comprehensive understanding of economics imperialism, along the lines of that offered by Uskali Mäki (Mäki 2009; Mäki and Marchionni 2011). Mäki identifies three forms of economics imperialism. First is imperialism of *scope*, which pertains only to the activity of seeking explanatory unification across disciplines. Second is imperialism of *style*, which pertains to the rhetorical practices and techniques of research. Third is imperialism of *standing*, which aims at displacing the intellectual and ultimately the political standing of another approach. To use Mäki's terms, Chicago neoliberals practiced not only imperialism of *scope*, but also the more objectionable imperialisms of *style* and *standing*.[52] As Mäki notes, these forms often go together; it is the latter upon which this paper has focused. Training one's focus on only the scope of the imperialists' analyses leads one to miss the point of some of the most significant aspects of imperialistic activities.

Finally, the previous analysis suggests that there are benefits to heeding Davis's recommendation to 'apply history to philosophy,' by using archival evidence to complement methodological studies of more recent developments in economics. While we do not deny the existence of some praiseworthy cases of communication between the members of the economics profession and other disciplines, one should not necessarily attribute changes to economic theory (for example, the innovations of Levitt) to this form of communication: it may turn out that the reports of the decline of economics imperialism have been greatly exaggerated.

Acknowledgements

We would like to thank the Roanoke College Faculty Scholar Program and the Center for the Humanities at the University of Rhode Island for research support. We thank Jeff Biddle, John Davis, Ross Emmett, Jean-Baptiste Fleury, Craig Freedman, Steve Medema and Philip Mirowski for their helpful suggestions. We are especially grateful to Roger Backhouse for his detailed comments on a previous draft and to Stephen Stigler for his permission to access the George J. Stigler Papers. Archival materials from the George J. Stigler Papers and the Henry Simons Papers, Special Collections Research Center, Regenstein Library, University of Chicago are quoted with permission.

Notes

1. Reactions to these events include Davis (2012), Fine (2002), Fine and Milonakis (2009), Frey and Benz (2004), Mäki (2009), Mäki and Marchionni (2011), and Vromen (2009). While not all of these pieces are 'in' economic methodology (i.e., the work of Ben Fine), all have influenced the discussion in economic methodology, a case we will make presently.
2. Vromen (2011), for example, makes the illuminating argument that Chicago economists resorting to biological concepts were not motivated by a wish to communicate with biology.
3. GSRL Box 19, File: Economics – The Imperial Science? Reproduced with permission from the Department of Special Collections, University of Chicago.
4. One might include Bruno Frey as a proponent of this intermediate position: 'The relationship between economics and psychology is characterized by a phase of economic[s] imperialism and psychological inspiration' (Frey and Benz 2004, p. 78).
5. More precisely, Davis's position is that 'imperialism' has existed, but 'economics imperialism' has not: '[P]articular episodes of economics-type imperialism associated with a particular economics research program (such as the Chicago School) cannot be labeled "economics imperialism," since "economics" could be inhabited by other research programs uninterested in and perhaps hostile to this particular economics research program's imperialism' (Davis 2012, p. 212).
6. We have documented in detail the rise of Chicago neoliberalism elsewhere. See Van Horn and Mirowski (2009) and Nik-Khah (2011a).
7. For details, see Caldwell (2007, pp. 18–23).
8. For more details about the relationship between Simons and Hayek, see Van Horn (2009).
9. Simons, for example, referred to the Study as the 'Hayek Project' (SPRL, September 4, 1945, Box 8, File 9). For biographical information on Director, see Van Horn (2010).
10. For a detailed look at the intellectual and political relationship of Hayek and Director, see Van Horn (in press).

11. For the details of how this project finally came to fruition, see Van Horn and Mirowski (2009).
12. 'Chicago University to Scan Free Market.' 1946, *The New York Times*, November 2, p. 31. For additional evidence of the desire to exert political pressure, see TSPR, May 23, 1946, Box 39 (addenda), Folder: Free Market Study.
13. The effort to reconstitute liberalism at Chicago was one part of a transnational effort to reformulate liberalism in connection with the Mont Pelerin Society. See Van Horn and Mirowski (2009) and Nik-Khah (2011a).
14. See Van Horn (2009) for an archival based account of Director's MPS address.
15. For a detailed look at how Viner's attitude toward concentrations of power was very similar to Director's attitude at this juncture, see Van Horn (2011).
16. The remainder of paragraph is based on Stigler (1982, p. 170), and Burgin (2007).
17. VPML, letter, June 9, 1947, Viner to Hayek, Box 39, Folder: Hayek, F.
18. For a detailed look at this position shift, see Van Horn (2009) and Van Horn and Klaes (2011).
19. For more on the Antitrust Project, see Van Horn (2009) and Van Horn and Klaes (2011b).
20. See Director ([1953] 1964).
21. For example, Bork maintained that '[vertical mergers added] nothing to monopoly power' (1954, p. 195), and his claim assumed that increased concentration resulting from a vertical merger was necessarily benign.
22. A tying arrangement is one form of vertical integration. Tying takes place when a seller stipulates that a buyer must purchase the 'tied' product in order to obtain the 'tying' product, the one the buyer wants. A tying arrangement is almost always imposed by the seller on the buyer. For example, if a retailer, a small business owner, runs a fishing boat business and if a manufacturer that commands monopoly in the fishing boat motor market demands that the retailer must purchase the manufacturer's motor oil in order to purchase its motors, then the manufacturer has tied its fishing motors (tying product) to its oil (tied product).
23. Hayek, as Director himself pointed out, attacked the views of a number of noneconomists in *Road*. In Director's words: '[R]eaders of *The Road to Serfdom* will be somewhat surprised by the selection of individual examples from among the pseudo-economists and no economists at all' (1945, p. 175).
24. For a detailed look at the rise of Chicago law and economics, see Teles (2008).
25. For an example of this view, see Posner (1979).
26. The following two paragraphs draw from (Nik-Khah 2010).
27. Letter of Stigler to Walgreen, December 28, 1959 (GSRL Box 13, File: Walgreen Correspondence).
28. In this book, Richard Posner portrayed his own work on politics as closely related to imperialistic projects undertaken by others at Chicago: 'With economists devoting increasing attention to the study of nonmarket activities and institutions – including the family, information and the law – the foundation is now in place for the thoroughgoing and unapologetic application of economic theory to the full range of primitive social institutions' (p. 151).
29. Ten contributions were funded by the CSES, four through the Walgreen Foundation and three were authored or coauthored by Stigler himself.
30. All memo citations discussed in this and the following two paragraphs are taken from GSRL Box 21, File: A Research Institute in Economics.
31. 'Professor Peltzman's study of the costs of the FDA's restriction and delay of new drugs is both pathbreaking and monumental, and I look forward confidently to the expansion of our knowledge of these costs of nonfeasance in regulation as other scholars follow his example and methods' (Stigler 1973, pp. 14–15).
32. GSRL Box 26, File: Mont Pèlerin Society 10th Anniversary Meeting.
33. Such a justification for imperialism is proffered in (Coase 1978, p. 210). While Stigler did at times speak in the same way, he was clearly motivated by political aims.
34. Available: http://freakonomics.blogs.nytimes.com/2008/06/23/david-warsh-on-the-new-milton-friedman-institute/ (accessed 4 April 2012).
35. Available: http://www.freakonomics.com/2005/04/ode-to-gary-becker.php (accessed 19 November 2010).
36. 'Honoring Gary Becker,' *Capital Ideas*, April 2006, available: http://www.chicagobooth.edu/capideas/apr06/intro.aspx (accessed 19 November 2010).

37. The Initiative on Chicago Price Theory operates in much the same way as it did before the merger. That it would is unsurprising since the Becker Center and the Milton Friedman Institute served complementary objectives, and had interlocking directorates and overlapping memberships (Nik-Khah 2011b).
38. Available: http://research.chicagobooth.edu/pricetheory/ (accessed 4 April 2012).
39. 'The idea for the Scholars Program grew out of Jesse Shapiro's visit to the University of Chicago in the fall of 2002, during which he participated in the Becker-Murphy price theory class. His exposure to the Chicago environment, and to price theory class in particular, gave Jesse a new perspective on economics that he took back with him to Harvard, where he finished his degree.' See the description of the Price Theory Scholars program, available: http://research.chicagobooth.edu/pricetheory/programs/ptscholars/index.aspx (accessed 4 April 2012).
40. Levitt, quoted in Michael Fitzgerald, 'Chicago Schooled,' *University of Chicago Magazine*, Sep-Oct 2009, available: http://magazine.uchicago.edu/0910/features/chicago_schooled.shtml (accessed 19 November 2010).
41. Available: http://freakonomics.blogs.nytimes.com/2007/05/08/economists-speak-out-on-prediction-markets/ (accessed 17 May 2010).
42. Available: http://freakonomics.blogs.nytimes.com/2007/03/03/lets-just-get-rid-of-tenure/ (accessed 17 May 2010).
43. Available: http://freakonomics.blogs.nytimes.com/2010/04/05/the-recent-health-care-bill/ (accessed 7 May 2010).
44. When challenged to account for his definition of incentives, Levitt retorted: 'for me (and I think this is the thing that makes me an economist ultimately) I just can't get away from the idea that people are active decision makers trying to get what they want in a reasonably sophisticated fashion.' 'Response of Steven Levitt,' available: http://crookedtimber.org/2005/05/23/response/#more-3340 (accessed 7 May 2010).
45. Furthermore, when viewed in light of his position on experts, Levitt's discussion of incentives offers a window into how Levitt views other disciplines such as criminology and education studies. Levitt presents himself as a 'third person … eager to explore the objective merits of interesting cases' (Levitt and Dubner 2006, p. 13), offering an 'honest assessment of data' (p. 11). It is difficult to avoid the impression that Levitt believes experts in other areas to be subjective and dishonest.
46. The Greatest Good describes itself as a 'unique firm formed with the goal of applying rigorous, cutting-edge data analysis and economic methods to the most salient problems in business and philanthropy.' Available: http://www.greatestgood.com/ (accessed 26 November 2010).
47. Creative brief for Freakonomics consulting Group, available: http://www.crowdspring.com/project/1268769_logo-and-stationery-needed-for-new-freakonomics-project/details/ (accessed 26 November 2010).
48. In commercializing an economic expertise that is inaccessible to the public, Levitt has followed a trail blazed by game theorists in the wake of the FCC spectrum auctions (Nik-Khah 2008), but has given it a Chicago twist by stressing Chicago price theory and 'natural experiments' over Bayes-Nash game theory.
49. The closest Levitt comes to a general statement about his approach to incentives is, 'People respond to incentives, although not necessarily in ways that are predictable or manifest' (Levitt and Dubner 2009, p. xiv), a statement that seems less to provide the reader with the key to solving our problems (say, a general policy science based on understanding incentives) than to persuade the reader that the only way to solve them is to consult with an certain kind of expert.
50. We believe this message is an underappreciated reason for why some find Levitt 'fun': while *Freakonomics* and *Superfreakonomics* do address serious matters (education, terrorism, global warming), he then assures us that we needn't worry about them. Because it issues no call for the public to do anything at all, *Freakonomics* sets a different tone than previous efforts to popularize Chicago Economics, such as *Capitalism and Freedom*, which neither the most enthusiastic admirer nor the staunchest critic would ever think of calling 'cute' or 'fun.'
51. A forthcoming paper by one of the authors (Mirowski and Nik-Khah 2012) argues that wavering between the 'trusting markets' and 'trusting economists' positions is an attribute of the contemporary economics profession.

52. 'Imperialisms of style and standing challenge the deeper values, social status, traditions, conventions, resources and life styles of researchers whose domains or disciplines are entered by the imperialists' (Mäki and Marchionni 2011, p. 648).

Works cited

Archival sources

SPRL Henry Simons Papers, Regenstein Library, University of Chicago.
GSRL George J. Stigler Papers, Regenstein Library, University of Chicago.
TSPR Theodore Schultz Papers, Regenstein Library, University of Chicago.
VPML Jacob Viner Papers, Mudd Library, Princeton University.

References

Bork, R. (1954), 'Vertical Integration and the Sherman Act', *University of Chicago Law Review*, 22, 157–201.

Burgin, A. (2007), 'A Prehistory of the Chicago School', paper Presented at the Rethinking the Chicago School Conference, University of Notre Dame.

Caldwell, B. (2007), 'Introduction', in *The Road to Serfdom*, ed. B. Caldwell, Chicago: University of Chicago Press, pp. 1–33.

Coase, R. (1978), 'Economics and Contiguous Disciplines', *Journal of Legal Studies*, 7(2), 201–211.

Davis, J. (2012), 'Mäki on Economics Imperialism', in *Economics for Real*, eds. A. Lehtinen, J. Kuorikoski and P. Ylikoski, New York: Routledge, pp. 203–219.

Director, A. (1945), 'Review of "The Road to Serfdom" by Friedrich A. Hayek', *The American Economic Review*, 35(1), 173–175.

——— (1950), 'Review of Charles E. Lindblom, Unions and Capitalism', *University of Chicago Law Review*, 18(1), 164–167.

——— (1951a), 'Conference on Corporation Law and Finance', *University of Chicago Law School*, 8.

——— (1951b), *Prefatory Note, in The Extent of Enterprise Monopoly in the United States*, Chicago: University of Chicago Press.

——— ([1953] 1964), 'The Parity of the Economic Market Place', *Journal of Law and Economics*, 7, 1–10.

Emmett, R. (2008), 'Chicago School (New Perspectives)', in *New Palgrave Dictionary of Economics* (2nd ed.), eds. S. Durlauf and L. Blume, Palgrave Macmillan: The New Palgrave Dictionary of Economics.

Fine, B. (2002), '"Economic Imperialism": A View from the Periphery', *Review of Radical Political Economics*, 34(2), 187–201.

Fine, B., and Milonakis, D. (2009), *From Economics Imperialism to Freakonomics*, New York: Routledge.

Frey, B., and Benz, M. (2004), 'From Imperialism to Inspiration', in *The Elgar Companion to Economics and Philosophy*, eds. J. Davis, A. Marciano and J. Runde, Northampton, MA: Edward Elgar, pp. 61–83.

Hammond, J.D. (2010), 'The Development of Post-War Chicago Price Theory', in *The Elgar Companion to the Chicago School of Economics*, ed. R. Emmett, Cheltenham, UK: Elgar, pp. 7–21.

Hirshleifer, J. (1985), 'The Expanding Domain of Economics', *American Economic Review*, 75(6), 53–68.

Lazear, E. (2000), "Economic Imperialism", *Quarterly Journal of Economics*, 115(1), 99–146.

Levitt, S., and Dubner, S. (2006), *Freakonomics* (rev. ed.), New York: William Morrow.

——— (2009), *Superfreakonomics*, New York: William Morrow.

Mäki, U. (2009), 'Economics Imperialism: Concepts and Constraints', *Philosophy of the Social Sciences*, 39(3), 351–380.

Mäki, U., and Marchionni, C. (2011), 'Is Geographical Economics Imperializing Economic Geography?', *Journal of Economic Geography*, 11(4), 645–665.

Medema, S. (2007), 'Introduction', in *Price Theory*, ed. M. Friedman, New Brunswick, NJ: Transaction Publishers, pp. vii–xiii.

Mirowski, P., and Nik-Khah, E. (2012), 'Private Intellectuals and Public Perplexity', paper presented at History of Political Economy Conference on Economists as Public Intellectuals.

Nik-Khah, E. (2008), 'A Tale of Two Auctions', *Journal of Institutional Economics*, 4(1), 73–97.

——— (2010), *George J. Stigler, in The Elgar Companion to the Chicago School of Economics*, Cheltenham, UK: Edward Elgar, pp. 337–341.

——— (2011a), 'George Stigler, the Graduate School of Business, and the Pillars of the Chicago School', in *Building Chicago Economics*, eds. R. Van Horn, P. Mirowski and T. Stapleford, New York: Cambridge University Press, pp. 116–147.

——— (2011b), 'Chicago Neoliberalism and the Genesis of the Milton Friedman Institute (2006–2009)', in *Building Chicago Economics*, eds. R. Van Horn, P. Mirowski and T. Stapleford, New York: Cambridge University Press, pp. 368–388.

——— (2012), 'The Intellectual Origins of Pharmaceutical Ignorance', paper presented at History of Political Economy Workshop, Duke University.

Nutter, G.W. (1951), *The Extent of Enterprise Monopoly in the United States*, Chicago: University of Chicago Press.

Peltzman, S. (1973), 'The Benefits and Costs of New Drug Regulation', in *Regulating New Drugs*, ed. R. Laudau, Chicago: University of Chicago Center for Policy Study, pp. 113–211.

Posner, R.A. (1979), 'The Chicago School of Antitrust Analysis', *University of Pennsylvania Law Review*, 127(4), 925–948.

Radnitzky, G., and Bernholz, P. (eds.) (1987), *Economic Imperialism*, New York: Paragon.

Stigler Center (2009), *2008-09 Annual Report*, available: http://research.chicagobooth.edu/economy/

Stigler, G. (1963), *The Intellectual and the Market Place*, New York: Free Press of Glencoe.

——— (1964), 'Public Regulation of the Securities Markets', *Journal of Business*, 37(2), 117–142.

——— (1966), 'The Economic Effects of the Anti-trust Laws', *Journal of Law and Economics*, 9, 225–258.

——— (1973), 'Regulation: The Confusion of Means and Ends', in *Regulating New Drugs*, ed. R. Laudau, Chicago: University of Chicago Center for Policy Study, pp. 9–18.

——— (1975), *The Citizen and the State*, Chicago: University of Chicago Press.

——— (1982), *The Economist as Preacher, and Other Essays*, Chicago: University of Chicago Press.

——— (1983), 'The Process and Progress of Economics', *Journal of Political Economy*, 91(4), 529–545.

——— (1984), 'Economics: The Imperial Science?', *Scandinavian Journal of Economics*, 86(3), 301–313.

——— (1988), *Chicago Studies in Political Economy*, Chicago: University of Chicago Press.

Stigler, G., and Friedland, C. (1962), 'What Can Regulators Regulate? The Case of Electricity', *Journal of Law and Economics*, 5, 1–16.

Teles, S. (2008), *The Rise of the Conservative Legal Movement*, Princeton, NJ: Princeton University Press.

Tullock, G. (1972), 'Economic Imperialism', in *Theory of Public Choice*, eds. J. Buchanan and R. Tollison, Ann Arbor: University of Michigan Press, pp. 317–329.

Van Horn, R. (2009), 'Reinventing Monopoly and the Role of Corporations', in *The Road from Mont Pèlerin*, eds. P. Mirowski and D. Plehwe, Cambridge, MA: Harvard University Press, pp. 204–237.

——— (2010), 'Harry Aaron Director', *History of Political Economy*, 42(4), 601–630.

——— (2011), 'Jacob Viner's Critique of Chicago Neoliberalism', in *Building Chicago Economics*, eds. R. Van Horn, P. Mirowski and T. Stapleford, New York: Cambridge University Press, pp. 279–300.

——— (in press), 'Hayek's Unacknowledged Disciple', *Journal of the History of Economic Thought*.

Van Horn, R., and Mirowski, P. (2009), 'The Rise of the Chicago School of Economics and the Birth of Neoliberalism', in *The Road from Mont Pèlerin*, eds. P. Mirowski and D. Plehwe, Cambridge, MA: Harvard University Press, pp. 139–178.

Van Horn, R., and Klaes, M. (2011), 'Intervening in Laissez-Faire Liberalism', in *Building Chicago Economics*, eds. R. Van Horn, P. Mirowski and T. Stapleford, New York: Cambridge University Press, pp. 180–207.

——— (2011b), 'Chicago Neoliberalism Versus Cowles Planning', *Journal of the History of Behavioral Sciences*, 47(3), 302–321.

Van Overtveldt, J. (2007), *The Chicago School*, Chicago: Agate.

Vromen, J. (2009), 'The Booming Economics-Made-Fun Genre', *Erasmus Journal for Philosophy and Economics*, 2(1), 70–99.

——— (2011), 'Allusions to Evolution: Edifying Evolutionary Biology Rather than Economic Theory', in *Building Chicago Economics*, eds. R. Van Horn, P. Mirowski and T. Stapleford, New York: Cambridge University Press, pp. 208–236.

The unbearable lightness of the economics-made-fun genre

Peter Spiegler

Department of Economics, University of Massachusetts-Boston, 100 Morrissey Boulevard, Boston, MA, USA

Several commentators have argued that the economics-made-fun ('EMF') genre contains very little actual economics. As such, it would seem that criticisms of EMF do not apply to economics more broadly. In this paper I take a contrary view, arguing that, in fact, at a deep conceptual level, the engine of EMF analyses is *precisely* the engine of mainstream economics. Specifically, I argue that both EMF and mainstream economics rest on a conceptual foundation known as the principle of the substitution of similars ('PSS'). Understanding how PSS leads EMF practitioners to make claims well beyond what is warranted by their analysis also offers insight into how PSS can put economists in danger of overestimating the power and scope of their analyses. I explore the consequences of such problems through examples of economic analysis of the US housing market in the lead-up to the recent financial crisis.

1 Introduction

In a famous scene from Monty Python's *Holy Grail*, a village wise man named Bedevere is called upon to adjudicate his fellow villagers' claims that a woman they have brought before him is a witch. After some thought and a bit of assistance from King Arthur, Bedevere devises a test and soon the villagers are gathered before an enormous balancing scale containing the woman and a duck, certain that they are about to receive definitive verification or refutation of their conjecture.

For fans of Monty Python's brand of humor, this scene bears the hallmark of what made Monty Python great: the juxtaposition of normalcy and absurdity. It is funny, in part, because the characters are completely committed to the logically sound and patently absurd elements of the situation in equal measure. This both highlights the absurdity and pokes fun at the human tendency to take our favored norms and beliefs, no matter how strange, as self-evidently right and true. When we laugh at Bedevere and the villagers, we are also laughing at our own all-too-human nature.

Lately, there has been a version of this comedic trope propagating through the popular non-fiction bookshelves in the guise of 'economics-made-fun' (EMF) writing. Like Bedevere, its authors claim to be revealing hidden aspects of the universe by interpreting superficial similarities between apparently unlike objects within the framework of a set of absurd assumptions to produce startling conclusions. For Bedevere and the villagers, the fact of the similar weights of a duck and woman means a witch roams among them.

For Levitt and Dubner (2005), the fact that some sumo wrestlers and some teachers sometimes cheat points to a deep underlying connection between the two.

EMF analyses, though, are marketed not as absurd comedy but rather as mostly straight-faced social analysis. Its practitioners do sometimes present their work as winking or tongue-in-cheek, but not in a sense that is meant to undermine the impression that their conclusions represent genuine and profound insights. For the most part, the work is meant to be a version of real economics and is put forth by unquestionably real economists, some of whom occupy prestigious chairs at elite institutions and regularly publish in the discipline's top journals.

Like many other critics of the EMF genre, I find the characterization of EMF work as even semi-serious social science to be misleading at best. Unlike other critics, however, I will not be taking issue here with the ways in which EMF work falls short of (or completely outside) the standards of contemporary economics.[1] Rather, I will be exploring the possibility that the central analytic principle of EMF work fits quite comfortably within the norms and standards of contemporary mainstream economics, and that by recognizing this we can better understand some of the serious methodological problems within mainstream economics that have led to its current state of turmoil. The analytic principle I have in mind is a particularly extreme (and logically flawed) version of metaphorical explanation called 'the principle of the substitution of similars' (PSS), which was first introduced into economics by the late nineteenth-century economist William Stanley Jevons. Put briefly, the PSS holds that if two objects are even superficially similar, they can be presumed to be identical with respect to certain (arbitrarily selected) essential features. I will argue below that the PSS is an important generator of many of the surprising (and unsupported) conclusions of EMF work, but that it is also a widely used generator of inferences in mainstream economics, with results similar to that which we encounter in EMF analyses. Worryingly, however, the version of PSS used in mainstream economics is generally more sophisticated than that used in EMF work, and so the faultiness of its procedure is more difficult to detect – not least because the currently accepted standards of model assessment in economics are not built to detect it. The result is that we have a strain of rot at the core of our methodology that has been doing damage for a long time, and continues to do so largely unabated. The solution to this problem must begin with identifying the exact nature of the problem to devise a targeted response. Since EMF work uses PSS in an exaggerated manner, it is an ideal laboratory for this exploration.

The paper will proceed as follows. In Section 2, I will discuss the standard analytic trope of EMF analysis and show how it produces ostensibly legitimate but actually unsupported inferences. In Section 3, I will argue that Jevons' PSS bears a strong resemblance to the standard trope of EMF analysis and can be helpful in understanding the relationship between EMF analysis and more rigorous academic economics. In Section 4, I present the more sophisticated version of the PSS used in current mainstream economics and argue – using examples from the literature on the housing market in the lead-up to the financial crisis – that its use can lead to problems similar to those encountered in EMF work. I conclude by suggesting that judicious use of interpretive methods can be used to protect economics against the nefarious influence of the PSS.

2 The standard trope of the economics-made-fun genre

Although the EMF genre has expanded prodigiously since the publication of *Freakonomics* (Levitt and Dubner 2005), the subtitle of that seminal work – *A Rogue*

Economist Explores the Hidden Side of Everything – still captures the genre's ethos quite well. The uncovering of previously hidden truths using economics in an unexpected way is the essence of the genre's self-understanding. I will argue in this section, however, that close inspection of EMF analyses reveals that the conclusions reached are generally not hidden truths uncovered by economic reasoning, but rather rational reconstructions of the phenomena under study that *assume* a deep structure (a.k.a. hidden order) binding the phenomena together. Put another way, EMF authors are not discovering hidden truths, but rather 'discovering' their own assumptions and reporting them as surprising insights.

The *Freakonomics* chapter 'What Do Schoolteachers and Sumo Wrestlers Have in Common?' provides a good example. The chapter is ostensibly about cheating. In it, the authors present a very broad picture of cheating – including everything from steroid use by athletes to a third grader copying from another student – and then recount several stories that are intended to be understood as instances of cheating. The story of the cheating teachers centers around the Chicago public school system's experience with 'high-stakes' testing – i.e., standardized tests on which students must achieve a passing score to advance to the next grade level, and for which teachers are rewarded for good performance in their classrooms. In a study of several years of student test scores (and of a re-test of a smaller sample of classrooms), Steven Levitt and his co-author Brian Jacob found evidence that some teachers had altered students' test responses after the fact to raise their scores (Jacob and Levitt 2003a,b). The story of the sumo wrestlers centers around some seemingly suspicious trends in match performance. Specifically, Levitt and his co-author Mark Duggan examined matches in which a win was extremely important for one wrestler but not for the other, and found that the wrestlers in need of a win performed much better in those matches than they did under similar circumstances in non-crucial matches (Duggan and Levitt 2002).

Levitt and Dubner suggest that the facts reviewed above are evidence that teachers and sumo wrestlers have something in common.[2] Before examining this claim in detail, we need first to make it more explicit. To dispense with a minimal reading of the title, we can simply note that there is no question that sumo wrestlers and teachers have *something* in common. Any two things have *something* in common.[3] But the authors' suggestion is clearly something more specific and contentious than this. As the stated intent of their book is to 'explore[] the hidden side of everything,' it seems appropriate to interpret the title of the chapter as a claim that there is a hidden connection between sumo wrestlers and teachers that the material covered in the chapter will expose.

To understand what would be necessary to make such a claim plausible, it is helpful to consider a literal reading of the stories and then trace the moves required to transform this reading into evidence of a hidden connection. What the stories indicate, literally, is that some members of a group of Chicago public school teachers and some sumo wrestlers, under a specific set of conditions, engaged in behavior that the authors believe was a violation of a set of rules the agents recognized as applying to them. If we give the authors the benefit of the doubt regarding their claims of cheating, then we could say that some Chicago teachers and some sumo wrestlers cheated under the specific circumstances reviewed in the stories.[4] The connection, so far, is a superficial similarity between an action taken by some of the wrestlers and some of the teachers.

The authors' transformation of this superficial connection between actions into a deep, hidden connection between people unfolds in two stages. First, they recast cheating (within whatever context it is encountered) as a uniform phenomenon: namely, as an outcome of incentive processing. The substance of the recasting involves first pointing out how important incentives are to our decision making, next describing various examples of behavior that would be commonly understood as cheating using the vocabulary of incentives, and finally concluding that '[c]heating is a primordial economic act: getting more for less' (Levitt and Dubner 2005, p. 25). This immediately changes the superficial similarity between the sumo wrestlers' and teachers' cheating into a deeper one: they are not merely engaging in activities that share some attributes, but, rather, are doing *the same thing*. To differentiate this meaning of cheating from the colloquial meaning (which is more capacious and nuanced), I will call the former 'freakcheating.'

The second stage in the transformation involves recasting freakcheating as the result of 'modular incentive processing activities' (this is my term, not Levitt and Dubner's). What I mean by this will be most easily explained by tracing out what Levitt and Dubner do to connect the uniform act of cheating to a kind of uniformity among cheaters. The first thing to note is that the uniformity of the act of freakcheating is immediately tied to a uniformity of internal process: it involves the processing of incentives by the individuals generating the activities. So the fact that wrestlers and teachers freakcheat tells us not merely that they have done the same thing, but that they have both done so as a result of the same type of action: processing incentives. But this is still not enough to support the claim of a deep, hidden similarity between the wrestlers and the teachers. For that we need the incentive processing activity undertaken by the two groups to be deeply similar as well – otherwise the appearance of freakcheating in both contexts could just have been coincidence. The authors do not explicitly argue for this last piece of the puzzle, leaving the reader to make the connection him/herself (or to reject it). But for those who are familiar with economic reasoning, the implication is fairly clear: if one holds all other differences equal, one can see that the offending teachers and offending wrestlers identically process similar circumstances to produce freakcheating. And this is where the notion of modularity is important. One way to understand this final step (and, I would suggest, the way that best fits Levitt and Dubner's meaning) is to imagine the wrestlers and teachers as bundles of incentive processing modules, where the actions of each module are analytically separable from all others. As such, although the teachers and wrestlers differ in many ways, and although their contexts differ in many ways, they share a particular element whose functioning manifests itself empirically if only we understand how to recognize it. This would allow us to interpret their freakcheating as evidence that each contains the module that processes similar antecedent freakcheating factors (i.e., high-stakes testing and crucial matches, respectively) identically. And this would, indeed, indicate that we had uncovered a previously hidden substantial connection.

In the foregoing description, for ease of exposition, I began with freakcheating and ended with the ontological position regarding action as the resultant of modular incentive processors. This is the order in which the elements of Levitt and Dubner's analytic process unfold to the reader. But from the point of view of the practitioner, the process unfolds in the opposite direction. Levitt and Dubner began with an ontological presumption, and it was within that ontology that their observations of the Chicago teachers and Sumo wrestlers acquired the meanings proposed in the chapter. This process can be stated in general form as follows:

(1) Begin with an unconventional ontological framework (e.g., the world is populated by a complex of separable incentives, incentive processing modules and resultants of this processing called 'actions').

(2) Reinterpret observed phenomena within the interpretive framework of that ontology (e.g., superficially similar actions are identical types that are the result of identical incentive processing modules acting in different contexts).

(3) Claim that this reinterpretation is evidence of the sort of deep connection envisioned in one's presumed ontology (e.g., the observation of cheating among teachers and sumo wrestlers is evidence of a deep similarity between them).

This explanatory strategy is an essential and pervasive trope of EMF work. Some of the other examples of the employment of this strategy are obvious, such as the *Freakonomics* chapter 'How is the KKK Like a Group of Real Estate Agents?' Using the same ontological framework as in the teacher–sumo wrestler chapter, the authors interpret their observation of superficially similar use of private information by Real Estate agents and the Ku Klux Klan as evidence of a deep connection between them. But it is not only these straightforward comparisons of types of people that follow the trope delineated above. In fact, virtually all EMF work employs this trope.

Take, for example, Tyler Cowen's (2008) *Discover Your Inner Economist: Use Incentives to Fall in Love, Survive Your Next Meeting, and Motivate Your Dentist.*[5] Although the book's chapters deal with a wide range of contexts and questions, the central message of the book is that there is something essentially identical about one's actions across all these contexts – namely, that one is processing incentives and that if one wants to do so properly, it helps to recognize that a generic processing module lies within the panoply of apparent diversity across all these contexts. The central metaphor that Cowen chooses for the book – one's 'inner economist' – is especially telling in this regard. The inner economist is the generic incentive processing module operating within each of us. And it is important to note that this metaphor must carry its home world along with it – i.e., that, as in the *Freakonomics* examples cited above, the deep similarities ostensibly discovered will only appear if one projects the imagined world of modular incentive processing units onto the world we actually experience. The idea of a generic incentive processing module within each of us is only intelligible within such an imagined world.

This explanatory trope has been a smashing success for EMF authors, judging not only by book sales, but also by the extent to which EMF thinking has become a 'meme' in popular culture and even an academic teaching tool.[6] But there are significant problems with the EMF trope, and to the extent that EMF authors want their work to be understood as semi-serious economics it is important to make these problems clear. DiNardo (2007) and Rubinstein (2006) have provided ample evidence of some of the methodological shortcomings of EMF work. DiNardo (2007), in particular, casts enough doubt on the claims of *Freakonomics* to place the burden of proof squarely on the shoulders of anyone who would claim that the claims should be understood as scientific results.

But there is an additional reason to question the legitimacy of EMF work that would remain even if the authors addressed the methodological issues identified by DiNardo, namely, that the central explanatory trope of EMF work is inherently question-begging. As discussed above, the observations that EMF authors present as evidence of deep connections between disparate phenomena could actually only count as such evidence *if we already presume the deep connections to exist*. As such, the evidence they adduce is incapable of answering the larger question of whether or not their claims are valid. For example, with respect to the teacher–sumo wrestler chapter in *Freakonomics*, the authors' empirical analyses that were meant to test whether or not the teachers and wrestlers were cheating could only be considered evidence of a deep connection between the two groups if we had already accepted the ontological presumption that turns these instances of cheating into freakcheating. This is why what the authors are actually doing is *not* discovering a previously hidden connection, but rather 'discovering' their initial assumptions and reporting them as such a discovery. And this is a general feature of EMF work: the surprising conclusions the authors reach are already contained in their assumptions, and the evidence they adduce to support the conclusions are only evidence of hidden connections if the assumptions are correct.

In this sense, EMF work bears a disturbingly strong resemblance to Bedevere's witch test. Bedevere claims that his proposed test – balancing the woman the villagers have brought to him against a duck – will reveal whether or not the woman is a witch. But seeing the results of the test as evidence of witchness (or lack thereof) only makes sense against the background of a set of ontological assumptions that include, *inter alia*, the existence of witches for whom floating in water is a constitutive property. We moderns can see that the villagers' focus on the balancing scales is misplaced. The ultimate answer to their question lies elsewhere – i.e., in an exploration of the question of the existence of witches – and that the testing methodology they have chosen is not equipped to produce the kind of information they need. They may come up with the right answer, but it will be for the wrong reason.

It is this latter problem of EMF analysis that has the most troubling implications. Unlike the problems identified by DiNardo and Rubinstein – the elucidation of which serves to separate contemporary economics from EMF – the problem I have raised is actually something that EMF *shares* with contemporary economics. Specifically, the philosophical justification for using the EMF trope as a means of (ostensibly) uncovering hidden patterns in the world is one that was originally also a part of the philosophical foundation of contemporary economics. This justification, the PSS, was the brainchild of William Stanley Jevons, and it is more than a mere historical curiosity. As I will argue in Section 4, it is an erroneous principle that not only allows EMF work to masquerade as semi-serious economics, but also provides cover for certain well-accepted methodological strategies within academic economics that actually possess the same essential flaw as EMF work. Before turning to this argument, however, it is necessary to give a brief review of Jevons' principle.

3   The principle of the substitution of similars

William Stanley Jevons is known to most contemporary economists as a member of the triumvirate of the marginalist revolution (along with Léon Walras and Carl Menger), but by his own reckoning his greatest contribution to knowledge came in the field of logic. The contribution, specifically, was the PSS, and it provided the analytic core of all of Jevons' scientific endeavors, including his seminal *Theory of Political Economy* (1871). Significantly, for the purposes of this paper, its imprint is still discernible today as an important part of the logic underpinning both EMF work and certain well-established methodological strategies in mainstream academic economics.

The PSS arose out of Jevons' engagement with mathematics and logic – a passion that predated by many years his interest in political economy. Although his university training centered around natural science, it was Jevons' studies in mathematics and logic with Augustus De Morgan that had the most profound impact on his scientific practice. In the late 1850s, Jevons began producing his first independent academic work – studies of cloud formation. In addition to yielding his first publications, this work also allowed Jevons to reflect concretely on the nature of scientific discovery and its relationship to methodology. He became convinced that the key to all scientific discovery was the recognition of similarities in apparently disparate objects – specifically, that when a heretofore obscure phenomenon is recognized as similar to a well-understood phenomenon, we may project what is known of the latter onto the former. Jevons felt that there was something very deep about this idea, and that although in some sense it was a commonplace its implications had not yet been fully explored. Further, he had a sense of how such exploration might be possible, and it hinged on an innovation in logic. On New Years' Eve, 1862, Jevons wrote in his journal, 'my logical speculations give me most confidence. I cannot disbelieve, yet I can hardly believe that in the principle of *sameness* I have found that which will reduce the whole theory of reasoning to one consistent lucid process' (Black and Könekamp 1972, p. 186).

Jevons' key logical innovation was to tighten the relationship between subject and predicate, specifically by replacing the standardly used copula – some form of the verb 'to be' – with the mathematical symbol ' = .' For Jevons, the standard copula was too ambiguous (1958, p. 16). It signaled only that the subject was included in a class of things denoted by the predicate. And this relationship could imply many different things, which made it a complicated matter to determine what precisely could be deduced from a series of statements expressed with the standard copula. Jevons believed (building on the innovations of George Bentham and George Boole) that by specifying precisely the part of the predicate to which the subject exactly agreed, one could express statements like 'A is B' as 'A = [some subset or aspect of B].'[7] The great advantage of this was that one could then use the rules of algebra to work out the implications of statements. All the complicated rules of syllogism in Aristotelian logic could thereby be done away with (Jevons 1869, p. 25).

As a practical matter, what Jevons was aiming for was a way to more accurately express his view regarding the power of deep similarity. Using the ' = ' symbol was a way of formalizing Jevons' belief that if one could establish a sufficient degree of similarity between two objects, then one ought to be able to conclude that *everything* that was true of the one would be true of the other – or, as he put it in his definition of the PSS, that a 'capacity of mutual replacement exist[s] in any two objects which are like or equivalent to a sufficient degree' (1958, p. 17).

An example from an early exposition of the PSS demonstrates how Jevons imagined the PSS would work in practice. Taking Nassau Senior's definition of wealth as the subject to be explored, he writes:

> Sometimes we may have two definitions of the same term, and we may then equate these to each other. Thus, according to Mr. Senior,
>
> (1) Wealth = whatever has exchangeable value.
> (2) Wealth = whatever is useful, transferable and limited in supply.
>
> We can employ either of these to make a substitution in the other, obtaining the equation,
>   *Whatever has exchangeable value = whatever is useful, transferable, and limited in supply.*
> (Jevons 1869, pp. 25–26)

The concluding statement follows from the preceding ones in precisely the same manner and for precisely the same reasons that '$y = 3$' would follow from the statements '$x = y$' and '$x = 3$.'

The primary problem with the PSS, as many of Jevons' contemporaries noted, is that transferring the notion of mathematical equality to a non-mathematical context is no simple matter. The fact that it is possible – in a purely mechanical sense – to *write* a statement in which two non-mathematical entities are joined by the ' = ' symbol does not entail that such a relationship is possible. At the very least, the intelligibility of such an expression would require the espousal of a radical social ontology – i.e., that either the social world is underlain with mathematical structure or that any non-mathematically structured elements are isolable from the mathematically structured elements. This would not be necessary if the ' = ' were understood more loosely, for instance by being interpreted as equivalent to ordinary language expressions like 'is similar to' or 'is the same as.' In this case, there would be no problem in interpreting sentences like the ones from Jevons' PSS example above. But Jevons intended to preserve the mathematical sense of the ' = ' symbol – indeed, this preservation of the mathematical sense was absolutely crucial to his goal of importing the algebraic operation of substitution into logic.[8]

Given the importance of providing some kind of philosophical grounding for the possibility of mathematical equivalence in non-mathematical settings, it is surprising that Jevons devoted nearly no space to the issue in *The Principles of Science*, focusing instead on the construction of a system to work out the logical implications of such similarity *assuming* that it was possible. To many of Jevons' contemporaries, this was simply question-begging, as they pointed out in reviews of *The Principles of Science* and in letters to Jevons. The eminent English scientist George Herschel, for example, expressed this objection trenchantly in an 1869 letter to Jevons:

> And then, after all, the difficulty of reasoning correctly lies not in the mechanical application of logical formulae ... but in the application of reason and observation to decide what things *are* similar: *so* similar as to admit of substitution for each other in the argument at hand; which is not a province of formal or Aristotelian logic, however largely supplemented by Dr Boole, Dr Thomson or yourself. (Cited in Maas 2005, p. 148)[9]

And Herschel was not alone in these concerns – John Stuart Mill and George Boole were also critical of this aspect of Jevons' philosophy of science.[10] And even Jevons' teacher and mentor Augustus De Morgan remained unconvinced, declining to adopt the replacement of the standard copula with the ' = ' symbol despite the fact that he, himself, was an early innovator in working out the connections between mathematics and logic.[11]

The reason for Jevons' relative neglect of this issue was not that he disagreed with these critics that it was important, but rather that he thought that it could be addressed quite straightforwardly. Specifically, Jevons held that all phenomena possess logical structure – which, because of Jevons' conflation of mathematics and logic, was equivalent to the position that all phenomena capable of varying in degree possess mathematical structure. And significantly for the purposes of this paper, this position was not an empirical finding or a position which Jevons supported with argument, but rather simply an article of faith.

We can see this by looking closely at Jevons' exposition of this position. He begins by proffering what he considers to be the fundamental laws of logic – i.e., 'the laws which express the very nature and conditions of the discriminating and identifying powers of the mind':

1. The Law of Identity. *Whatever is, is.*
2. The Law of Contradiction. A thing cannot both be and not be.
3. The Law of Duality. *A thing must either be or not be.* (Jevons 1958, p. 5)

Next, he makes the radical inference that these laws are not merely laws of thought, but further are an expression of the structure of all existence. Significantly, he does so not through rigorous argumentation, but through a dialog with an imagined interlocutor:

> Are not the Laws of Identity and Difference the prior conditions of all consciousness and all existence? Must they not hold true, alike of things material and immaterial? and [*sic*] if so can we say that they are only subjectively true or objectively true? I am inclined, in short, to regard them as true both 'in the nature of thought and things,' ... and I hold that they belong to the common basis of all existence. (Jevons 1958, p. 8)

And this helps us to make sense of the following general description of phenomena that appears several pages earlier:

> In the material framework of this world, substances and forces present themselves in definite and stable combinations ... The constituents of the globe, indeed, appear in almost endless combinations; but each combination bears its fixed character, and when resolved is found to be the compound of definite substances. (Jevons 1958, p. 2)

From the previous quotation, we can see that the 'framework' of which Jevons writes above encompasses *all* things, material and immaterial. What Jevons is expressing in these passages is nothing less than a thoroughgoing rationalist ontology.

Jevons does not provide an account of *why* he holds this ontological position, but the fact that he does hold it takes us a long way in understanding why he would have considered the PSS to be well founded despite his critics' misgivings. Herschel's concern that Jevons had not paid sufficient attention to the question of how one determines *what* things are similar is addressed by Jevons' ontological assumptions. For Jevons, *all* things are deeply similar structurally; specifically, they are modular complexes of definite substances. And this is precisely the kind of similarity we need to get the principle behind the PSS off the ground. Based solely on this, we need not worry if statements like 'Wealth = whatever is useful, transferable and limited in supply' are *intelligible*, but rather only whether or not – *given that they are of an appropriate form* – they are correct.

We are now prepared to see the deep parallels between the PSS and the standard trope of EMF work discussed above. As with the EMF trope, the PSS involves beginning with an unconventional ontological position and reinterpreting observed phenomena within the interpretive framework of that ontology, and, once one successfully 'tests' the description against a relevant set of data, claiming that the reinterpretation is evidence of the sort of deep connection envisioned by the presumed ontology. But just as with the EMF trope, the test that ostensibly vindicates the proposition of a deep connection between the phenomena under study will be question-begging – specifically, it will be a test conducted entirely within the presumed ontology, will never touch the question of the plausibility of the ontology and will end only in 'discovering' one's initial assumptions.

We can see this by turning to another example - Jevons' application of his logic to the following statement made by Augustus De Morgan: 'He must have been rich, and if not absolutely mad was weakness itself, subjected either to bad advice or to most unfavourable circumstances.'[12] Jevons claims that the statement can be equivalently understood as follows (note that the symbol $\cdot \mid \cdot$ is, roughly, Jevons' representation of 'and/or'):

> If we assign the letters of the alphabet in succession, thus,
>
> A = he
> B = rich
> C = absolutely mad
> D = weakness itself
> E = subjected to bad advice
> F = subjected to most unfavorable circumstances,
>
> the proposition will take the form
>
> $$A = AB\{C \cdot \mid \cdot D(E \cdot \mid \cdot F)\}\ (1958, p.\,76)$$

This is a decomposition of the subject of De Morgan's sentence into a modular complex of attributes. To the extent that such attributes are also observed in other subjects, the latter's decomposition would include the same letters which, by Jevons' account, would not only have to mean precisely the same thing, but would also have to be associated with the subjects in precisely the same way. Whatever else might be true of disparate subjects containing some identical attribute, they are all deeply connected by being associated with that identical attribute in an identical manner. This is precisely what Levitt and Dubner implicitly claim by interpreting the cheating of teachers and sumo wrestlers as freakcheating generated by an identical incentive processing module, and it is logically unsound for precisely the same reason. The 'discovery' of that deep connection was not established through observation, but rather was something that was embedded in the analysis by assumption.

4   The PSS and contemporary academic economics

Unfortunately, the logic of the PSS underpins not only EMF analysis, but also some ostensibly legitimate analytic strategies that are pervasive in contemporary academic economics. In brief, the principle that the only valid test of a hypothesis is its empirical success (and, therefore, that the realisticness *per se* of the hypothesis is irrelevant) allows EMF-type methods to masquerade as legitimate methods by obscuring their illegitimacy through inadequate testing procedures. In this section, I will argue for this claim and provide as support the example of academic economic writing on the housing market in the lead-up to the recent financial crisis. I will proceed by first discussing (1) the relation between PSS and contemporary economic methodology, and (2) the safety net that is supposed to prevent the PSS from causing EMF- and Bedevere-type problems. I will then argue that the safety net is porous in that it is insensitive to certain kinds of important problems for the same reason that the standard EMF trope reviewed above is logically flawed.

The philosophical framework of the PSS is present in contemporary economics on two levels – first, with respect to ontological presuppositions and second, with respect to the manner in which these presuppositions are ostensibly rendered harmless. To what extent contemporary economics is committed to a rationalist ontology is a matter of controversy.[13] The discipline's methodological and epistemological commitment to mathematical modeling, however, is clear. Economic analysis of social phenomena today *means* creating a mathematical representation (implicitly or explicitly, though usually explicitly) of the phenomena as a means of proposing and testing possible explanations of the nature and dynamics of those phenomena. Economic knowledge is the product of proper application of this methodology. As such, a milder form of the Jevonian ontological position is implicitly espoused by contemporary economics, at least provisionally – namely, that mathematical representations of (any) social phenomena are a potentially useful explanatory mechanism for those phenomena and, further, that explaining social phenomena *only and always* through mathematical representation does not limit the potential scope of one's social explorations. A rationalist ontology is a sufficient grounding for such a belief, though not a necessary one. Still, although a practicing economist can be ontologically agnostic to some extent, that agnosticism must be bounded to exclude the position that the phenomena of the social world are *definitely not* rationally structured. Such a position would be directly at odds with the standard practice of carrying only mathematical tools in one's toolkit.

What is supposed to keep this ontological commitment from being a rationalist blemish on the economist's pure empiricism is the principle that the only relevant thing about a hypothesis is its agreement with empirical observation (and not, therefore, its origin). Milton Friedman's 1953 essay provided the canonical statement within economics of this principle, but Jevons had anticipated Friedman's position in 1874, stating quite clearly in the first edition of *The Principles of Science* that '[*a*]*greement with fact is the one sole and sufficient test of a true hypothesis*' (1874, p. 138, italics in original).[14] This principle is meant to provide protection against the kinds of problems that the ontological elements of PSS thinking could otherwise cause. Unlike in much EMF work, in proper science (the thought goes) one cannot view deductions made from within one's ontological presumptions as results in themselves. Rather, they must be treated as hypotheses to be rigorously tested and to the extent they agree with empirical observation the presumed ontology can be treated merely as a creative source of theory. In effect, the ontological presumption is rendered invisible.

The central problem with this position is succinctly articulated by the two prongs of the Duhem-Quine thesis.[15] First, since one can never test hypotheses in isolation, any hypothesis test is actually a test of the hypothesis along with all of its framing assumptions. Second, the test itself is never a comparison of the hypothesis with brute facts of nature, but, rather, a comparison of the former with empirical observations that have already been parsed into the categories of the theory. Put another way, the test must occur entirely *within* the presumed ontology and, as such, is merely a test of whether an internally consistent rational reconstruction of empirical observations is possible. What is left aside is the question of whether the presumed ontology itself is plausible, and this is the door through which EMF-type problems can enter into contemporary academic economic practice.

To explain precisely how his happens, I need to be a bit more precise about the current model assessment standards of contemporary economics. The basic tenets can be distilled into three principles:

(1) *The empirical consequences principle (ECP)*: The only real kind of problem that an economic model can have is one that has empirical consequences – e.g., it makes bad predictions.

(2) *The econometrics sufficiency principle (ESP)*: All modeling problems with empirical consequences – i.e., all *real* modeling problems – can in principle be detected econometrically.

(3) *The Friedman Principle (FP)*: Economists need recognize no constraints in their model creation besides the ECP and ESP.

This statement of the model assessment standards is just an expansion of the Jevons–Friedman standard cited above to include the type of testing that is considered necessary and sufficient within contemporary economics – namely, econometric methods.

What is left out in these standards is a recognition of the role of ontological background assumptions not only as creative sources of hypotheses, but also as the scaffolding within which one's data is created and one's empirical testing occurs.[16] Ignoring this role puts one in danger of mistakenly endorsing explanations that take superficial similarities to be evidence of deeper, more essential connections. The problem is that, based on the model assessment standards above, we have no way of verifying whether such deep connections actually exist, and if they do, whether the particular deep connection we've projected onto the data is the right one. In his essay 'Is a Science of Comparative Possible?' Alasdair MacIntyre put the point cogently with respect to positive political science work:

> [I]f we identify behavior except in terms of the intentions and therefore of the beliefs of the agents we shall risk describing what they are doing as what we would be doing if we went through that series of movements or something like it rather than what they are actually doing. Nor do we avoid this difficulty merely by finding *some* description of the behavior in question which both the agents themselves and the political scientist would accept. (1978, p. 264)

As such, using the ECP–ESP–FP complex as one's assessment standards casts a shadow over one's conclusions, regardless of whether or not they have met those standards. By extension, if these are used as the assessment standards for an entire discipline, then that discipline will have an *a priori* credibility problem with respect to any of its results.[17]

This is not merely a theoretical problem. If one's model assessment standards leave one blind to important misunderstandings, then empirical consequences that are missed by one's empirical testing procedures may end up making their first appearance as live problems in actual reality that one has failed to anticipate. This could manifest itself, for example, as a realization of a particular event that is well outside of one's predictions, or as the failure of a policy designed on the basis of one's models. These problems can occur because of modeling problems that are within the province of the ECP–ESP–FP complex, but can just as easily occur for reasons outside it.

The recent global financial crisis and its relationship to the US housing market provides one concrete example of the types of things that can be missed by the ECP–ESP–FP complex and the consequences that can result. As we now know, the central cause of the financial crisis was the concentration of investment in the US housing market, particularly through derivative securities (e.g., credit default swaps and various forms of collateralized debt obligations and mortgage backed securities). The massive inflow of investment during the late 1990s and throughout most of the 2000s inflated a bubble in US (and eventually non-US) housing and related assets that unraveled and burst when, in 2007, housing prices began to level off and mortgage defaults began to rise. When the bubble had burst and losses began to be realized, it became clear that the use of opaque derivatives on a massive scale to take and hedge positions in the mortgage-related asset market had intertwined the fate of a large portion of the international financial industry.

What has also become clear is that this was no simple speculative bubble. Rather, it was a bubble created and sustained in part by a politico-commercio-regulatory (hereinafter 'PCR') environment created by, *inter alia*, private financial institutions, legislators, the Federal Reserve and the Treasury department. Among the primary elements of this environment were regulatory decisions that allowed OTC derivatives markets such as those for credit default swaps to remain non-standardized and opaque; a problematic framework for relations between credit rating agencies and their clients that encouraged misleading ratings of complex mortgage derivative products; severe moral hazard problems on the part of mortgage originators caused by massive demand for securitization of mortgages; and the spread of accounting and compensation practices that encouraged short-term thinking and high degrees of leverage in the creation and marketing of highly complex structured finance products. Although presumably it was not the intent of the agents involved in creating this environment to cause a financial crisis, there *was* a clear intent to remove barriers to highly leveraged investment strategies using lightly regulated and unregulated derivates.[18] One result of this was that the US housing market in the late 1990s and 2000s did not conform to the standard economic picture of a housing market – i.e., it was not *simply* a market for an asset delivering a certain type of service with attendant financing issues analyzable through the standard model of financial assets. Rather, it was a part of a PCR gambit and, significantly, this characteristic was *constitutive* of the late 1990s–2000s US housing market in the sense that failing to understand this fact meant failing to understand the phenomenon.

The unprecedented rise in US housing prices in the 2000s was apparent to economists concerned with such issues, and not surprisingly many papers were written on the subject. What *is* surprising is the almost complete lack of connection in the academic economic literature between the dynamics of the housing market, the activity in the related securities markets and the political and regulatory environment that was fueling the interplay between the two. A review of six of the discipline's most prestigious generalist journals and three specialist journals related to housing, banking and finance from 2003 to 2008 turns up no papers that explicitly sought to connect these dots.[19,20] Faccio, Masulis and McConnell (2006) and Schneider and Tornell (2004), two papers that explore the link between political connections and bank bailouts, are possible exceptions, though their focus is largely or entirely non-US and they do not address the specific dynamics of the PCR environment (in the USA or elsewhere). It is significant that this relative silence on the matter from academic economists extends well into 2008 when the crisis had already begun to unfold and journalistic accounts of the connections between the housing market, derivatives market and deregulation were being minutely covered in the financial press.

How should we interpret this? Was this lack of focus on the PCR environment a failing? If so, what kind of failing? If not, is this for ontological, epistemological or methodological reasons? – i.e., was it acceptable to ignore these factors because they are not a part of the economic universe; because, although they are a part of this universe it is impossible to detect them *ex ante*; or because although they are a part of the universe and detectable *ex ante*, economists need not take account of them directly to achieve their (and the discipline's) illuminatory goals?

The basic premise of these questions – i.e., that the discipline may have been blind to factors crucial to the financial crisis – has been debated voluminously in various post-mortem panels, symposia, hearings, academic articles, journalistic articles and opinion pieces. Any kind of comprehensive account of these debates is well beyond the scope of this paper, and I will not attempt one here. Rather, in the remainder of this section, I will briefly put forth and defend one possible answer to these questions – namely, that the neglect of the PCR environment was indeed a failing, and, moreover, was an example of the kind of problem reviewed above (i.e., of blind spots resulting from the confluence of PSS theoretical foundations and ECP–ESP–FP assessment methodology).

In general, what we find in the mainstream literature in the lead-up to the crisis are analyses of the housing market and its attendant financial markets from within the perspective of existing economic models. As such, there is an implicit presumption that the particular markets and institutions under study are not substantially different in nature from other such markets and institutions that have been the subject of similar models. For example, with respect to the behavior of housing prices, we generally see papers examining the impact of specific individual factors in isolation from broader consideration of the broader PCR environment. Several papers addressed the narrow question of whether or not there was a bubble in housing prices by regressing prices against 'fundamental' factors and exploring the extent to which the residual contained a substantial amount of the variation (and also, in some cases, gauging the psychology of home buyer expectations through surveys).[21] Other papers examined the role of land use and construction regulation on home prices.[22] Many papers explored the question of house price dynamics in the abstract by developing general models. Some of these did integrate financial and policy factors – e.g., collateral requirements, borrowing constraints, the secondary mortgage market, monetary policy – but none made specific reference to the peculiar PCR environment of the 2000s market in particular.[23] Another group of papers examined the risk in the financial system in general, with several focusing on the role of liquidity in banking crises and others focusing on other issues in bank risk.[24] But, again, none of these incorporated wider PCR factors.[25] As PCR factors were not included in the models and econometric specifications, they also were not explicitly included in the data used to test the models. Consequently, the generation of hypotheses and the assessment of those hypotheses were completely orthogonal to PCR considerations. The methodology, then, created a blind spot with respect to the effects of PCR factors: even if such factors had significant empirical consequences, these consequences would have been attributed to some other factor that existed within the ontology of the model.

In arguing that PCR considerations were absent from these analyses, I am not claiming that economists would have predicted the financial crisis if only they had taken the PCR into account. My claim is that a class of relevant information was systematically excluded from these analyses *not* by a conscious and informed choice, but *implicitly*, because it lay outside of the models' presumed ontology. This is not to say (because it would not be true) that the PCR environment was invisible to economists. (Consider, for example, Raghuram Rajan's (2005) explicit warning, at the 2005 Fed symposium at Jackson Hole, that the confluence of regulatory, technological and culture changes in the financial industry posed a threat to the economy.) The problem is not that economists *qua individuals* did not recognize these factors, but that economic methodology allowed such factors to remain invisible to them *qua economists*.

The way to address this kind of systematic exclusion is to reform the methodology to make it sensitive to features that are empirically important, but may be outside of what is currently considered economically relevant. This suggestion is in keeping with the general tenor of many of the reform proposals that have emerged from the numerous recent post-mortem analyses of economics' performance in the lead-up to the financial crisis – for example, those calling for more agent-based modeling or a deepening of the behavioral content of models to recognize currently excluded complexity; or those calling for changes in the institutional structure and/or culture of academic economics to encourage a more diverse discourse.[26] To address the kinds of concerns I have discussed above, however, the necessary methodological reform would be more substantial. To be able to assess the plausibility of one's ontological presumptions, it is necessary to have methods for discovering the nature of one's subject matter 'from the bottom up' – that is, to allow for the subject matter itself to reveal its nature, even if that nature is different from or even contrary to that presumed by one's existing models.[27]

To accomplish this, economics would need to incorporate research methods that elicit a more fine-grained portrait of empirical reality. Whether or not this would require major methodological innovation is up for debate. We have examples both within and without the discipline of what such work might look like. Within the discipline, for example, there are calls for such reform along the lines of fine-grained institutional economics (Hodgson 2008, 2009), Post-Keynesian economics (Davidson 2009; Leijonhufvud 2009; Taylor 2010) and critical realist economics (Lawson 2009). And Bewley (1999) provides a concrete example of fine-grained economics specifically tailored to enhance our approach to macroeconomics. From outside the discipline, we have examples of what a more ethnographic style of economic inquiry might look like from recent work in the anthropology of finance.[28] While interpretive methods are not a panacea, and their integration into economics will require considerable effort, I would argue they have the potential to play an important role in covering the blind spots of current economic methodology.

5   Conclusion

The EMF genre of economic writing has been both commercially successful and influential in popular discourse. Careful examination of one of its central explanatory tropes, however, reveals that it is fundamentally misleading. Rather than revealing a hidden structure of everyday life, it presumes that structure, interprets empirical reality from within the framework of that presumed structure and takes this reinterpretation as evidence of the existence of the presumed structures.

Many critics of EMF writing portray it as a bastardized form of economics, implying that its methodological problems are not relevant to mainstream academic economic work. I have argued, on the contrary, that EMF and ostensibly legitimate economic work share a common root in William Stanley Jevons' PSS, and that this common root has infected legitimate economics with some of the same problems bedeviling EMF. Specifically, the PSS allows ontological presuppositions to masquerade as empirically established economic facts. Although academic economics includes rigorous testing standards that ostensibly insulate it from this problem, I have argued that these standards are porous enough not only to let the problem persist, but also to render it invisible. The most direct way to address this problem is to introduce methods that can shine a light upon and directly assess the validity of these ontological presuppositions. Although such methods are not currently in use in mainstream economics, they are a standard tool in the anthropological toolkit, and have been put to good use in exploring, among other things, the nature of financial markets. Because of the seriousness of the lapses that PSS-type problems can cause, it would be beneficial for economists to explore the integration of such anthropological methods into standard economic practice.

Acknowledgements

I am grateful to the participants in the Erasmus Institute for Philosophy and Economics Symposium on the Economics-Made-Fun Genre, December 2010, Rotterdam, for their comments. I also thank Arjun Jayadev and Heike Schotten for helpful comments on an earlier draft. All mistakes are, of course, the responsibility of the author.

Notes

1. This point has been made most forcefully and comprehensively by DiNardo (2007). Rubinstein (2006) offers a brief critique in a similar vein.
2. This is suggested by the title of their chapter, though they do not explicitly state this claim anywhere in the chapter.
3. For example, sneezes and the Crimean War share the common trait that both can be the subjects of sentences.
4. This is not a trivial concession, and DiNardo (2007) offers compelling reasons against making it (with respect to the finding of teacher cheating as well as many of the other findings in *Freakonomics* ostensibly supported by rigorous statistical analysis). I make the concession only to indicate that the points I make here are not dependent upon a critique of the authors' empirical testing methods. If the concession is not made, then my argument in this section would hold even more strongly.
5. Numerous other examples could have been chosen as well – e.g., Harford (2009), Landsburg (1993) or Friedman (1997). Each of these employs the same basic logic as that discussed here.
6. Harper Collins, the publisher of *Freakonomics* and *Superfreakonomics* (Levitt and Dubner 2009), offers a range of companion teaching materials and study guides (see http://files. harpercollins.com/OMM/freakonomics_teaching_materials.html).
7. The specific innovation of Bentham and Boole referenced here is the 'quantification of the predicate.' See Jevons (1869, p. 4).
8. This is a somewhat contentious claim, as Jevons does seem to argue in *The Principles of Science* for a broader understanding of the '=' symbol, noting that 'the meaning of the sign has … been gradually extended beyond that of common [i.e. mathematical] equality' (1958, p. 15). However, he goes on to state that there is 'some real analogy between its diverse meanings' (Jevons 1958, p. 16), and his subsequent discussion is most consistent with the view that it is the non-mathematical uses that conform with the mathematical rather than vice versa. In any event, the mathematical usage is the most restrictive of all the senses of equality he discusses,

and so in order for that sense to be included among the many senses of equality expressed by ' = ' it must be the case that if there is something extra-mathematical about his meaning of ' = ' it could not obviate any of the mathematical meaning of the symbol.

9. The Boole and Thomson referred to in the quotation are the English logician and mathematician George Boole (referred to above in connection with the quantification of the predicate) and the Scottish mathematician and physicist William Thomson, Lord Kelvin.

10. Mill expressed his objections to Jevons' logic directly in a letter to John Elliott Cairnes in December 1871, criticizing Jevons for having 'a mania for encumbering questions with useless complications, and with a notation implying the existence of greater precision in the data than the questions admit of' (Mill 1963, XVII, pp. 1862–1863; cited in Maas 2005, p. 97). For Boole's critique, see Grattan-Guinness (1991).

11. For De Morgan's review of Jevons' logic, see Sánchez Valencia (2001).

12. The statement is taken from De Morgan (1858).

13. I have argued elsewhere (Spiegler 2005) that contemporary economic methodology is incoherent in the absence of such a commitment. See also Spiegler and Milberg (2009) for an application of this argument to a recent example taken from the institutional economics literature.

14. The position has a much longer history that predates economics. Descartes was, famously, comfortable with unrealistic assumptions, holding the predictive and postdictive power of hypotheses as the only legitimate measure of their adequacy. Frustration with this position was the source of Newton's quip *hypotheses non fingo*.

15. See Duhem (1962, esp. p. 185) and Quine (1963, esp. chap. II, secs. 5–6).

16. Suppes (1962) referred to this mediated version of the data as a 'model of the data.' For a discussion of the role of models of data in scientific explanation, see also Suppes (1967).

17. This is not to say that no results coming from such a science could be legitimate and/or correct. Rather, it is to say that since the discipline's standards are blind to the difference between legitimate and (certain types of) illegitimate results, the discipline's stamp of approval alone cannot inspire much confidence.

18. This story has been covered in many venues. See Johnson and Kwak (2010) for a good overview with historical perspective.

19. The journals in question are *The American Economic Review, The Journal of Economic Literature, The Journal of Economic Perspectives, The Journal of Finance, The Journal of Housing Economics, The Journal of Money, Credit and Banking, The Journal of Political Economy, The Quarterly Journal of Economics* and *The Review of Economic Studies*.

20. In the remainder of the paper, I will take these papers to be a proxy for mainstream writing on the housing and financial markets in the lead-up to the crisis.

21. See, e.g., Case and Shiller (2003), Shiller (2007), Goodman and Thibodeau (2008), Himmelberg, Mayer and Sinai (2005) and Smith and Smith (2006). There are also several papers examining the phenomenon of bubbles in general, either through historical review (e.g., LeRoy 2004) or through the construction of a theoretical model of bubbles (e.g., Scheinkman and Xiong 2003).

22. See, e.g., Glaeser, Gyourko and Saks (2005) and Quigley and Raphael (2005).

23. See, e.g., Peek and Wilcox (2006), Iacoviello (2005) and Ortalo-Magné and Rady (2006).

24. In the former group, see, e.g., Diamond and Rajan (2005), Ericsson and Renault (2006) and Gorton and Huang (2004). In the latter group, see, e.g., Morrison and White (2005), Dell'Ariccia and Marquez (2006), Krishnan, Ritchken and Thomson (2005) and Van Order (2006).

25. For the sake of brevity, I do not discuss here the mainstream literature on the macroeconomy in general. The general tenor of this literature was quite upbeat during the 2000s (see, e.g., Chari and Kehoe 2006), though the excessive abstraction of dynamic stochastic general equilibrium modeling during this time has subsequently come in for significant criticism (see, e.g., Colander, Howitt, Kirman, Leijonhufvud, and Mehrling 2008 and Colander et al. 2009).

26. For the first class of proposals, see, e.g., Colander et al. (2009), Shiller (2005) and Allied Social Sciences Association (2009, 2010); for the second class see, e.g., Besley and Hennessey (2009, 2010).

27. See Piore (1979) for a particularly instructive example of this in an economic setting.

28. See, e.g., MacKenzie's (2006, 2009), Zaloom's (2006), Lepinay's (2011) and Ho's (2009) works in the anthropology of finance, Riles' (2011) work in the anthropology of legal

communities supporting financial regulation, and Holmes' (forthcoming) work on the anthropology of central banking.

References

Allied Social Sciences Association (2009), 'Panel Discussion: Recent Financial Crisis', ASSA Annual Meeting, January 3, http://www.aeaweb.org/webcasts/2009/Recent_Financial_Crisis_ Jan_3_2009/Player.php

Allied Social Sciences Association (2010), 'Panel Discussion: How Should the Financial Crisis Change How We Teach Economics?', ASSA Annual Meeting, January 3, Part 1: http://www. aeaweb.org/webcasts/2010/fin_crisis_1/ Part 2: http://www.aeaweb.org/webcasts/2010/fin_ crisis_2/

Besley, T., and Hennessy, P. (2009), 'The Global Financial Crisis – Why Didn't Anybody Notice?', *British Academy Review*, 14, 8–10.

——— (2010), 'Financial and Economic Horizon-Scanning', *British Academy Review*, 15, 12–14.

Bewley, T. (1999), *Why Wages Don't Fall During a Recession*, Cambridge, MA: Harvard University Press.

Black R.D.C., Könekamp R., (eds.) (1972), *Papers and Correspondence of William Stanley Jevons*. (Vol. I: Biography and Personal Journal). London: Macmillan.

Case, K.E., and Shiller, R.J. (2003), 'Is There a Bubble in the Housing Market?', *Brookings Papers on Economic Activity*, 2003(2), 299–342.

Chari, V.V., and Kehoe, P.J. (2006), 'Modern Macroeconomics in Practice: How Theory is Shaping Policy', *Journal of Economic Perspectives*, 4, 3–28.

Colander, D., Goldberg, M., Haas, A., Juselius, K., Kirman, A., Lux, T., and Sloth, B. (2009), 'The Financial Crisis and the Systemic Failure of the Economics Profession', *Critical Review*, 21(2–3), 249–267.

Colander, D., Howitt, P., Kirman, A., Leijonhufvud, A., Mehrling, P., and Beyond, D.S.G.E. (2008), 'Models: Toward and Empirically Based Macroeconomics', *American Economic Review*, 98(2), 236–240.

Cowen, T. (2008), *Discover Your Inner Economist: Use Incentives to Fall in Love, Survive Your Next Meeting, and Motivate Your Dentist*, New York: Plume Books.

Davidson, P. (2009), *The Keynes Solution: The Path to Global Economic Prosperity*, New York: Palgrave Macmillan.

De Morgan, A. (1858), *On the Syllogism, No. III and on Logic in General*, London: Pamphlet.

Dell'Ariccia, G., and Marquez, R. (2006), 'Lending Booms and Lending Standards', *Journal of Finance*, 61(5), 2511–2546.

Diamond, D.W., and Rajan, R.G. (2005), 'Liquidity Shortages and Banking Crises', *Journal of Finance*, 60(2), 615–647.

DiNardo, J. (2007), 'Interesting Questions in *Freakonomics*', *Journal of Economic Literature*, 45(4), 973–1000.

Duggan, M., and Levitt, S.D. (2002), 'Winning Isn't Everything: Corruption in Sumo Wrestling', *American Economic Review*, 92(5), 1594–1605.

Duhem, P.(P.P. Weiner,trans.) (1962), *The Aim and Structure of Physical Theory* ((2nd ed.)), New York: Atheneum.

Ericsson, J., and Renault, O. (2006), 'Liquidity and Credit Risk', *Journal of Finance*, 61(5), 2219–2250.

Faccio, M., Masulis, R.W., and McConnell, J.J. (2006), 'Political Connections and Corporate Bailouts', *Journal of Finance*, 61(6), 2597–2635.

Friedman, M. (1953), *Essays on Positive Economics*, Chicago: University of Chicago Press.

Friedman, D. (1997), *Hidden Order: The Economics of Everyday Life*, New York: Harper Business.

Glaeser, E.L., Gyourko, J., and Saks, R.E. (2005), 'Why Have Housing Prices Gone Up?', *The American Economic Review*, 95(2), 329–333.

Goodman, A.C., and Thibodeau, T.G. (2008), 'Where are the Speculative Bubbles in US Housing Markets?', *Journal of Housing Economics*, 17, 117–137.

Gorton, G., and Huang, L. (2004), 'Liquidity, Efficiency, and Bank Bailouts', *The American Economic Review*, 94(3), 455–483.

Grattan-Guinness, I. (1991), 'The Correspondence Between George Boole and Stanley Jevons, 1863–1864', *History and Philosophy of Logic*, 12, 15–35.

Harford, T. (2009), *Dear Undercover Economist: Priceless Advice on Money, Work, Sex, Kids and Life's Other Challenges*, New York: Random House Trade Paperbacks.

Himmelberg, C., Mayer, C., and Sinai, T. (2005), 'Assessing High House Prices: Bubbles, Fundamentals and Misperceptions', *Journal of Economic Perspectives*, 19(4), 67–92.

Ho, K. (2009), *Liquidated: An Ethnography of Wall Street*, Durham, NC: Duke University Press.

Hodgson, G.M. (2008), 'After 1929 Economics Changed: Will Economists Wake Up in 2009?', *Real-World Economics Review*, 48, 273–278.

———— (2009), 'The Great Crash of 2008 and the Reform of Economics', *Cambridge Journal of Economics*, 33, 1205–1221.

Holmes, D.R. (forthcoming), *Economy of Words: How Central Banks Underwrite the Future with Faith and Credit*, Chicago, IL: University of Chicago Press.

Iacoviello, M. (2005), 'House Prices, Borrowing Constraints, and Monetary Policy in the Business Cycle', *American Economic Review*, 95(3), 739–764.

Jacob, B.A., and Levitt, S.D. (2003a), 'Rotten Apples: An Investigation of the Prevalence and Predictors of Teacher Cheating', *Quarterly Journal of Economics*, 118(3), 843–877.

———— (2003b), 'Catching Cheating Teachers: The Results of an Unusual Experiment in Implementing Theory', *Brookings-Wharton Papers on Urban Affairs*, 4, 185–209.

Jevons, W.S. (1869), *The Substitution of Similars*, London: Macmillan.

———— (1871), *The Theory of Political Economy*, London: Macmillan.

———— (1874), *The Principles of Science: A Treatise on Logic and Scientific Method*. (American ed.). New York: Macmillan.

———— (1958), *The Principles of Science: A Treatise on Logic and Scientific Method*. (Reprint of 1887 reprint of 2nd (1874) ed., Introduction by Ernest Nagel). New York: Dover Books.

Johnson, S., and Kwak, J. (2010), *13 Bankers: The Wall Street Takeover and the Next Financial Meltdown*, New York: Pantheon.

Krishnan, C.N.V., Ritchken, P.H., and Thomson, J.B. (2005), 'Monitoring and Controlling Bank Risk: Does Risky Debt Help?', *Journal of Finance*, 40(1), 343–378.

Landsburg, S.E. (1993), *The Armchair Economist: Economics and Everyday Life*, New York: Free Press.

Lawson, T. (2009), 'The Current Economic Crisis: Its Nature and the Course of Academic Economics', *Cambridge Journal of Economics*, 33, 759–777.

Leijonhufvud, A. (2009), 'Out of the Corridor: Keynes and the Crisis', *Cambridge Journal of Economics*, 33, 741–757.

Lepinay, V.A. (2011), *Codes of Finance: Engineering Derivatives in a Global Bank*, Princeton, NJ: Princeton University Press.

LeRoy, S. (2004), 'Rational Exuberance', *Journal of Economic Literature*, 42(3), 783–804.

Levitt, S.D., and Dubner, S.J. (2005), *Freakonomics: A Rogue Economist Explores the Hidden Side of Everything*, New York: William Morrow.

———— (2009), *Superfreakonomics: Global Cooling, Patriotic Prostitutes, and Why Suicide Bombers Should Buy Life Insurance*, New York: William Morrow.

Maas, H. (2005), *William Stanley Jevons and the Making of Modern Economics*, New York/Cambridge: Cambridge University Press.

MacIntyre, A. (1978), 'Is a Science of Comparative Politics Possible?', in *Against the Self-Images of the Age: Essays on Ideology and Philosophy*, Notre Dame, IN: University of Notre Dame Press, pp. 0.

MacKenzie, D.A. (2006), *An Engine, Not a Camera: How Financial Models Shape Markets*, Cambridge, MA: MIT Press.

———— (2009), *Material Markets: How Economic Agents are Constructed*, New York: Oxford University Press.

Mill, J.S. (1963), *Collected Works of John Stuart Mill*. (33 Vols.). ed. J.M. Robson, Toronto: University of Toronto Press.

Morrison, A.D., and White, L. (2005), 'Crises and Capital Requirements in Banking', *The American Economic Review*, 95(5), 1548–1572.

Ortalo-Magné, F., and Rady, S. (2006), 'Housing Market Dynamics: On the Contribution of Income Shocks and Credit Constraints', *The Review of Economic Studies*, 73(2), 459–485.

Peek, J., and Wilcox, J.A. (2006), 'Housing, Credit Constraints and Macro Stability: The Secondary Mortgage Market and Reduced Cyclicality of Residential Investment', *The American Economic Review*, 96(2), 135–140.

Piore, M. (1979), 'Qualitative Research Techniques in Economics', *Administrative Science Quarterly*, 24(4), 560–569.

Quigley, J.M., and Raphael, S. (2005), 'Regulation and the High Cost of Housing in California', *The American Economic Review*, 95(2), 323–328.

Quine, W.V. (1963), *From a Logical Point of View* ((2nd ed.)), New York: Harper & Row.

Rajan, R.G. (2005), 'Has Financial Development Made the World Riskier?', Symposium Proceedings: The Greenspan Era – Lessons for the Future, Federal Reserve Bank of Kansas City. http://www.kansascityfed.org/publicat/sympos/2005/pdf/Rajan2005.pdf

Riles, A. (2011), *Collateral Knowledge: Legal Reasoning in the Global Financial Markets*, Chicago, IL: University of Chicago Press.

Rubinstein, A. (2006), 'Freak-freakonomics', *The Economists' Voice*, 3, 9, Article 7.

Sánchez Valencia, V. (2001), 'An Athanaeum Curiosity: De Morgan's Reviews of Boole and Jevons', *History and Philosophy of Logic*, 22(2), 75–79.

Scheinkman, J.A., and Xiong, W. (2003), 'Overconfidence and Speculative Bubbles', *Journal of Political Economy*, 111(6), 1183–1219.

Schneider, M., and Tornell, A. (2004), 'Balance Sheet Effects, Bailout Guarantees and Financial Crises', *The Review of Economic Studies*, 3, 883–913.

Shiller, R.J. (2005), *Irrational Exuberance* ((2nd ed.)), Princeton, NJ: Princeton University Press.

——— (2007), 'Understanding Recent Trends in House Prices and Home Ownership', *Proceedings: Housing, Housing Finance and Monetary Policy Symposium, Federal Reserve Bank of Kansas City*, http://www.kansascityfed.org/publicat/sympos/2007/PDF/Shiller_0415.pdf

Smith, M.W., and Smith, G. (2006), 'Bubble, Bubble, Where's the Housing Bubble?', *Brookings Papers on Economic Activity*, 2006(1), 1–50.

Spiegler, P. (2005), 'A Constructive Critique of Economics', unpublished Ph.D. dissertation, Harvard University, Dept. of Economics.

Spiegler, P., and Milberg, W. (2009), 'Taming Institutions in Economics: The Rise and Methodology of the "*New* New Institutionalism,"', *Journal of Institutional Economics*, 5(3), 289–313.

Suppes, P. (1962), 'Models of Data', in *Logic, Methodology and the Philosophy of Science: Proceedings*, eds. E. Nagel, P. Suppes and A. Tarski, Stanford, CA: Stanford University Press, pp. 252–261.

——— (1967), 'What is a Scientific Theory?', in *Philosophy of Science Today*, ed. S. Morgenbesser, New York: Basic Books, pp. 55–67.

Taylor, L. (2010), *Maynard's Revenge: The Collapse of Free Market Macroeconomics*, Cambridge, MA: Harvard University Press.

Van Order, R. (2006), 'A Model of Financial Structure and Financial Fragility', *Journal of Money, Credit and Banking*, 38(3), 565–585.

Zaloom, C. (2006), *Out of the Pits: Traders and technology from Chicago to London*, Chicago, IL: University of Chicago Press.

The evolving notion of relevance: an historical perspective to the 'economics made fun' movement

Jean-Baptiste Fleury

THEMA - Université de Cergy-Pontoise, Cergy-Pontoise, France

This paper aims to study the 'economics made fun' literature with regard to its main purpose: popularizing economics. We shed an historical light on such literature by showing that its main strategy for introducing economics to non-specialists had already been tried in the 1970s in what were described as "issues-oriented" textbooks. We show that both literatures, as introductory enterprises, were responses to similar challenges. The first one is the problem of economic illiteracy, a problem that has concerned teachers in economics since the early 1960s. Both literatures did offer an interesting response to perceived shortcomings of introductory courses. The second challenge came from the attacks on economics and its teaching for their lack of relevance. We explore how the notion of relevance evolved in time and how both literatures attempted to respond to the criticisms of their time accordingly. By addressing these questions, our study explores how economists used these introductory enterprises to disseminate a certain image of them and their discipline in comparison to other social scientists and non-specialists, and how these representations evolved in time.

1 Introduction

The literature that has been called 'economics made fun' (EMF) has, among others, two important goals: one is to boost the public image of economics; the other is to make its reader more economically literate. So far, the EMF literature has been criticized for its choice of topics, too 'freaky,' too 'cute,' and too far away from 'big' (macro)economic problems (e.g. Vromen 2009). Yet, there has been no examination of the EMF literature with regard to its main purpose: popularizing the economic mode of thinking for the non-specialist. This paper examines how this genre faced many challenges that such purpose raised in time, through a comparison with previous introductory endeavors.

To address a non-scholarly audience, EMF books have chosen to introduce a few basic principles and apply them to a host of issues, carefully chosen to stimulate the interest of the reader (Vromen 2009). Interestingly, although the EMF appears as a brand new genre, the same strategy for introducing economics to non-specialists had already been tried in the 1970s in what were described as 'issues-oriented' textbooks. Comparing the two literatures proves very interesting, since both, as introductory enterprises, were responses to similar challenges. The first one is the problem of economic illiteracy. Both literatures chose to introduce a few basic principles in a non-formal way so that the reader could master them fully, to better disseminate the 'economic way of thinking.' Although EMF books are not textbooks *per se*, we will show that they, like the 1970s textbooks, can be understood as a powerful response to perceived shortcomings of introductory courses, especially at the undergraduate level, at different periods of time.

The second challenge has come from the attacks on economics and its teaching for its lack of relevance. In this paper, we investigate how the understanding of what is and is not relevant in economics has shifted. Then, we analyze how the issues-oriented textbooks and the EMF literature responded to this evolving problem, through, for example, the way they chose their topics and how they depicted the economist vis-à-vis other social scientists and common wisdom. In the context of social unrest of the late 1960s, economics and its teaching were thought as lacking relevance because they failed to address the social issues of the day, which lay outside the traditional boundaries of economics. The 1970s issues-oriented courses responded to these criticisms by depicting economics as a policy science applicable to these problems. In the 1980s and 1990s, however, the understanding of relevance shifted. Economics and its teaching, once again, were under fire for lacking relevance but now it was because they failed to relate to the observation of the real world, especially the students' everyday life. In such context, the EMF – notably through its emphasis on 'naturalism' – can be understood as a response to these criticisms, and, in the meantime, a way to boost the image of economics to the general public.

In Section 2, we study the context of the 1960s and the innovative attempts to reshape introductory courses so as to make them effective and relevant. In Section 3, we study the evolution of the notion of relevance in the 1980s and 1990s and analyze the EMF literature in the light of this changing context. Finally, Section 4 offers concluding remarks.

2　Facing the problems of relevance and illiteracy in the 1970s

Many commentators agree that from the mid-1960s on, the unprecedented increase of the student–faculty ratio in universities profoundly transformed the task of teaching. The lack of 'flexibility to accommodate the diverse interests and abilities of students' that arose out of mass education raised dissatisfaction among both professors and students (Mandelstamm, Petr and Segebarth 1971; Phillips 1971; Wallis 1973, p. 26). Dissatisfaction was also fueled by the student unrest starting in the mid-1960s. Student activists pointed out the seemingly paradoxical conduct of two wars, one in Vietnam against communism and another within the USA against poverty (Phillips 1971; Bender 1997). Their involvement in the 'movement' reinforced the domestic tensions within the USA at the time.

At a time when Civil rights demonstrations made the headlines, students attacked the ivory-tower behavior of scholars and protested against the 'lack of relevance' of many academic disciplines. Economics, political science, literary analysis and many other disciplines found themselves at odds with students' demands (McCleery and Parente 1968, p. 316; Metzger 1969; Solow 1970, p. 94; Gallagher 1997, p. 145). Considering economics only, these criticisms did not imply that traditional macroeconomics had never been relevant: inflation, employment and the growth of national product had been considered relevant in the 1930s, but the meaning of relevance had changed and in the 1960s a leading macroeconomist (Solow 1970, p. 96) could write, 'the macroeconomic problems now seem ... less urgent than the problems of war, poverty, racial discrimination, urban decay, traffic congestion ....' Traditional introductory courses in economics typically stood in stark contrast with students' demands for 'subjects like the draft, the war in Vietnam, ethnic problems, drugs, the generation gap, and so on' (Blyth 1970, p. 380; Heilbroner 1970).

Students' concerns were not completely homogeneous, but among them, radicals were very influential in their challenge to traditional academic disciplines and teaching. They were responsible for the development of student-initiated courses, for instance in Harvard, to overcome the alleged inability of the establishment to address 'relevant' issues (Mata 2009). Their attacks on teaching could not be separated from their attacks on scholarly research, which, likewise, pointed out the neglect of such topics. During the summer 1968, they asked both the American Political Association and the American Sociological Association meetings to state their official position regarding the pressing social issues, and, in the case of economics, radicals organized an alternative to the meeting of the American Economic Association (AEA) (McCleery and Parente 1968; Mata 2009). These attacks on the discipline's lack of relevance echoed a profound conflict within the social sciences (McCleery and Parente 1968, p. 318). For instance, these years of social unrest challenged the leading approaches in political science, behavioralism, which studied the democratic process and its stability drawing from the leading framework in sociology, structural functionalism (Smith 1997, p. 260; Backhouse and Fontaine 2010). Mainstream economists themselves came to realize that although economics had secured important achievements regarding its own traditional problems, they had failed to address the burning social issues of the day (e.g. Schultze 1971).

Yet, in the late 1960s, a number of economists interested in educational methods rejected the idea that economics could not handle 'relevant' issues, and debated the possibility of redesigning the content of introductory courses. However, in doing so, they faced another important problem: these courses did not appear to have any lasting effect on the students who took them. Although this was not a new problem, the mid-1960s witnessed the emergence of studies that tested what was labeled the 'Stigler hypothesis' – that after a while, college students who had followed an introductory course in economics were as economically illiterate as other students (Stigler 1963, p. 657). Such an approach called for a nationwide objective test of student's knowledge and teaching effectiveness, and in 1963, the Test of Economic Understanding was created and used to gather data at the high school level. In 1965, leading economists such as Paul Samuelson and Stigler, as well as leading scholars in economic education, such as Rendigs Fels, took part in the design of a Test of Understanding in College Economics (Villard 1969). These tests would be extensively used to evaluate of the efficiency of new teaching styles and methods developed in the late 1960s and during the 1970s.

Fels, Stigler and many others were convinced that introductory courses covered too much material, an encyclopedic aspect that was 'fashionable' among economists, but that eroded the lasting effect of the course. The average student felt 'hopelessly swamped' and could not properly master basic economic principles (Mandelstamm et al. 1971). For these specialists in economic education, illiteracy was thus to be fought by reducing the amount of material covered during the first semesters.

Debating and evaluating various teaching methods was, essentially, the *raison d'être* of the nascent subfield of economic education. Despite the attacks on the relevance of economics and its teaching, economic education did not aim to redefine economics on new foundations. Many agreed with Fels (1969) that the field should apply the same techniques as were employed in standard research in economics. This ambitious program explains why economists, unlike other social scientists, took a leading role in the development of innovative teaching methods (Lumsden 1969).[1] In 1969, the Joint Council on Economic Education (JCEE) followed the recommendations of the AEA and created the *Journal of Economic Education* (JEE), with Fels sitting on editorial board (Fels 1969). The creation of the journal marked the beginning of a creative decade, favorable for experimenting with new styles of teaching economics to respond more efficiently to the problems of relevance and economic illiteracy. In particular, the JCEE, in a joint effort with the AEA's Committee on Economic Education, supported the development of experimental courses soon labeled 'issues-oriented' (Welsh 1974). Most experiments, such as Leftwich and Sharp's three-year test program at Oklahoma State University starting in 1973, shared a concern for limiting the set of principles introduced. Mastery would only arise out of relentless application of these principles to various relevant problems. Some of these experiments drew explicitly on psychological analysis of learning behavior. At Vanderbilt University in the early 1970s, Fels and Ewing P. Shahan redesigned the course in favor of a combination of the case method (used in Law schools) and the personal self-paced instruction (PSI) method, the latter comprising the supervision by a proctor of various assignments and, later, oral and written tests (Fels 1974).[2] Here too, the consequence of this approach was the reduction of the amount of material covered in a semester, and prioritizing to full mastery of the material: students could only move on to new material only after they had passed the exam with a sufficiently high grade. Phillip Saunders's four-terms experiment at the University of Indiana, based on an experimental course delivered in the mid-1960s at Carnegie-Mellon, also relied on psychology. Saunders (1975, p. 5) insisted on giving the student a firm grasp of the 'few basic principles and analytical tools they need' and, consequently, on learning to think about economic problems.

Meanwhile, textbooks pertaining to this approach emerged. Some were directly related to these experiments, as with Fels and Uhler's *Casebook of Economic Problems and Policies* ([1969] 1976), and Leftwich and Sharp's *Economics of Social Issues* ([1974] 1976). Some others were inspired by experiments in other disciplines, for instance *The Economist Looks at Society* (1973), coauthored by the Northeastern University economist Gustav Schachter and the *New York Times* journalist Edwin Dale, which adapted the experimental course in biology by Herman Epstein at Brandeis University (Eberhard 1969). More generally, the number of issues-oriented textbooks rose in the first half of the 1970s, while the 'increasing number of pages devoted to issues in principles textbooks' testified to the interest generated by the approach (Leftwich and Sharp 1974, p. 3).[3]

By reducing the content covered, the proponents of the 'issues-oriented' approach agreed that the most important thing for the student to learn was to think like an economist. As a consequence, this definition of the purpose of teaching influenced the content of the economics chosen, with the result that the subject matter of economics becoming the means to the end – that is, improving the student's intellectual skills (Mandelstamm et al. 1971). Many issues-oriented books defined economics to reflect this: economics was defined as 'a mental skill that incorporates a special view of human behavior characteristic of economists' (McKenzie and Tullock 1975, p. 5; see also Fels and Uhler [1969] 1976; Saunders 1975). A relevant course would introduce in mostly non-technical language the basic features of this mode of thinking, i.e. scarcity, opportunity costs, supply and demand, marginal analysis, market clearing, elasticity and efficiency. This approach to teaching was reminiscent of the Chicago view of economics, which considered the discipline as a set of tools to be applied to real-life and policy problems, not a game played by clever academics. Although this approach was not consensual in the early 1950s, it was less idiosyncratic two decades later.

This mental skill was systematically applied to concrete problems, thereby addressing the criticism that economics lacked relevance.[4] Most textbooks explored pressing social issues, and some also explored problems related to everyday life, but they all shared an interest in topics considered to be outside the traditional scope of economics. Some of them addressed almost exclusively noneconomic topics. For instance, Leftwich and Sharp's *Economics of Social Issues* ([1974] 1976), Culyer's *The Economics of Social Policy* ([1973] 1975), Miller and North's *The Economics of Public Issues* ([1971] 1976), Dale and Schachter's *The Economist Looks at Society* (1973) and McKenzie and Tullock's *The New World of Economics* (1975). These textbooks hoped to depart from the usual depiction as 'dull,' 'dry,' and 'difficult' and a number of them were written entertainingly, by, for instance, introducing chapters with fictitious stories involving students and marijuana (Leftwich and Sharp 1974), or provocative statements like: '[f]or 1974, New York City chose to permit 1,555 murders, 77,940 robberies, 158,321 burglaries, and 26,084 assaults as well as various numbers of lesser crimes' (Miller and North 1976, p. 119).

A few textbooks (Fels 1969) understood relevance as a set of practical issues belonging *only* to the traditional domain of economics, because studying topics too far from economics would only reinforce the criticisms against the lack of relevance of the discipline. Yet, in between these two extremes, most courses included real-world examples both inside and outside the traditional scope of economics. They depicted economists as policy advisers claiming practical relevance on a well-defined set of topics: population growth, income redistribution, higher education, health care, pollution and environmental problems. Crime was generally addressed, but other burning topics, such as abortion, prostitution, marriage and the family, political behavior, as well as racial and gender discrimination, were addressed in only a few texts (see also Feiner and Morgan 1987). During the 1970s, this expanded view of the scope of economics progressively permeated 'regular' textbooks as well.

This new scope of analysis called for some justification and, in providing one, these books offered a favorable depiction of the economist and his role in relation to 'others.' In Culyer's book, economists and their scientific outlook were opposed to practitioners of public policy, who were said to be entangled in party politics. Dale and Schachter (1973, p. v) considered that economists were able to measure the effect of discrimination better than any 'decent American.' Other texts were less clear as to whom economists were being compared: Leftwich and Sharp's experimental classes would begin, for instance, with a comparison between economics and so-called 'common wisdom.' Aggregating the views of the layman, journalists and other social scientists into such a common wisdom provided a powerful rhetoric with which to criticize other social sciences and underline the power of economics. Sociologists, journalists and others, including old-fashioned economists who did not believe in the relevance of economic analysis outside its traditional boundaries, were often portrayed refusing either to investigate 'real' questions or to seek realistic answers. They opposed, for instance, the use of dollar values to evaluate human life, or the use of the rationality assumption to study criminal behavior (McKenzie and Tullock 1975). In contrast, the economist did not offer a 'simpleminded' solution nor did he rely on Utopias (Dale and Schachter 1973, p. vi).[5] Showing every characteristic of true scientific behavior, the economist alone stood against the many attempts to prevent scientific reasoning from prevailing.

The scientific character of economics rested in its complexity and its counterintuitive results. Economic education was important because it introduced marginal analysis that was not found in other disciplines but was very important for dealing with public policies. In the context of domestic crisis, the economist was pictured as a savior, a scientific superhero who used a 'more comprehensive' approach 'than any other' (Culyer [1973] 1975, p. 260).[6] It is thus not surprising to find that several of these textbooks were authored by economists responsible for expanding the scope of economics during the 1960s, including North, Culyer, Tullock, Simon Rottenberg, and Phillips and Votey. Given that those involved in 'economics imperialism' had not yet convinced the economics profession as a whole, the 'issues-oriented approach' provided an opportunity to demonstrate the relevance of their work and to disseminate their message about disciplinary boundaries to a wider audience. They echoed the struggles at the scholarly and political levels about the role of economics in social policy making, illustrated by the early 1970s debates on the possible creation of a Council for Social Advisers (see Fleury 2010). Yet, more 'traditional' economists also contributed to this textbook literature, which, added to its relative success at the time, provided evidence the profession's growing acceptance of its expanded domain of expertise.

3 Relevance, economic education and the EMF movement

In the 1980s, the impetus for reshaping introductory courses lost momentum, as did issues-oriented pedagogy, which was progressively dropped in favor of more traditional introductory courses (Grimes 2009). One reason is these experiments produced no significant differences in tests scores or lasting effects (Leftwich, Sharp and Bumpass 1975; Siegfried and Strand 1976; Leftwich 1977). Another is that, from the late 1970s to the mid-1990s, there was considerably less interest in developing new teaching methods at the undergraduate level: economists progressively lost their lead in that domain and were 'noticeably absent from groups formed to advance college teaching' (Becker 1997, p. 1351). Moreover, according to a few proponents of issues-oriented courses, these required far more work than a traditional course (Grimes 2009). Finally, the 1980s witnessed an increase in graduate education at the expense of liberal arts type of education, concomitant to a strong emphasis on research at the expense of teaching, which increased the technical prerequisites of the undergraduate level (Becker 1997).

In conjunction with the increasing specialization of research in 1980s and 1990s, this context contributed to the growing content covered during introductory courses. This development was regularly criticized during the period, in particular during the 1987 conference on principles of economics textbooks and by the 1991 Commission on Graduate Education in Economics.[7] Most specialists agreed that the best-selling textbook at the time, *Economics,* by Paul Samuelson and William Nordhaus, was having a bad influence on the market for textbooks (e.g. Shaw Bell 1988; Dolan 1988). The rise of conglomerates in the higher education publishing industry during the 1980s played a major role in developing a fierce non-price competition (the 'package war') over content, coverage, printing quality and supplementary material, which also led to a great deal of homogeneity (Thompson 2005). As a consequence, it was generally considered, until the early 2000s, that principles textbooks were not introductory anymore (e.g. Case 1988). Once again, specialists in economic education missed the intuitive Chicago style of economic analysis, which managed to link theories to the real world through stories (Case 1988; Krueger 1991).

Scholarly research faced similar criticisms. In the 1980s and 1990s, relevant economics no longer meant the study of social issues but had come to mean the study of the 'real world,' taken to imply an emphasis on observation and empiricism. Economics had become very technical, fascinated by model building (Solow 1997), which could appear as an irrelevant intellectual exercise.[8] Moreover, critiques lamented that economists did not act as biologists and other natural scientists, that is, they (allegedly) did not spend time observing the world to gather data (Colander 1998; Bergmann 2005). Graduate programs were also attacked for not rewarding creative thinking (Colander 1998).

From the mid-1990s onwards, macroeconomics was criticized for failing to consider well-established phenomena such as involuntary unemployment, financial bubbles and banking collapses (e.g. Akerlof 2002; Bergmann 2005). Relevance in macroeconomics was argued to require observing the actual behavior of agents and the institutional settings in which they operated. Thus, some critiques welcomed the new theoretical insight drawn from behavioral economics, which introduced sociological and anthropological insights to better understand real-world observations, as well as the experimental economics of Daniel Kahnemann, Amos Tversky, and Vernon Smith, and the revival of survey methodology on actual business behavior by Alan Blinder and Truman Bewley.

These criticisms were permeated by a new ideal for scientific investigation as defined by a particular view of the natural scientist. It emphasized empiricism and observation at the expense of pure deductive reasoning (drawn from physics), and advocated open-mindedness to sociological and psychological insights (e.g. Kreps 1997; Colander 2000). That David Card and Steven Levitt were awarded the Bates Clark Medal illustrates the renewed interest, since the late 1980s, for natural experiments, i.e. situations 'where the forces of nature or government policy have conspired to produce an environment somewhat akin to a randomize experiment' (Angrist and Krueger 2001, p. 73).

In contrast, for undergraduate students of the 1980s and 1990s, relevance was defined not in terms of empiricism but in relation to the student's own life, a life that had evolved since the late 1960s. Students of the early 1980s were generally described as self-concerned, career-driven, choosing safe curricula (sciences, pre-law) in a context of sluggish economy. In sum, students turned inward and when they wished to tackle real-world social problems, they did it from the point of view of their own everyday life, their town or their neighborhood, by engaging in community service (Altbach and Cohen 1990; Hirsch and Levine 1991). With the fading of student unrest, economics and its teaching faced less incentive to adapt to students' demands; this helps explain why the discipline remained 'consistently at the bottom of both course and instructor effectiveness scales' when compared to 45 other disciplines (Becker 1997, p. 1369).

Not only had economists been criticized for the dry, technical and overloaded content of their teaching: they had also neglected their role as public intellectuals (Solow 1983). Apart from a few books, such as Heilbroner's *Worldly Philosophers,* there were no books equivalent to the bestsellers that popularized physics or the natural sciences, such as the ones by Albert Einstein and Richard Dawkins (Day 1989). Until the late 1980s, economists were unable or unwilling to provide the general population with books that would convey their passion for the distinctiveness and rigor of their discipline (Day 1989). So far, the way economics was popularized in newspapers overemphasized the differences in opinion among economists. Regarding popular books, they were either highly critical of the 'fallacies' of the discipline, or viewed as ideological enterprises (e.g. Milton Friedman's *Capitalism and Freedom*). Economists had failed to develop a suitable style with which to address the general population, which required stories, actors and 'events in the real world' (Lamm 1989, p. 96). Consequently, economics books were progressively ignored by reviewers in the most important newspapers, for instance the *New York Times Book Review.*

Yet, economists saw their influence as public intellectuals rise and faced an increased demand in economic expertise. They also adapted to the evolutions of mass media in the 1980s: shorter columns in newspapers and magazines led to an increase in the number of columnists and diversity of topics addressed. To respond to the perceived changes in their audience's demand, newspapers asked for Black voices, women's voices, sexual experts, etc. Lifestyle became an important and relevant subject for the audience, and consequently, 'fun' was a word that increasingly described 'the mind state of readers and writers' (Joffe 2003). That Gary Becker pioneered in addressing an impressive variety of topics with provocative recommendations in his columns for *Business Week* from the mid-1980s on is only one illustration of this change.

Thus, in the early 1990s, introducing economics to non-specialists had to take into account this changed view of relevance. Moreover, given the state of the textbook market, smaller commercial publishers and university presses reoriented part of their resources toward the publishing of trade books and academic trade books (Thompson 2005). In such context, Steven Landsburg's 1991 book proposal, 'Prospectus for The Economic Naturalist,' might appear as an opportunistic move. The book aimed to offer a consensual view of the economic mode of thinking that would compete with other science popularization books in the shelves of popular bookstores. That Landsburg was not initially trained in economics, but mathematics, and yet enjoyed the conversations with Chicago economists during lunch breaks, might explain his motivation. Landsburg's book project applied a few basic economic principles to provide insights into the real world the same way that popular writers on biology applied natural selection (Landsburg 1991, p. 1). Landsburg's *Economic Naturalist* eventually turned into the best-selling *The Armchair Economist* (1993). Its publication soon prompted Landsburg's friend, David Friedman, to publish a similar book, *The Hidden Order* (1996). The genre boomed only a few years later, in the early 2000s, with the publications (among others) of Coyle's *Sex, Drugs, and Economics* (2002), Charles Wheelan's *Naked Economics*, Tim Harford's *The Undercover Economist* – a project that began in 2001 under the advice of a science writer friend, eventually published in 2006. Finally, Stephen Dubner's 2003 paper on Steven Levitt for the *New York Times Magazine* eventually lead to the best-selling *Freakonomics* (2005).

As Vromen (2009) noted, these popularization books were not all written for the exact same purpose. Some aimed at mastery of the economic way of thinking (Landsburg, Harford, Frank), some offered an overview of recent developments in economics (Coyle), Tyler Cowen's was a self-help book and *Freakonomics* only exposed Levitt's work. Yet, they all focused on a limited set of basic principles, which included most of the microeconomics principles found in the issues-oriented literature of the 1970s, i.e. opportunity costs, equimarginality, supply and demand, externalities, and price discrimination. To this list, the 2000s literature added recent development in economics such as information asymmetries as well as insights from behavioral and experimental economics, sociology and psychology. Like the 1970s textbooks, this literature applied those principles to issues relevant to the targeted audience, but left aside the graphs in favor of an entertaining writing style. These books are, thus, quite similar to Miller and North's *The Economics of Public Issues* ([1971] 1976), written as a complement to introductory courses. That Miller and North's other book, *Abortion, Baseball and Weed* (1973), was one of the books that had the most influence on Cowen as a student is of no surprise.

This approach was instrumental in fighting the negative image of economics and promoting its scientific character. The limited content was an integral part of the economist's way of thinking, separating them from other scientists and uniting them around a rigorous approach (e.g. Landsburg 1993; Wheelan 2002). Moreover, to both remain fun and provide a consensual depiction of the results and applications of economics, these books avoided important macroeconomic issues, contrary to the issues-oriented textbooks that covered poverty, growth and involuntary unemployment. For Landsburg (1993), modern macroeconomics was only two decades old and had yet to succeed. This did not mean, though, that pop-economists did not address the 'big' issues facing society at all, but rather that these issues were tackled using entertaining stories about the riddles of everyday life. For instance, the environmental question of endangered species would be studied through the answer to the funny question 'Why are whales in danger of extinction, but not chickens?' (Frank [2007] 2008).

The economic mode of thinking remained the main theme that writers wanted to popularize, but the pop-economics books depicted economics and its practitioners slightly differently from the way their 1970s counterparts did. Economics was not introduced as a toolbox for analyzing public policy issues, but as a set of patterns useful for understanding situations of everyday life and human behavior in society. Economics was now defined as the study of how human behavior responds to incentives, and, as Landsburg ([1993] 2009, p. 3) wrote 'the rest is commentary.' Observation was emphasized much more than in the 1970s textbooks, as is illustrated by the emphasis on naturalism by Landsburg and Frank. Economics consisted in 'observing the world with genuine curiosity,' to unravel hidden patterns, that is, to use Cowen's words, to discover one's own 'Inner Economist' through practice.

Like Levitt, some of these authors would characterize themselves broadly, as social scientists. The study of incentives was not necessarily limited to monetary ones, and could extend to reputation and social norms (e.g. Cowen 2007). References to the pioneering work of Akerlof, Kahneman and Tversky, and Thomas Schelling showed that although rational choice remained at the heart of their approach, most authors considered the possibility of groups deviating from the optimal solution. In comparison to the 1970s textbooks, one finds a description of the economist as being much less arrogant vis-à-vis the other social sciences.[9] Consequently, the way economics was compared to common wisdom evolved. Authors had to solve a complex problem: for economic reasoning to be accessible, the arguments should be concise and clear (e.g. Frank's 500-word assignment, discussed below, or Cowen's 'postcard' test), sometimes jargon-free, but in the meantime, the counterintuitive nature of economic reasoning still grounded its scientific character.[10] Thus, arguments needed to make sense when confronted to real-world situations *and* common sense, while unraveling some hidden truth.[11]

Changing the practice of the economist came with a change in its representation. Aware of the negative image of economics, most writers did not write about the average dismal scientist, and chose rather to tell stories about an 'armchair economist,' a 'freakonomist,' an 'undercover economist,' an 'inner economist' and, of course, an 'economic naturalist.' The economist depicted here was not interested in pure mathematics and technical analysis, but curious about the real world and clever in his analysis of observations. Levitt was depicted approaching the world 'not so much as an academic, but as a very smart and curious explorer – a documentary filmmaker, perhaps, or a forensic investigator or a bookie whose markets ranged from sports to crime and pop culture' (Dubner and Levitt [2005] 2009, p. xii). This representation can be understood a timely response to the criticisms against the lack of relevance of economics, as well as the shortcomings of its popularization until the mid-1990s.

Given the state of economic education in the 1990s, this pop-economics literature also performed promising pedagogical functions, and, indeed, emerged in conjunction with a new impetus for teaching economics at a time of an apparent decrease in the enrollment of economics majors (Becker and Watts 2001; Becker 2003). Once again, specialists in economic education actively engaged in the fight against the encyclopedic character of textbooks as with the creation in 1997 of the Voluntary National Content Standards in Economics by Michael Salemi and John Siegfried (Hansen, Salemi and Siegfried 2002).[12] Frank (2002) himself added to the laments on the state of teaching and introduced his 'Economic Naturalist' course as an effective solution. Students had to write a 500-word paper in which they were required to apply the basic principles studied in class to a real-life paradox. The collection of the best papers eventually became Frank's *Economic Naturalist*. Likewise, Coyle's 2002 book was written for an audience of undergraduate students (Coyle to the author, 2010). Criticisms against economics 101 were also found in Wheelan's book as well as in *Freakonomics*, echoing Becker's (2003) lament about the neglect of sexy topics that, according to him, accounted for the decrease in enrollment in economics majors. Many agreed on opportunities opened up by the use of 'sexy' research for teaching (e.g. Hamilton 2003), precisely the kind of natural experiments and applications of economics to 'outlandish' phenomena on which the pop-economics literature drew heavily. Many illustrations used in the EMF literature – such as the story of Feldman and his bagels, the story of delays in Israeli day care centers, the observations that popcorn cost more at the movies, that sometimes criminal behavior is not very rewarding, that splitting the bill at the restaurant can lead a group to order more food than desired, and that gym memberships are often underused – fitted the requirements of a standard course in microeconomics.

Given the fact that this literature performed similar pedagogical functions as the introductory textbook that was missing on the market, it is not surprising that some reactions from the academia and the blogosphere were related to the state of the discipline's teaching. Mangiero's (1994, p. 1530) review of *The Armchair Economist* recommended the book for 'any professor seeking to complement his course text with a book that provides some real-world examples of economics and financial principles.' As McAfee (2006, p. 726) wrote about Harford's *Undercover Economist*:

> Introductory textbooks now seem more appropriate for physically beating the students into submission, or perhaps being thrown like a discus at somnambulant tardy students, and it takes a football coach just to lift one. Compared to these miserable doorstops, *The Undercover Economist* … offers a more appealing paradigm. (McAfee 2006, p. 726)

4 General conclusion

This paper has documented the challenges facing a number of endeavors to introduce economics to an audience of non-specialists, from the 1960s to the present. Be they textbooks in the 1970s or popularization books in the 2000s, they all aimed to improve economic literacy in the long run, by applying a limited range of economic principles to numerous problems that were of direct relevance for their audience. It remains true that nowadays, in the aftermath of the subprime crisis, the EMF books ignore questions related to macroeconomic policy, such as unemployment and regulation of the banking system, that are thought highly relevant. But this only emphasizes that relevance is an ever-changing notion, depending on the problems of the day as well as on the current state of economics and its teaching. Relevant economics in the 1960s and 1970s implied addressing the noneconomic issues of crime, pollution, discrimination, etc. Later, when the first EMF books were published, relevance had a very different meaning: it referred to observation, empiricism and the everyday life problems of the students. After the subprime crisis it changed again.

Thus, there is a sense in which the label 'economics made fun' is misleading, since it does not characterize this literature with regard to its purpose, i.e. popularization. Moreover, its considerable success in the 2000s might be explained by its ability to face these challenges. These books filled a void in the popularization literature, offering a long-awaited passionate depiction of economics and its rigor. Their focus on observation, through the figure of the 'economic naturalist,' answered the growing criticisms of both scholars and students against economics' disconnection from the real world. Finally, it carried on the pedagogic method of the issues-oriented textbooks of the 1970s, which still appeared as an innovative and more effective way to disseminate the economic mode of thinking to a wider audience of non-specialists.

Acknowledgements

Previous drafts benefited from the comments of Roger E. Backhouse, Peter J. Boettke, Yann B. Giraud, Steven G. Medema, Philippe Fontaine, the attendees of the History of Postwar Social Science workshop at the LSE (1 November 2010) and the attendees of the "Economics Made Fun in the Face of the Economic Crisis" symposium held in Rotterdam in December 2010. I also wish to thank Diane Coyle, Robert H. Frank, Paul Grimes, Tim Harford, Hirshel Kasper and Steven E. Landsburg for answering various queries.

Notes

1. *Improving College and University Teaching* was created in 1960. *The American Educational Research* Journal was created in 1964 and was devoted to study educational problems from primary school to college. *Teaching Sociology* was created as late as 1973. Note that *Change* was a very influential journal, where teachers from various disciplines exposed their experiments and reforms.
2. The PSI method was developed by the Columbia experimental psychologist Fred S. Keller and involved no lectures or class discussions, only assignments.
3. The eighth edition of the famous *Economics: An Introduction to Analysis and Policy* (1974) by George Leland Bach provides another illustration of this point: 27 problem-cases were added 'to improve it further as a problem oriented text' (Leamer 1974, p. 52).
4. 'This book has been written from the pragmatic viewpoint that the student is entitled to a justification of the relevance of a particular scientific approach before he can be expected to embrace it with enthusiasm. We have attempted to establish the relevance of economics as a logical approach to decision making by providing a sampling of the broad spectrums of problems with which economists deal ... We hope that the student, as he gains in understanding of the tools of economic analysis, will discover that there are other social problems that are amenable to solutions with those same tools' (Phillips and Votey 1974, p. v).
5. Mancur Olson's archives at the University of Maryland provide an interesting illustration of this. He was very critical of some sociologists, whom he often portrayed as utopians.
6. 'Reading the daily newspapers, one is bound to get the feeling that the country is in a state of crisis ... While the substance of the problems may change, their nature will generally be such that from the point of view of analysis and evaluation, there is certain constancy about them ... Economics, which is a science of decision-making, provides us with basic concepts and tools that are needed for the task' (Phillips and Votey 1974, p. 1).
7. Members of the commission were, among others: Kenneth Arrow, Robert Lucas, Anne Krueger, Lee Ansen and Joseph Stiglitz.
8. In France, the most radical critiques created the Post Autistic Movement and the *Real World Economics Review.*
9. Arguably, it might also reflect the evolution of the discipline described by Ben Fine as moving toward a new form of economics imperialism, grounded on the asymmetric information paradigm.
10. Although Landsburg's and Wheelan's books echoed Frank in the use of precise terminology, Cowen's and Harford's books generally do not focus much on introducing the concepts of economics as economists would name them ('opportunity costs,' etc.) and uses parables to expose a specific type of reasoning.
11. *Freakonomics* and *The Armchair Economist* are a bit different and closer to the 1970s textbooks rhetoric. Landsburg, for instance, clearly associates common wisdom with journalism, religion and more generally unscientific approaches.
12. Negative reactions to this endeavor (for instance, Lucas's or W. Becker's) showed that although there was widespread consensus on the need to reduce the content of introductory courses, there was no consensus on the principles to be chosen.

References

Akerlof, G.A. (2002), 'Behavioral Macroeconomics and Macroeconomic Behavior', *The American Economic Review*, 92(3), 411–433.

Altbach, P.G., and Cohen, R. (1990), 'American Student Activism: The Post-Sixties Transformation', *Journal of Higher Education*, 61(1), 32–49.

Angrist, J.D., and Krueger, A.B. (2001), 'Instrumental Variables and the Search for Identification: From Supply and Demand to Natural Experiments', *The Journal of Economic Perspectives*, 15(4), 69–85.

Backhouse, R., and Fontaine, P. (2010), *The History of the Social Sciences Since 1945*, New York: Cambridge University Press.

Becker, W.E. (1997), 'Teaching Economics to Undergraduates', *Journal of Economic Literature*, 35, 1347–1373.

——— (2003), 'How to Make Economics The Sexy Social Science (From Chronicle of Higher Education)', *Southern Economic Journal*, 70(1), 195–198.

Becker, W.E., and Watts, M. (2001), 'Teaching Methods in U.S. Undergraduate Economics Courses', *Journal of Economic Education*, 32(3), 269–279.

Bender, T. (1997), 'Politics, Intellect, and the American University, 1945–1995', *Daedalus*, 126(1), 1–38.

Bergmann, B. (2005), 'The Current State of Economics: Needs Lots of Work', *Annals of the American Academy of Political and Social Science*, 600, 52–67.

Blyth, M.D. (1970), 'A Case for Irrelevance', *The English Journal*, 59(3), 380–386.

Case, K. (1988), 'Observations on the Use of Textbooks in the Teaching of Principles of Economics: A Comment', *Journal of Economic Education*, 19(2), 1988.

Colander, D. (1998), 'The Sounds of Silence: The Profession's Response to the COGEE Report', *Journal of Agricultural Economics*, 80(3), 600–607.

——— (2000), 'New Millennium Economics: How Did It Get This Way, and What Way is It?', *The Journal of Economic Perspectives*, 14(1), 121–132.

Cowen, T. (2007), *Discover Your Inner Economist*, New York: Dutton.

Coyle, D. (2002), *Sex, Drugs, and Economics*, London: Texere.

Culyer, A. ([1973] 1975), *The Economics of Social Policy* (2nd ed.), London: M. Robertson.

Dale, E.L., and Schachter, G. (1973), *The Economist Looks at Society*, Lexington, MA: Xerox College.

Day, C. (1989), 'Journals, University Presses, and the Spread of Ideas', in *The Spread of Economic Ideas*, eds. A.W. Coats, D. Colander, New York: Cambridge University Press.

Dolan, E.G. (1988), 'Observations on the Use of Textbooks in the Teaching of Principles of Economiçs: A Comment', *The Journal of Economic Education*, 19(2), 169–170.

Dubner, S.J., and Levitt, S.D. ([2005] 2009), *Freakonomics: A Rogue Economist Explores the Hidden Side of Everything*, New York: Penguin Books.

Eberhard, E.G. (1969), 'An Upside-Down Thing', *The English Journal*, 58(8), 1192–1193.

Feiner, S., and Morgan, B. (1987), 'Women and Minorities in Introductory Textbooks: 1974 to 1984', *Journal of Economic Education*, 18(4), 376–392.

Fels, R. (1969), 'Hard Research on a Soft Subject: Hypothesis-Testing in Economic Education', *Southern Economic Journal*, 36(1), 1–9.

——— (1974), 'The Vanderbilt-JCEE Experimental Course in Elementary Economics', *Journal of Economic Education*, 6(2), 3–94.

Fels, R., and Uhler, R.G. ([1969] 1976), *Casebook of Economic Problems & Policies: Practice in Thinking* (4th ed.), New York: West Publishing.

Fleury, J.-B. (2010), 'Drawing New Lines: Economists and Other Social Scientists on Society', *History of Political Economy*, 42(Number Suppl 1), 315–342.

Frank, R.H. (2002), 'The Economic Naturalist: Teaching Introductory Students How to Speak Economics', *The American Economic Review*, 92(2), 459–462.

Frank, Robert H. ([2007] 2008), *The Economic Naturalist*, London: Virgin Books.

Gallagher, C. (1997), 'The History of Literary Criticism', *Daedalus*, 126(1), 133–154.

Grimes, P. (2009), 'Reflections on Introductory Course Structures', in *Educating Economists: The Teagle Discussion on Re-Evaluating the Undergraduate Economics Major*, eds. D. Colander and K.M. McGoldrick, Northampton, MA: Edward Elgar.

Hamilton, J. (2003), 'Improving the Principles of Economics Course', *Southern Economic Journal*, 70(1), 198–201.

Hansen, W.L., Salemi, M.K., and Siegfried, J.J. (2002), 'Use it or Lose it: Teaching Literacy in the Economics Principles Course', *The American Economic Review*, 92(2), 463–472.

Harford, T. (2006), *The Undercover Economist*, London: Little Brown.

Heilbroner, R. (1970), 'On the Limited Relevance of Economics', *The Public Interest*, 21, 80–93.

Hirsch, D., and Levine, A. (1991), 'Undergraduates in Transition: A New Wave of Activism on American College Campus', *Higher Education*, 22(2), 119–128.

Joffe, J. (2003), 'The Decline of the Public Intellectual and the Rise of the Pundit', in *The Public Intellectual, Between Philosophy and Politics*, eds. A. Melzer, J. Weinberg and M.R. Zinman, Lanham, MD: Rowman & Littlefield.

Kreps, D.M. (1997), 'Economics: the Current Position', *Daedalus*, 126(1), 59–85.

Krueger, A.O. (1991), 'Report on the Commission on Graduate Education in Economics', *Journal of Economic Literature*, 29(1), 1035–1053.

Lamm, D. (1989), 'Economics and the Common Reader', in *The Spread of Economic Ideas*, eds. A.W. Coats and D. Colander, New York: Cambridge University Press.

Landsburg, S. (1991), 'Prospectus for The Economic Naturalist', Unpublished document.

Landsburg, S. ([1993] 2009), *The Armchair Economist*, New York: Free Press.

Leamer, L. (1974), 'A Guide to College Introductory Economics Textbooks', *Journal of Economic Literature*, 6(1), 46–56.

Leftwich, R. (1977), 'The Issues Approach to Economic Literacy', *Change*, 9(1), 18–19.

Leftwich, R., and Sharp, A.M. ([1974] 1976), *Economics of Social Issues,* Dallas, Texas: Business Publications.

———— (1974), 'Syllabus for an "Issues Approach" to Teaching Economic Principles', *Journal of Economic Education*, 6(1), 2–32.

Leftwich, R., Sharp, A.M., and Bumpass, D.M. (1975), 'An Examination of Trade-Offs in Teaching Economics Principles', *Journal of Economic Education*, 7(1), 56–58.

Lumsden, K.G. (1969), 'Where We Now Stand', *Journal of Economic Education*, 1(1), 12–19.

Mandelstamm, A.B., Petr, J.L., and Segebarth, D.C. (1971), 'The Principle Course Revisited', *Journal of Economic Education*, 3(1), 41–48.

Mangiero, S.M. (1994), 'Review of The Armchair Economist', *Journal of Finance*, 49(4), 1527–1530.

Mata, T. (2009), 'Migrations and Boundary Work: Harvard, Radical Economists and the Committee on Political Discrimination', *Science in Context*, 22(1), 115–143.

McAfee, R.P. (2006), 'Review of The Undercover Economist', *Journal of Economic Literature*, 44(3), 722–726.

McCleery, M., and Parente, W. (1968), 'Campus Radicalism and a Relevant Political Science: Channel Undergraduate Interests Constructively', *Journal of Higher Education*, 39(6), 316–325.

McKenzie, R.B., and Tullock, G. (1975), *The New World of Economics*, Homewood, IL: Richard D. Irwin, Inc.

Metzger, D. (1969), 'Relevant "Relevance"', *College Composition and Communication*, 20(5), 339–342.

Miller, R., and North, D.C. ([1971] 1976)), *The Economics of Public Issues* (3rd ed.), New York: Harper & Row.

———— (1976), *Abortion, Baseball, and Weed*, New York: Harper and Row.

Phillips, J.A. (1971), 'Student Unrest and Relevant Education', *Improving College and University Teaching*, 19(3), 250–251.

Phillips, L., and Votey, H.L. (1974), *Economic Analysis of Pressing Social Problems*, Chicago: Rand McNally.

Saunders, P. (1975), 'Experimental Course Development in Introductory Economics at Indiana University', *Journal of Economic Education*, 6(4), 2–128.

Schultze, C.L. (1971), 'The Reviewers Reviewed', *The American Economic Review*, 61(2), 45–52.

Shaw Bell, C. (1988), 'The Principles of Economics from Now Until Then', *Journal of Economic Education*, 19(2), 133–147.

Siegfried, J., and Strand, S.H. (1976), 'An Evaluation of the Vanderbilt-JCEE Experimental PSI Course in Elementary Economics', *Journal of Economic Education*, 8(1), 9–26.

Smith, R.M. (1997), 'Still Blowing in the Wind: The American Quest for a Democratic, Scientific, Political Science', *Daedalus*, 126(1), 253–287.

Solow, R. (1970), 'Science and Ideology in Economics', *The Public Interest*, 21, 94–107.

———— (1983), 'Teaching Economics in the 1980s', *Journal of Economic Education*, 14(2), 65–68.

Solow, R.M. (1997), 'How Did Economics Get that Way and What Way Did it Get?', *Daedalus*, 126(1), 39–58.

Stigler, G.J. (1963), 'Elementary Economic Education', *American Economic Review*, 53(2), 653–659 *(Papers and Proceedings of the 75th Annual Meeting of the American Economic Association)*.

Thompson, J.B. (2005), *Books in the Digital Age*, Malden, MA: Polity Press.

Villard, H.H. (1969), 'Where We Now Stand', *Journal of Economic Education*, 1(1), 60–66.

Vromen, J. (2009), 'The Booming Economics-Made-Fun Genre: More than Having Fun, but Less than Economics Imperialism', *Erasmus Journal for Philosophy and Economics*, 2(1), 70–99.

Wallis, G.W. (1973), 'Improving the Teaching of Introductory Sociology by an Innovative Classroom Organization', *Teaching Sociology*, 1(1), 25–37.

Welsh, A.L. (1974), 'Foreword', *Journal of Economic Education*, 6(1), 1.

Wheelan, C. (2002), *Naked Economics*, New York: Norton & Co.

Economic page turners

Björn Frank

Department of Economics, University of Kassel, Kassel, Germany

Economic page turners like *Freakonomics* are well written and there is much to be learned from them – not only about economics, but also about writing techniques. Their authors know how to build up suspense, i.e., they make readers want to know what comes. An uncountable number of pages in books and magazines are filled with advice on writing reportages or suspense novels. While many of the tips are specific to the respective genres, some carry over to economic page turners in an instructive way. After introducing some of these writing tools, I discuss whether these and other aspects of good writing lead to a biased presentation of economic theory and practice. I conclude that whatever the problems with certain economic page turners may be, they are not due to the need to write in an accessible, appealing way.

1 Introduction

So you have read *Freakonomics*. Did you like it? You didn't like it? If your answer to both questions is yes, then you must be Gregory Mankiw. I am guessing this because he (you?) expressed both his critical concern and admiration for *Freakonomics* in one short blog entry:

> '[M]ore young economists today are doing Levitt-style economics and fewer are studying the classic questions of economic policy. That is disconcerting, to a degree. It could be especially problematic twenty years from now, when President Chelsea Clinton looks for an economist to appoint to head the Federal Reserve, and the only thing she can find in the American Economic Association are experts on game shows and sumo wrestling'.

Then, after arguing that this will not happen anyway, Mankiw concedes that

> '*Freakonomics* has made many laymen appreciate that economics is a broader discipline than they had thought, and it has attracted many students to the field. That is a great service. On the first day of ec 10, I asked the students who had read *Freakonomics*. About a third to a half raised their hands'.[1]

The latter point is well taken. *Freakonomics* did not steal time from students who would otherwise have read the *General Theory* or the *Journal of Economic Perspectives*. *Freakonomics* competes with *How to Win Friends and Influence People* by Dale Carnegie, *Sh*t My Dad Says* by Justin Halpern and *The 7 Habits of Highly Effective People* by Stephen R. Covey, among others (suggestions from Amazon's 'Customers Who Bought This Item Also Bought' section). Hence, the relevant question is not whether (and if so, how much) harm is done when people read *Freakonomics* instead of serious economic research. Relevant questions are: would we prefer people to read *Freakonomics* instead of wasting their time? I presume, without further argument, that this is so. Then the next question is whether it would be possible to write a book that is as readable, and possibly as popular, as *Freakonomics*, but less susceptible to criticism like that by Mankiw quoted above?

As a modest initial step toward answering this question, I will offer a number of storytelling device suggestions, which successful authors apply in order to turn a book on economics into a page turner. I prefer the terms 'economics made exciting' or 'economic page turners' over 'economics-made-fun' (Vromen 2009) because I focus on the way these books are written, rather than their subject (such as the grotesque side of certain bits of economic research featured by some). Freaky subjects alone make a nice contribution to any campus magazine, but not a memorable book. The real difficulty is to write in an enthralling way, making readers want to read on and on. Economic page turner writers are a bit like crime writers, who 'have taken a decision that, even though they may feel they have something to say, they will subordinate the saying of it where necessary to the simple task of keeping their readers' noses stuck in the pages' (Keating 1986, p. 1). This marks the difference between my approach and that of McCloskey's investigations on the rhetoric of economics: McCloskey (1994, 1998) asks how economists try to persuade. A typical economists' audience consists of either fellow economists or people like politicians who are wondering whose advice to follow; in any case, the audience is interested in understanding who is right and who is wrong. An economist who convinces these audiences that he is right can gain academic reputation, or maybe consulting contracts. The general audience, the typical *Freakonomics* readers, cannot provide these benefits, but they can make a book a best seller through word-of-mouth. Convincing them that you are right will not do the job. My neighbor, who is a retired double bass player, will not recommend *Freakonomics* to my other neighbor, who is a pediatrician, just because he thinks that Levitt and Dubner (2005) are right. The main point is that he will recommend the book if he enjoyed reading it.

A second difference between the 'rhetoric of economics' research and this paper is that economists, when writing research papers, inevitably use rhetoric devices like metaphors (Klamer and Leonard 1994), but, as argued by McCloskey (1998, p. 5), they need not be aware of doing so, just like birds can fly without understanding aviation. On the other hand, probably all authors of economic page turners are aware of the tools they are using for increasing the joy of reading.

In Section 2, I will describe some of these tools that are mastered by successful (fiction and nonfiction) authors, illustrating these general points with examples from various economic page turners. In Section 3, I will discuss whether the necessity to apply at least some of these devices leads to biases in the representation of economic research in economic page turners. Section 4 concludes the paper.

And finally: STOP READING NOW if you agree with Robert Louis Stevenson, who began his essay 'On Some Technical Elements of Style in Literature' with the warning that there 'is nothing more disenchanting to man than to be shown the springs and mechanisms of any art'.[2]

2 Storytelling devices

It would be hard to detect an essential difference between economic page turners and other writings on economics as long as you only look at the way authors put their sentences together. You could take almost any single sentence out of *Freakonomics* and imagine that it is from an *AER* paper.[3] Many (although not all) successful academic authors, whether intuitively or as a result of training, write their sentences according to the rules that are also applied by journalists or crime fiction writers (e.g., if they produce too long a sentence, they split it up into two, and they carefully check whether pronouns are really unequivocally referring to the noun that they are intended to replace).

However, successful writers do not just follow (and sometimes, when appropriate, intentionally break) rules on writing style (e.g., McCloskey 1999b, 2000). And they are not just aware that economists are often using an insiders' jargon (see Klamer 2007), which, of course, must be avoided as far as possible in popular writings. An essential ingredient of economic page turners, and one that is missing in purely academic writing, is a structure that makes the readers want to continue reading. This makes a 'good story', a term that I (following DiNardo 2006) use in a more colloquial way than McCloskey (1990, 1998, 1999a) who argues that also economists who are building models are thereby telling stories.[4] Apart from structure, there are specific writing tools that serve the same purpose, but that are not found in academic journals because they do not exactly contribute to informing researchers, who are only interested in scientific content.

In Subsections 2.1 and 2.2, I sketch writing devices that apply to all genres, and maybe a bit less to economic page turners than to other kinds of fiction and nonfiction. On the other hand, the devices described in Subsections 2.3–2.7 are of particular importance to economic page turners, and some (in particular that described in Subsection 2.3) are applied to a lesser extent elsewhere.

2.1 Show, don't tell

When the ghost of Banquo enters (in *Macbeth*, Act III, Scene IV), this *shows* how horrified Macbeth, who had ordered his killing, is, which is much more impressive than any moral reasoning in a Macbeth monologue could be. 'Show, don't tell' is a piece of advice that professional writers often come across (e.g., Stein 1995, chap. 12): Novelists set up a stage, so to say, in their readers' minds, show things to their readers, allow them to get involved, and to draw their own conclusions. Authors of economic page turners are following the same advice.

However, novelists and academics differ in the way they write when they are violating the 'show, don't tell' principle. When novelists and journalists tell, rather than show, they typically do it via adjectives: 'he became a *fearful* person'. Compare this to 'he gave up his large ground floor apartment for a smaller one on the second floor, replaced the wooden entrance door by a steel door and stopped leaving the house after dark'.

In academic writing, it is taboo to claim in adjectives what you have not shown. But the information given is reduced to what is relevant for replication. Economists often claim to have 'shown' something, but that refers to regression results, not to something lively that they have shown on the stage in the reader's mind.

A simple example for something written with the general reader in mind is this: instead of telling him that tariffs lead to incentives for smuggling, Fisman and Miguel (2010, p. 58) show this point: 'Travelers returning to the United States can bring up to $800 of foreign goods into the country duty-free. (...) Suppose you bought a $2,000 Gucci handbag in Italy and want to avoid the 10 percent duty (...). You have a couple of options as you nervously shuffle toward the green or red signs at customs'.

In fiction, authors no longer have to tell what they have already shown. This is not a rule in nonfiction writing. One might do both, working the 'ladder of abstraction'

(Clark 2006, p. 107) up and down: showing examples and telling what the reader might take home as the general point. Take the well-known case study of the day-care center that introduced a fine for parents who picked up their children late, only to find that the fine led to more, rather than less, cases of late pickups (Gneezy and Rustichini 2000). It is used by both Levitt and Dubner (2005, chap. 1) and Cowen (2007, pp. 36–37) to *show* something. However, they also *tell* their readers what they conclude: that motivating people extrinsically does not leave everything else unchanged; that it is often hard to get the incentives right because they might backfire.

A final example: Harford (2008, pp. 33–50) *tells* us that some 'poker hustlers', those who play more or less instinctively, are making rational decisions; his argument is that it turned out to be extremely difficult to beat them, even with a computer-supported game-theoretic preparation. He also *shows* this by describing – in very lively detail – the final of the 2000 World Series between the experienced, more intuitive player T.J. Cloutier, who looked back on many great successes at the poker table, and Chris 'Jesus' Ferguson, an applied game theorist. It was an extremely tense battle; finally, Ferguson needed – and did have – a lot of luck when Cloutier went 'all in'. No doubt readers now *see* the point.

2.2   *Writing for all senses*

Just like 'show, don't tell', 'writing for all senses' is a creative writing classic. It is stunning how dull pieces of prose come to life as soon as authors revise them and pay attention to describing how people or things not only look, but also smell, taste, sound or feel. It is difficult, often even unnatural, to follow this advice when writing about economics, or about the economy; but if you think that economic page turner authors never write for the senses, then you have not read *SuperFreakonomics* yet, or you would not have forgotten[5] the description of a preautomobile metropolis:

> The noise from iron wagon wheels and horseshoes was so disturbing – it purportedly caused widespread nervous disorders – that some cities banned horse traffic on the streets around hospitals and other sensitive areas. (...) In vacant lots, horse manure was piled as high as sixty feet. It lined city streets like banks of snow. In the summertime, it stank to heavens; when the rains came, a soupy stream of horse manure flooded the crosswalks and seeped into people's basements. (Levitt and Dubner 2009, pp. 9–10)

2.3   *Addressing the reader*

Novelists can involve the reader through emotional identification with a protagonist, such as Oliver Twist. This is not possible for economic page turners. In single economic page turner chapters, the reader might feel empathy for real people whose fate is described, such as Kitty Genovese, whose killing is the prime example of the 'bystander effect', reconsidered in Levitt and Dubner (2009, chap. 3).[6] However, I know of only one economic page turner in which the reader accompanies the protagonist through the *whole* book: Russell Roberts' clever novel *The Invisible Heart* (Roberts 2001).[7] Instead, economic page turner authors have found another way to get the reader involved: they address him directly. This is rarely found in (post-Victorian[8]) fiction, but Landsburg (2007) does it in every one of his page turner's 16 chapters. To do so is natural in economics, as economics is about choices, including those of you, the reader. Landsburg (2007) is particularly instructive as he uses a great variety of possibilities to address the reader; Table 1 gives an example for each of these.

Table 1. Ways of addressing the reader directly.

The reader as a ...	Example
detective	'Why does the practice of check splitting cause people to spend more at restaurants?' (Frank 2007, p. 101).
person who knows something (but not quite everything)	'You've read elsewhere about the sin of promiscuity. Let me tell you about the sin of self-restraint' (Landsburg 2007, p. 9).
hypothetical example	'If you're 6 feet tall, you probably earn about $6000 more per year than the equally qualified 5-foot-6-inch shrimp in the next office' (Landsburg 2007, p. 53).
receiver of externalities	'[W]hen *I* decided to have a child, *you* were a winner' (Landsburg 2007, p. 33), emphasis in original.
witness	'Come out to my suburban neighborhood on any crisp October Saturday, and I will show you a minor tragedy: on every lawn a man with a blower, blowing his leaves onto the next man's lawn' (Landsburg 2007, p. 3).
decider in a real choice situation	'When you snack at midnight, you get most of the benefits, but your spouse (who has good reason to care about your health and appearance) shares many of the costs' (Landsburg 2007, p. 180).
decider in a hypothetical choice situation	'Suppose we were offered the option of surgery, or a pill, to correct our self-deception ... All of our beliefs would be brought into line with the facts. Don't take that pill' (Cowen 2007, p. 120).

Almost every economic page turner author uses this technique, although not as intensely as Landsburg. In two cases listed in Table 1, I picked an example not from Landsburg (2007), but from another book. Frank (2007) relies heavily on using questions to which the reader might try to find solutions on his own; I am quoting only one of hundreds of questions he addresses to the reader. Cowen (2007) is interesting in his way of often using 'we' (i.e., you and I) instead of 'you', which is quite appropriate, as he often discusses human weaknesses.

2.4 Controlling the reader's pace

In Gerard Donovan's highly acclaimed novel *Julius Winsome*, two men, who are definitely not friends, are facing each other; one has a rifle while the other has had to give up his own and is now trying to save his life by talking. We do not know whether he will survive or not – the one with the rifle is the narrator, and he has shot six other men before. The tense situation is described in short sentences, about one line each. ('And if he moved he was a dead man in that second'.) But then, all of a sudden, the narrator thinks back:

> When I was young I heard a visitor to the farm point to the ducks we kept and say to my father that they were being unnaturally protected against predators, that in the real world they fend for themselves, that the laws of nature favor the strong. The sun was shining that day and the ducks were in the water of the upturned basin lid they had crowded into, corded their necks together and slept. (Donovan 2007, p. 198)

With two sentences in eight lines, Donovan takes tempo out of the story, and he does it on purpose. Eco (1994) devotes a large part of a book to demonstrating how great authors vary the relation between story time on the one hand (i.e., an hour that passes in *Ulysses*), and

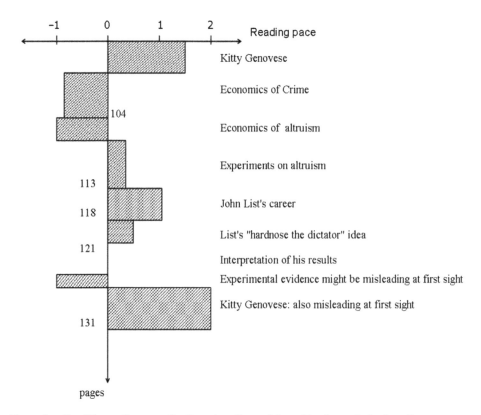

Figure 1. Possible reading pace for the subsections of *SuperFreakonomics'*, chap. 3.

discourse time (possibly proxied as the length of the written text) and reading time on the other hand.[9] Can economic page turner authors learn from that? Often there is no such thing as story time, except in economic history or adventures such as that of Sudhir Venkatesh and the drug dealing gang, retold in *Freakonomics* (and very briefly further below). However, there is always a stream of marginal increases of the reader's knowledge. In academic publishing, referees and editors would object to attempts to insert digressions that serve no other purpose than to comfort the reader. Furthermore, reading time is impossible to control in academic writing anyway, as it very much depends on the single reader's foreknowledge and ambition. Not so with economic page turners. Figure 1 shows how the reading pace varies within Chapter 3 of *SuperFreakonomics*, on a scale from − 1 to 2. It is my subjective account of possible reading pace, or of the ease with which a subsection can be read out, but I tried to make it replicable[10]: a score of 2 is given for a page devoted to personal anecdotes or personal historical accounts, a score of 1 for a historical account or an easily comprehensible result, and a score of − 1 for the introduction of a new concept, hypothesis or method, for the need to keep numbers in working memory, for a sophisticated result and for the introduction of experimental designs (or rules). It is unavoidable that some topics reduce the reading pace; hence, negative and positive scores are not at all intended to correspond to 'bad' and 'good' writing, respectively. It is good to vary the reading pace, however, and one can learn from most economic page turners how to achieve this.

The most noteworthy thing in Figure 1 is that it shows something happening in the middle of the chapter: the digression on John List's career has absolutely no function for the economic argument – it does not matter that he is a truck driver's son, or that the dean of some university thought the budding superstar could be replaced for $63,000. Nevertheless, this subsection helps the readers through the economics. They pick up pace after a discussion of conventional behavioral economics and altruism, and before the way List challenged these views is introduced. Furthermore, this chapter structure appeals to readers' sense of variety.

2.5   Getting the reader hooked

How can you draw the reader into the paper, so to say, with a stunning beginning of the text, by making it immediately clear that the author is about to answer an interesting and important question? This is no trade secret that only economic page turner writers know; in fact, one finds many good examples in the first paragraphs of leading journals. Compare the first sentence in Chapter 1 of *Freakonomics* with the first sentence of the journal paper to which it refers:

> Imagine for a moment that you are the manager of a day-care center. (Levitt and Dubner 2005, p. 19)

> Suppose you are the manager of a day-care center for young children. (Gneezy and Rustichini 2000, p. 1)

In top journals, many more good examples for clever ways of opening a text can be found, like: 'One of the biggest risks in life is the family one is born into' (Farhi and Werning 2010, p. 635). This is the nicely laconic opening line of a *Quarterly Journal of Economics* paper, which of course is less easy to read in later sections, written for specialized economists and for no one else. Nevertheless, the authors of many research papers bother to write a nice introduction. Why? I only have one explanation: because this is a way to signal that their research matters, that the math relates to real life.

I do not suggest that economic page turner authors deal with highly relevant questions just because they manage to get their readers hooked. But at least it is easier to write a convincing first paragraph if the chapter deals with a topic that is indeed relevant, in one way or the other, for the reader. (This is a recurrent theme: whatever the problem might be with some economic page turners, it is not due to the fact that economic page turners need to be well written.)

2.6   Keeping the reader hooked

Closely related to the task of getting the reader on the hook is that of not letting him off the hook. The standard technique used for thrillers, but also for many other novels, is the cliffhanger, so well known that it needs no introduction. Here is an example from Harford's (2006) *The Undercover Economist*, where Chapter 2 ends as follows:

> When PillCorp changed its global pricing policy, it did something that was not only profitable but also both efficient and fair. Can we say anything more generally about when private greed will serve the public interest? For the answers to all these questions, and more … read on. (p. 59)

In typical economic page turners, however, there is only a loose connection between the single chapters. Often they could even be placed in a different order without the need to rewrite. This is why the introductions to *Freakonomics* and *SuperFreakonomics* are so long: they serve as a collection of cliffhangers, so to say, for all the chapters in the book.[11]

2.7   Combining tools

Merely applying well-known principles is maybe not enough. Economic page turner authors combine the writing tools discussed above in a way that is appropriate for these authors' topic (i.e., economics). In fact, the first example given in Subsection 2.5 already demonstrated this, getting the reader hooked by addressing him directly. Frank (2007) appears to be an exception in his way of using exactly one tool: addressing the reader as a detective. The 'solutions' are presented immediately thereafter, and it requires a good deal of self-discipline for a reader not to read on immediately after each question, but to pause and try to work out the economics on his own. For readers of other economic page turners, it is easier to get the satisfaction of independently solving the case because writing tools like 'show, don't tell' and also varying the reading pace make them think for themselves. However, there is a trade-off involved: Frank (2007) presents more problems than the number of pages in his book. This is only possible when writing rather straightforwardly.

3 Biases

One thing, and possibly the only thing, that all economic page turners I have referred to above have in common is that they are extremely well written. In Section 2, I have discussed various aspects of good writing. Now the critical question is whether the need to write well (i.e., to serve the reader) leads to a biased presentation of economic theory and practice. Three possible biases are the ratio of 'freaky' to 'normal' research topics, over-representation of certain research methods and microeconomics versus macroeconomics.

Concerning the freaky subjects, I submit that economic page turners give a fair impression of how popular these subjects are in academic research (note that *Freakonomics* is largely based on first-class journal publications). Whether academic research itself is biased (i.e., more freaky than it ought to be) is another question. Concerning the method, it might well be that experimental research is more attractive to economic page turner writers (e.g., Häring and Storbeck 2007; Ariely 2008) than the amount of scientific progress generated by experiments would suggest. This is due to 'the performativity of experiments and their spectacular nature' (Kübler 2010), in line with the 'show, don't tell' principle. Nevertheless, this does not blind the readers to the way contemporary economists think and practice; after all, experimental results have long begun to influence research by economists who consider themselves as theorists and who are not doing their own experiments. The greatest concern, I think, is the micro–macro bias.

Milton Friedman's famous list of things that realistically describe the wheat market, but that we safely can, and in fact should, leave out of economic models, includes 'the personal characteristics of wheat-traders such as the color of each trader's hair and eyes, his antecedents and education, the number of members of his family, their characteristics, antecedents, and education, etc.' (Friedman 1953, p. 32). This is intended to sound absurd, but compare Friedman's list to the information given in *Freakonomics* on the personal characteristics of the researcher who collected data on a drug gang: 'Sudhir Venkatesh – his boyhood friends called him Sid, but he has since reverted to Sudhir – was born in India, raised in the suburbs of upstate New York and southern California, ... he had just spent three months following the Grateful Dead around the country' (Levitt and Dubner 2005, p. 93).[12] Although these bits of information are irrelevant in a narrow sense, there is a justification for including them. It shows the reader (rather than telling him) how different Venkatesh is from the black members of the drug gang he more or less stumbles into. Apart from being enthralling in itself, this story also demonstrates that sometimes research requires a good deal of luck in order to be successful (first, finding the gang and, second, surviving the meeting). And as far as the eyes and hair of Friedman's trader are concerned, they might indeed be irrelevant for the Chicago wheat exchange, but they do possibly matter when he negotiates with his neighbors over the price of an acre of land, or with his employer (for an experimental investigation of the effects of beauty in wage negotiations, see Mobius and Rosenblat 2006).

Now, what is the problem with writing like this? One might argue that the likelihood of finding something that can be shown (rather than just told), thus attracting readers, is much more likely for micro than for macro topics. Showing the reader how *one* subject made his decision is often appropriate for microeconomic topics, yet typically misleading for macroeconomics (take the 'paradox of saving' as an example). Furthermore, it is much easier to vary the pace and develop subplots for micro 'stories'; trying the same trick in macroeconomics would run a high risk of confusing and losing readers.

Indeed, the micro-to-macro ratio is much higher in economic page turners than in academic research, and also higher than the ratio of micro- to macro-phenomena that really change people's lives. However, it would be futile to complain that macroeconomists are facing 'unfair' competition in this respect. In fact, macroeconomists have already taken up the challenge and applied some of the writing tools discussed above:

- Kay (2003) compares living standards not only by numbers but also by exemplary people from various countries. Unfortunately, and by no means necessarily, these are stereotyped cardboard cutouts – for example, he writes about Heidi and Hermann, a Swiss couple: she a primary school teacher, he a Zurich bank manager.
- Coyle (2007), surely aware of the difficulty of letting the objects of research come to life in the macroeconomic parts of her book, draws a lively picture of the actors in research, i.e., the economists. For example, she gives a colorful description of the geographical and social background of Angus Maddison (Coyle 2007, pp. 11–12), reveals what motivated Heckman, Krugman and Stiglitz to become economists (pp. 33–34, 147) and starts one chapter with scurrilities from Bentham's life and afterlife (chap. 4).
- Taking up a suggestion by Paul Krugman, Quiggin (2010) personifies macroeconomic and finance theories in a way that creates a sense of thrill – his book is entitled *Zombie Economics: How Dead Ideas Still Walk among Us*, and he uses the Zombie metaphor throughout, e.g., 'The ultimate zombie is one that is completely invulnerable. Neither special bullets nor hammer blows nor even decapitation can finally lay this undead being to rest. (...) Supporters of the Efficient Market Hypothesis have sought a redefinition that would make it invulnerable to refutation' (p. 64).
- Finally, most readers know, however vaguely, how difficult it is to find a fable that is accessible to the general audience, but still useful for demonstrating macroeconomic principles. Consequently, someone who succeeds receives much admiration – like Paul Krugman, who popularized the fable of the baby-sitting co-op (first in Krugman 1994). In other words, the incentives are high for writing a macroeconomic page turner.

Hence, macroeconomics is not completely unlikely to be featured in future economic page turners. (I admit that macroeconomics will remain underrepresented, but on the other hand, isn't macroeconomics, compared to modern microeconomics, overrepresented in newspaper reporting?)

4 Conclusion

Every economic page turner needs some of the ingredients described in this paper. The ingredients do not suffice; I own a number of cookbooks, but I cannot cook. And this is not intended to be an economic page turner cookbook anyway. Rather, I inspected the ingredients (i.e., the writing tools) in order to answer the question: is their use responsible for the criticism some economic page turners have received? My answer is no. Good writing, even entertaining writing, and good economics are no enemies.

Acknowledgements

I am indebted to participants of the EIPE Symposium *Economics Made Fun in the Face of the Economic Crisis* for helpful comments and to Adriana Kramer for polishing the style of a previous draft.

Notes

1. http://gregmankiw.blogspot.com/2007/04/is-steve-levitt-ruining-economics.html, posted 24 April 2007; retrieved on 12 September 2010.
2. In Robert Louis Stevenson, 'The Art of Writing', quoted from the Penn State Electronic Classics Series at http://www2.hn.psu.edu/faculty/jmanis/rlsteven/art_writ.pdf.
3. This implies that there are some sentences in AER papers that one can imagine to be part of *Freakonomics*; here is an instant classic as an example from Akerlof's (1991) discussion of procrastination: 'Each morning for over eight months I woke up and decided that the *next* morning would be the day to send the Stiglitz box' (p. 3, emphasis in original). Scheiber (2007) is so consequent as to extend his criticism of *Freakonomics* to the fanciness of nontraditional topics in AER and JPE.
4. Besides fact and logic, 'a serious argument in economics will use metaphors and stories as well – not for ornament or teaching alone but for the very science' (McCloskey 1998, p. 19).
5. There is a reason why using different senses makes texts that are not easily forgotten: 'Writing that honors the senses (. . .) engages not only the logical mind but also our visual, physical and emotional intelligences. Sensory-rich writing awakens the full spectrum of consciousness and our myriad ways of knowing' (Hiestand 2007, p. 201).
6. Another example is Ngugi Wa Thiong'o, a novelist who returned to his home country Kenya after a promising political change, and was then brutally assaulted, most probably in an act of revenge ordered by 'Economic Gangsters' (Fisman and Miguel 2010, pp. 1–3).
7. The Marshall Jevons detective stories featuring Harvard professor Henry Spearman (e.g., Jevons 1993) are entertaining as well, but hardly provide an opportunity for readers to really get emotionally involved. But after all Spearman serves as the reader's proxy.
8. I owe this qualification to Lodge (1992), chap. 17.
9. Jute (1999, p. 75) doubts that this can consciously be planned, but advises writers to avoid 'bad rhythm'. See Stein (1995, chap. 20) for more ambitious advice on pace variation.
10. Details on the construction of Figure 1 are available from the author, or in the manuscript version of this paper at http://www.uni-marburg.de/fb02/makro/forschung/magkspapers/26-2011_frank.pdf.
11. After subsections on opening a book and on keeping the readers from stopping to read, it seems natural to insert one on ending a book (or a chapter). However, this is a point where writing a journal paper and writing an economic page turner are almost indistinguishable. By training, academic writers are always looking for a powerful, well-founded conclusion to end their paper. However, there is one trick of the trade that economic page turner writers might have learned from other successful nonfiction writers, and this is the *full circle ending*, according to Hart (2007, p. 235) the 'most satisfying story ending, it gives the sense that the story has come back to where it began'. For example, Landsburg (1993) starts his Chapter 16 like this: '"They *pay* you to think about things like that?" My airline seatmate didn't come right out with the question, but despite his best efforts, his expression revealed all". And then, after 11 pages reflecting on why popcorn pricing in cinemas is only seemingly trivial, he elegantly ends: 'It might have been fun to discuss these questions with my neighbor on the airplane. But I decided to let him sleep'. Note that Levitt and Dubner (2009) also bring their Chapter 3, summarized in Figure 1 above, full circle.
12. The Grateful Dead reappear in *SuperFreakonomics* (Levitt and Dubner 2009, p. 69), which suggests that Lodge's (1992, p. 168) conjecture 'Symmetry (. . .) matters more to writers of fiction than readers consciously perceive' extends to some cases of nonfiction.

References

Akerlof, G.A. (1991), 'Procrastination and Obedience', *American Economic Review*, 81(2), 1–19.
Ariely, D. (2008), *Predictably Irrational*, New York: HarperCollins.
Clark, R.P. (2006), *Writing Tools: 50 Essential Strategies for Every Writer*, New York, Boston and London: Little, Brown and Company.
Cowen, T. (2007), *Discover Your Inner Economist*, London: Plume.

Coyle, D. (2007), *The Soulful Science*, Princeton, NJ: Princeton University Press.

DiNardo, J. (2006), 'Freakonomics: Scholarship in the Service of Storytelling', *American Law and Economics Review*, 8, 615–626.

Donovan, G. (2007), *Julius Winsome*, London: Faber and Faber.

Eco, U. (1994), *Six Walks in the Fictional Woods*, Cambridge, MA: Harvard University Press.

Farhi, E., and Werning, I. (2010), 'Progressive Estate Taxation', *Quarterly Journal of Economics*, 125, 635–673.

Fisman, R., and Miguel, E. (2010), *Economic Gangsters*. (2nd printing with new postscript). Princeton, NJ: Princeton University Press.

Frank, R. (2007), *The Economic Naturalist: In Search of Explanations for Everyday Enigmas*, New York: Basic Books.

Friedman, M. (1953), *Essays in Positive Economics*, Chicago, IL: University of Chicago Press.

Gneezy, U., and Rustichini, A. (2000), 'A Fine Is a Price', *Journal of Legal Studies*, 29, 1–18.

Harford, T. (2006), *The Undercover Economist*, London: Little, Brown.

——— (2008), *The Logic of Life*, London: Abacus.

Häring, N., and Storbeck, O. (2007), *Ökonomie 2.0.99 überraschende Erkenntnisse*, Stuttgart: Schäffer-Poeschel.

Hart, J. (2007), 'The Storyteller's Lexicon', in *Telling True Stories*, eds. M. Kramer and W. Call, London: Plume, pp. 235–239.

Hiestand, E. (2007), 'On Style', in *Telling True Stories*, eds. M. Kramer and W. Call, London: Plume, pp. 198–202.

Jevons, M. (1993), *Murder at the Margin*, Princeton, NJ: Princeton University Press.

Jute, A. (1999), *Writing a Thriller* (3rd ed.), London: A&C Black.

Kay, J. (2003), *The Truth About Markets*, London: Allen Lane.

Keating, H.R.F. (1986), *Writing Crime Fiction*, London: A&C Black.

Klamer, A. (2007), *Speaking of Economics*, London/New York: Routledge.

Klamer, A., and Leonard, T.C. (1994), 'So What's an Economic Metaphor?', in *Natural Images in Economic Thought*, ed. P. Mirowski, New York: Cambridge University Press, pp. 20–51.

Krugman, P. (1994), *Peddling Prosperity*, New York: W.W. Norton.

Kübler, D. (2010), 'Experimental Practices in Economics: Performativity and the Creation of Phenomena', Discussion Paper SP II 2010–01, Wissenschaftszentrum Berlin.

Landsburg, S.E. (1993), *The Armchair Economist*, New York: Free Press.

——— (2007), *More Sex Is Safer Sex*, New York: Free Press.

Levitt, S.D., and Dubner, S.J. (2005), *Freakonomics*, New York: HarperCollins.

——— (2009), *SuperFreakonomics*, London: Allen Lane.

Lodge, D. (1992), *The Art of Fiction*, London: Penguin.

McCloskey, D.N. (1990), 'Storytelling in Economics', in *Narrative in Culture*, ed. C. Nash, London/New York: Routledge, pp. 5–22.

——— (1994), 'How Economists Persuade', *Journal of Economic Methodology*, 1, 15–32.

——— (1998), *The Rhetoric of Economics* (2nd ed.), Madison, WI: University of Wisconsin Press.

——— (1999a), *If You're So Smart*, Chicago, IL: The University of Chicago Press.

——— (1999b), 'Economical Writing: An Executive Summary', *Eastern Economic Journal*, 25, 239–242.

——— (2000), *Economical Writing* (2nd ed.), Prospect Heights, IL: Waveland Press.

Mobius, M.M., and Rosenblat, T.S. (2006), 'Why Beauty Matters', *American Economic Review*, 96, 222–235.

Quiggin, J. (2010), *Zombie Economics: How Dead Ideas Still Walk among Us*, Princeton, NJ: Princeton University Press.

Roberts, R. (2001), *The Invisible Heart*, Cambridge, MA: MIT Press.

Scheiber, N. (2007), 'Freaks and Geeks: How Freakonomics Is Ruining the Dismal Science', *The New Republic*, April 2 27–31.

Stein, S. (1995), *Stein on Writing*, New York: St. Martin's Griffin.

Vromen, J.J. (2009), 'The Booming Economics-Made-Fun Genre: More Than Having Fun, but Less Than Economics Imperialism', *Erasmus Journal for Philosophy and Economics*, 2, 70–99.

Economics made fun, and made fun of: how 'fun' redefines the domain and identity of the economics profession

Erwin Dekker[a] and Paul Teule[b]

[a]Erasmus School of History, Culture & Communication, Erasmus University, Rotterdam, The Netherlands; [b]European Studies Department, University of Amsterdam, The Netherlands

This paper compares two aspects of the use of 'fun' within the economics profession. It analyzes the way in which a recently emerged genre of economics-made-fun uses fun and surprising insights to reach new audiences. And it also analyzes the way in which humor is used within and from outside the economics profession to criticize certain practices and characteristics of economists. It argues that the economics-made-fun genre, 'Freakonomics' being the prime example, not only redefines the domain of economics, as is widely acknowledged, but also changes the identity of economists. In a similar way, humor is used by both insiders and outsiders to (re)define the appropriate identity and domain of economists. It draws on recent work in the history of science which distinguishes between various professional identities of scientists, such as the quirky genius and the intuitive and playful amateur. We argue that Levitt and other authors within this new genre redefine the identity of economists toward this latter type. On the other hand, humor is often used by critics of this economistic outlook on life to show the limitations of this perspective and to delineate its appropriate domain.

1. Introduction

The past decade we have seen a surge of successful books that popularize economics by taking its principles and concepts into 'uneconomic' areas. Levitt and Dubner's *Freakonomics* (2005) and *Superfreakonomics* (2009) stand out, selling millions of copies, but Harford's *The Undercover Economist* (2005) and *The Logic of Life* (2008) or Frank's *The Economic Naturalist* (2007), among many other titles, have generated widespread attention for the dismal science.

Vromen (2009) even makes out a new genre, 'economics-made-fun', where the fun lies in exploring the hidden side of everyday phenomena, in solving the unsettling mysteries that defy conventional wisdom – under the guidance of the master economist.[1] For Vromen, this type of fun should not be equated with 'trivial' or 'funny'. Economics-made-fun is to be taken very seriously, by its authors and its fans. At least critics do so and view the genre as economics imperialism at work (Rubinstein 2006; Fine and Milonakis 2009). Fun in the sense of 'funny' is for Vromen something completely different. Mocking papers and jokes, often by economists themselves, are part of the 'economists-can-be-funny' genre, a genre 'not to be taken seriously'.

We argue that both the 'economics-made-fun' and the 'economists-can-be-funny' should be taken seriously – though we prefer to rename the latter genre 'economics-made-fun-of' to distinguish it from the economists putting on a funny hat, or pulling a weird face. We claim both genres serve well in redefining economics. Together they offer an interesting methodology to see where economics is fruitfully exploring new areas, and where it is going astray. But 'economics-made-fun' and 'economics-made-fun-of' also help in defining what it means, or should mean, to be an economist. We argue that 'fun' lies at the heart of the controversy about the identity of economists, and we draw from recent work by Steven Shapin on the identity of natural scientists in the twentieth century to clarify this.

Klamer (2007) and McCloskey (1990, 2001) are engaged in a continued attempt to characterize the culture of the economic conversation, of which jokes are indeed an essential part, both in their analysis of the economic conversation and in their own work. Implicitly they have already paid much attention to the identity of the economist, and especially his persuasion strategies. We hope to show that 'economics-made-fun' and 'economics-made-fun-of' add another dimension to this effort. The 'fun' or 'funniness' in economics is much more than just a matter of rhetoric, and more than just a way of being an economist. It actually serves to settle the domain and identity of the economics profession – something quite substantive and serious.

2. Economics-made-fun and made-fun-of

Delineating genres is always somewhat arbitrary, but Vromen is right in seeing a few striking similarities in the above mentioned titles of the economics-made-fun genre: (1) they are all written in an entertaining and accessible (though not infantile) way; (2) they all use (basic) economics to explain topics of interest for a broad (non-economist) audience, e.g. sports, dating, drive-in restaurants; and (3) they break with conventional wisdom, where the economics prism reveals what's 'underneath'.

In our view, the real fun of economics-made-fun lies in (2) and (3), in the new, surprising insights economic analysis can offer. When Levitt and Dubner (2005) show why drug dealers still live with their moms, the surprise lies in that they in fact do. Isn't crack cocaine a lucrative business? It is not, at least not for the better part of the gangs. When Frank (2007) asks why 24-hour shops have locks on their doors, our curiosity is sparked. Why would they need them if they never close?

Looking at economics-made-fun-of, we aim to show that the fun actually stems from quite the same surprise. The genre, consisting of all literary means of making fun of economics and economists, is in fact quite old and venerable, going from the *Economic Sophisms* of Bastiat (1909), the satire of Veblen, to the mocking papers of the last decades, like Blinder's 'The Economics of Brushing Teeth' (1974) or Leijonhufvud's 'Life Among the Econ' (1973). But to explain how it mirrors economics-made-fun, we focus on the vast stock of jokes that have targeted economists and their profession.[2]

'Many a true word is spoken in jest', Dow (2002) writes as she starts off her inquiry into economic methodology by looking at economists' jokes. But some jokes, of course, bear more truth than others. Jokes that give economic concepts a playful twist (e.g. 'Economists do it with Slutsky matrices') do not tell us much about the economics profession *per se*. Most other jokes do. They portray economists as being dull (e.g. 'An economist is someone who didn't have enough charisma to become an accountant'), hopelessly inconclusive (e.g. 'How has the French revolution affected world economic growth? Economist: Too early to say'[3]) and so divided that they can win Nobel Prizes for saying opposite things and, individually, are unable to hand out 'one-handed' advice.

Economists are thus quite useless, it seems ('Q: What does an economist do? A: A lot in the short run, which amounts to nothing in the long run').

Another set of jokes make fun of their *déformation professionnelle*. Sometimes economists clearly take their views and assumptions too far, and miss out on reality:

> An economics professor and a student were strolling through the campus.
> 'Look', the student cried, 'there's a $100 bill on the path!'
> 'No, you are mistaken', the professor replied, 'that cannot be. If there were actually a $100 bill, someone would have picked it up'.

Sometimes they also take their professional habits too far. Being overly calculative and prudent does not always work outside the economics department:

> You might be an economist if ...

> (1) you spent one hour in a toy shop making up over 20 bundles of toys that could be purchased for $25 and then ask your daughter to select one of these bundles;
> (2) you refuse to sell you children, only because they will be worth more later;
> (3) you have a bumper sticker that says 'I'm an economist so I don't vote'.

Real life and economics clash here. Humor research indeed suggests that the basis for a joke lies in its surprise, caused by frames (patterns, logics or views) coinciding, with the punch line marking the point of collision. Beeman (1999), for instance, asserts it is the tension between 'cognitive frames' that drives humor: a message is contextualized within one cognitive frame, and suddenly one or more additional cognitive frames are presented that are in conflict with the original frame and the sudden reframing provokes an emotional release that is experienced as amusing (and shown by smiles or laughter). Meyer (2000) says an accepted pattern is violated by another in a not too shocking or threatening, but also not too mundane, way. Veatch (1998) sees humor as 'affective absurdity' where a perceiver has two conflicting views in mind: one that seems normal and one that violates the moral or natural order. The situation seems normal, yet something is wrong, which results in humor.

In the case of the $100 bill joke mentioned above, the two conflicting frames are clear. The frame of reality and that of the economists' assumption collide. The $100 bill on the path is real for any normal person, but not for the economist who abides by his unrealistic assumptions. Also the case of the economist treating his children as utility maximizers under constraints or investment goods, or taking his cost–benefit analysis to the voting booth, exhibits this 'incongruity' – the economic frame clashes with reality.

Economists are mocked so widely, because its frames are so widely perceived to clash with the real world. Economists share this with, among others, lawyers, politicians, and to a lesser extent, civil servants, accountants, statisticians, philosophers and psychotherapists – who all have dozens of websites full of jokes dedicated to them. Sociologists, biologists, pilots, nurses or kick boxers do not get this type of attention. There would not be any demand for a stand-up anthropologist or web designer.[4] Of course, almost all professions do feature in jokes, but only few are mocked for the flaws and vices of the profession *per se*.[5]

In addition, economics jokes are funny because economists have authority and power. Authority is a perpetual source of humor.[6] Imagine that economists would seldom hold high positions in government or business, or were never listened to by journalists and policy makers. Would economist jokes be as funny as they are now? And if, on top of this, economists would always show extreme modesty about explanatory or prophetic abilities, would economics jokes make any sense?

What is interesting is that the same conditions – controversy and (perceived) authority – also create the fun in the economics-made-fun genre. There are no rogue sociologists or historians, and no political scientist has been accused of imperialism, because their disciplines are somewhat less controversial and authoritative.

Moreover, the 'fun' of both genres actually stems from the same clash of frames. Just imagine for a second that the economist of the $100 bill joke was in fact right, that the $100 bill was in fact not there or that picking it up would have had bad consequences (offsetting the $100 gain). Then the situation would all of a sudden fit economics-made-fun and the deformed professor would suddenly be the rogue economist that explains how, contrary to common wisdom, $100 bill on the path is not what it seems.

When an economist reveals what is hidden, what lies underneath, showing what's *really* real, it is often fun. When his views are trumped by reality, it is funny. It's a matter of which of the two frames is the 'real' one. The type of fun tells us if economists have gone astray or not, which helps to make sense of the 'economics imperialism' discussion.

3. 'Fun' and economics imperialism

The sheer fact that economics has pushed its borders is not disputed. Nobel Prize laureate Gary Becker led the 'successful' expansion of economic analysis of traditionally noneconomic subjects like family, love, parenting, suicide, linguistics, sports and education. Becker also succeeded in getting the notion of 'human capital' universally accepted (1964). He admitted: '"Economic imperialism" is probably a good description of what I do' (Becker 1990, p. 39). Becker has been dubbed the Old Imperialist, and Levitt, his apprentice, the New Imperialist.

The term 'imperialism' has been appropriated by those who hail Becker, and those who loath his work. 'Imperialist' can be an insult, or a 'Geuzennaam' (a label bestowed by your critics, but then adopted as honorary title). Critics gratefully make use of the negative connotations one might have with 'imperialism', e.g. 'colonization', 'exploitation', 'occupation' and 'aggression' (e.g. Stigler 1984; Fine 2000; Rubinstein 2006). But 'imperialism' also gives its practitioners its rogue status, with Becker being the old crusader, and Levitt his maverick apprentice. Imperialists are doing God's work and should be applauded. In fact, the first mention of 'economic imperialism', in the Ph.D. thesis of Souter in 1933, aims at this enlightened despotism serving no less than the salvation of all:

> The salvation of Economic Science in the twentieth century lies in an enlightened and democratic 'economic imperialism' which invades the territories of its neighbors, not to enslave them or to swallow them up, but to aid and enrich them and promote their autonomous growth in the very process of aiding and enriching itself. (Souter 1933, p. 97)

One recent proponent, Lazear (2000), admits that economics has been imperialistic, and rightfully so, because economics is the most successful social science. A qualitative proof of this claim is not given – he lets 'the market' decide, pointing to the fact that economics 'attracts the most students, enjoys the attention of policy-makers and journalists, and gains notice, both positive and negative, from other scientists' (Lazear 2000, p. 99). What 'markets' apparently appreciate, according to Lazear, is the methodological rigor of economics, its efficiency and simplicity. Economists produce the most 'answers'. Other disciplines, sociology, anthropology or psychology, might be better in 'identifying issues', because they are 'broader-thinking'. Yet they need economists to provide the concise answers.[7]

Some say economists just impoverish other social sciences by exploiting their questions (i.e. their natural resources; cf. Rubinstein 2006). We argue that these answers should be scrutinized on a case-by-case basis. Should their answers spark excitement, then that would probably mean they provide new and useful insights. If they make us laugh, the economist has gone too far. It all depends, so to say, on the $100 bill actually lying there or not. In this way, economics-made-fun and economics-made-fun-of may provide a new methodology to help settling the border disputes of economics with its neighbors.

Obviously, whether or not an answer given by an economic imperialist is considered fun or funny, or neither, depends on who is considering. It depends not only on his knowledge whether or not he gets the joke, but also on his views and values whether or not he can appreciate the answers the economics-made-fun genre provides. And economists have praised and opposed economics-made-fun books, not only based on what answers are provided, but also on the questions that are asked and even on who is asking – so, the identity of the economist is also at stake.

4. 'Fun' and the identity of economists

At a relatively early stage, before the publication of *Freakonomics*, Dubner published an interview with Levitt in the *New York Times Magazine*.[8] The interview starts on a high: Levitt is the most brilliant young economists of America, referring to the John Bates Clark medal Levitt won in the same year. What makes Levitt different is that 'he sees things differently than the average person. Differently, too, than the average economist'. Average economists 'wax oracularly' about monetary policy and other boring topics. Levitt brushed traditional economics aside, admitting that he is not even good at it:

> I don't know very much about the field of economics. I'm not good at math, I don't know a lot of econometrics, and I also don't know how to do theory. If you ask me about whether the stock market's going to go up or down, if you ask me whether the economy's going to grow or shrink, if you ask me whether deflation's good or bad, if you ask me about taxes – I mean, it would be total fakery if I said I knew anything about any of those things. (Dubner 2003)

This is quite radical for a John Bates Clark medal winner in economics, the most prestigious prize for young economists. He is clearly distinguishing himself from the older generation of economists. The interview continues with stating that many of Levitt's peers do not recognize his work as economics at all. If not economics proper, than what is Levitt doing, and why is he so successful at it?

According to Levitt, it is because he asks a different type of questions and employs different methods. He is not afraid to use his personal observations and curiosities. The article uses the term 'intuitionist' to refer to Levitt's style of economics. He is able to turn everyday observations into serious science – driven by curiosity and a good intuition. 'He [Levitt] was the guy who, in the slapstick scene, sees all the engineers futzing with a broken machine and then realizes that no one has thought to plug it in' (Dubner 2003). In fact, he is not that special, he is just like someone who is very good with computers. And his looks confirm this: 'his appearance is High Nerd: a plaid button-down shirt, nondescript khakis and a braided belt, sensible shoes. His pocket calendar is branded with the National Bureau of Economic Research logo' (Dubner 2003). Levitt is a master at being an amateur economist. He is not interested in politics or moralizing, let alone Big Science. He is the different, new type of intellectual, departing from the deep thinking and big ideas of the Old University of Chicago. Though his economics is about empiricism and portrays clever thinking, it ultimately deals with insubstantial ideas – something of a postmodern joke on Big Science in its great bastion itself, the University of Chicago.

This new image of the smart amateur having fun is appealing and attractive to new students. Economics-made-fun is the genre that celebrates this new image. Both Levitt and Dubner are very aware of this and capitalize on it, other economists have mixed feeling about it – but all changes of identity in all sciences draw mixed reactions. Recent work of Shapin (2008), *The Scientific Life*, testifies to this.

Shapin analyzes the professional identity of natural scientists throughout the nineteenth and twentieth century. This identity has shifted dramatically from Big Men doing Big Science to regular guys pursuing their curiosity. Some scientists have applauded this, but others lamented this change. The evolutionary biologist Steven Pinker, for example, complained: 'The old notion of scientist as hero has been replaced by the idea of amoral nerds at best' (quoted in Shapin 2008, XV). Immediately we are reminded of Levitt, who was described precisely as such by Dubner in the article.

What Shapin does, instead of praising or condemning this change, is to try to distill some ideal types[9] from these changes. His focus is mainly historical, but we think these types can be observed simultaneously, they are:

(1) The eccentric and heroic individual.
(2) The competitor.
(3) The playful type.[10]

The first image is perhaps the most traditional notion of the scientist, to which Pinker longs back. Typically this type of scientists is an outsider, a quirky eccentric individual who is usually quite unsocial. Although they are eccentric and hard to deal with, they are also geniuses. Einstein and Newton are perhaps the typical examples of scientists who are commonly described as such. Biographies portrayed them as uncompromising individuals, with great visions. Heilbroner's 'Wordly Philosophers' features the Great Economists from Smith to Schumpeter, all outstanding individuals with great visions. These kinds of histories are nowadays often derogatorily referred to as Big Man Histories. Heilbroner, like Pinker, has repeatedly lamented the disappearance or marginalization of this type of individuals from economics (e.g. Heilbroner and Milberg 1995).

In the postwar era, another image of the scientist emerges. James Watson's *The Double Helix* sketches a picture of scientists working in close-knit groups who are in heavy competition – in search of not only for the origins of life or other big answers (e.g. Manhattan Project) but also motivated by fame and stardom. Watson's account of the discovery of *The Double Helix* was shocking to many. Scientists were not virtuous, collaborative intellectuals, but competitive, sometimes ruthless truth-seekers, with little concern for the scientific commons. As such Stanislaw and Yergin's account of the battle for the 'Commanding Heights' of the economy is similar: economists are in competition with one another, but ultimately they compete to answer the fundamental economic questions (Yergin and Stanislaw 1998).

Shapin's third type of the natural scientist, the playful type, is personified by Richard Feynman. Feynman is a physicist who portrayed himself as a witty, funny person for whom playing the bongo or juggling were the same type of activity as doing physics. His books written for a popular audience were as much about his daily life and hobbies as they were about science, and with great success. Feynman was celebrated for having shown that doing physics was fun, but critics accused him of degrading the serious subject of physics and distorting the truth about the hard hours of work in the lab. Feynman not only showed that physicists were 'normal' people, as we already learned from Watson, but also that science was a 'normal' activity. Science was just another human activity, no different from his other hobbies and thus accessible to large groups. But the fun of his science also consisted of the counterintuitive and striking scientific results he presented. His favorite of the kind is undoubtedly the 'double-slit experiment', which shows that light is both a particle and a wave at the same time, which figures prominently in many of his popular books.

Feynman's popular books resemble the economics-made-fun genre. They use simple intuitive insights combined with some experimental or empirical results, to show counterintuitive aspects of reality. The reader becomes a discoverer along with the scientist, who can follow him at every step – contrary to the hermetic nature of much of scientific literature. And they blur the distinction between the public and the private nature of science. Whereas the scientists in other accounts are objective disinterested observers, the scientists in these stories are participants, involved at every stage.

Levitt neatly matches this profile. He and other authors of the economics-made-fun genre are turning economics into a type of play and in this play they draw a wide audience to their books. People are able to identify with Levitt, personally. He does not portray himself as superior in knowledge or even intelligence. Instead of being the omnicognescent teachers to their audience, they become one of them, mainly through their self-depreciative humor. In the recent 'Freakonomics' movie this comes out very clearly. Toward the end of the movie Dubner states:

> We give people permission to challenge conventional wisdom sometimes. And to ask a different kind of question entirely. And a lot of times, these are the sorts of question you ask as children, and people kinda chuckle at you. But once in a while they are really good. The problem is that when you get older (. . .) and people laugh at you hard, you just stop asking these questions entirely. (Ewing et al. 2010)

Levitt and Dubner claim that they are asking the basic human questions everyone asks as a child. The similarity to Feynman's self-description again is striking: 'When I was a kid I had a lab. It wasn't a laboratory in the sense that I would measure, or do important experiments. Instead I would play' (Feynman 1985, p. 91). What Levitt and Feynman have in common is the stress on the play element in science, the curiosity aspect of it. The reason to do science does not lie outside of them in political goals, economic rewards or aspirations of fame, but in the fun of doing it. Therefore, the comparison of science to juggling and playing the bongo by Feynman are apt. They are all noninstrumental activities, pursued for their own good. The implicit message is that economics can be done by everyone, because it is about basic human questions about everyday life (and about fun answers). And as everyone can be an economist, economists are just like everyone – or as Shapin observes, the playful type not only normalizes science as practice, but it also normalizes its practitioner.

Levitt and Dubner stress their lack of political convictions, their lack of adherence to theory and stress their human side, while at the same time they argue that everyone deep inside is an economist, as the title of the book by Cowen (2007), *Discover Your Inner Economist*, suggests. So they extend the group of economists enormously, everyone who has asked smart questions as a child, can now be an economist. In other words, the profession is open to amateurs, to all.

This in itself of course is a threat to the ethos of the professional economist (he did get a Ph.D. in economics for something, right?) and might also explain some of the moral outrage in the profession. What the economics-made-fun genre does is not simply extending the domain of economics, but it also changes the identity of the profession, and its practitioners. The imperialist is not the same guy as the old economist. He has freed himself from theory, politics and mathematical models, but equipped himself with a fresh intuition and a new set of questions. The professional economist in the meanwhile is mainly puzzled about what's economic about explaining why milk cartons are square, while soda bottles are round (to name one example from Frank's book).

As it determines the domain of economics, humor also shows how the playful identity has its limits. The professionally deformed economist featuring in the 'You might be an economist if . . . ' is ridiculed since he clearly went astray. Interestingly, the Levitt we see in the Freakonomics film shows signs of deformation himself, when we see how he is raising his daughter Amanda. He is potty training her using, of course, incentives. Amanda is rewarded with candy every time she uses the toilet. But soon the daughter figures out that by going to the toilet much more often than she really needs to, she can get extra candy. Incentive scheme failed. The fun of Freakonomics turns into the funny of economics-made-fun-of.

Here, another function of humor also comes into play. As humor results from two cognitive frames clashing, solving for the 'real one' so to say, it also reduces the distance between speaker and audience. Meyer sees humor as (also) serving to defuse tense situations. Humor causes 'the release [of] nervous energy' (Meyer 2000, p. 312), which, like economics-made-fun, helps to bond master and amateur economists. It helps to bring the 'outsiders' in, especially when the joke is told by an 'insider'. Understandably, the first thing that Yoran Bauman, the stand-up economist, makes clear is that he has done a Ph.D. in economics himself. As an insider, he has more ethos – his jokes are appreciated more than perhaps the same jokes made by an anthropologist. An economist mocking himself releases more tension than an anthropologist mocking economists. Leijonhufvud's paper 'Life among the Econ' (1973) or Blinder's 'The Economics of Brushing Teeth' (1974), but also similar efforts made by important insiders like George Stigler, Kenneth Boulding, Paul Samuelson, Paul Krugman and Martin Feldstein, are all funnier, and more easily accepted because they jokes are made by insiders.

The status of the speaker is thus important to understand a particular remark, is it funny, rude or serious? And so, Levitt is able to use the failed incentive scheme for his daughter to make the point that setting up incentive schemes is not a simple task. But he does so safely at the end of the movie, when the audience understands the power of incentives, and has sufficiently identified himself with Levitt. Nevertheless the expansion of the domain of economics has its dangers. Would Blinder's paper on the economics of brushing teeth – associate professors brush 2.14, full professors 1.47 times a day – still be understood as economics-made-fun-of? Or would it be considered as evidence, that yes, incentives matter even in the unexplored territory of personal hygiene?[11]

5.   Conclusion

The general question lurking underneath the EIPE Conference 'Economics made fun in the face of the economic crisis' was how to appreciate the 'economics-made-fun' genre. Should we welcome it as a valuable addition to economics or should we look at it as the denial or degradation of a serious subject? We think economics-made-fun should not be dismissed out of hand. It has drawn in millions of new amateurs into the field, and helped regular economics students to make sense of their subject (Frank wrote his book, knowing how regular economics classes usually do not stick in student's minds for long). It has quite successfully expanded the audience of economics. But is has also shifted the domain of economics, and the professional identity of the economist – changes that will accompanied with a certain degree of moral indignation.

These changes are far from inconsequential, if for no other reason than shaping the expectations of our future students. They also mean a change in what it means to be an economist; he is not just the policy advisor commuting between Cambridge and Washington, but possibly also the clever guy full of clever anecdotes based on intuitive empirical research. As such what Levitt and other authors in the genre are doing is posing a challenge to the professional establishment, both in terms of what they do and who they are. And hence they deserve to be taken quite seriously.

One surprising finding of this paper is that to keep economics-made-fun in check, economics-made-fun-of might have a role to play. Making fun of economists helps to keep economics from trespassing, from entering the noneconomic areas where its principles and assumptions have no value. Especially economists can successfully do this mocking, they know the theories from the inside and have the professional ethos to successfully mock the trespassing imperialists.

One such attempt is a recent article by Rubinstein (2006), who suggests to apply the principles of the genre back onto its authors. This could, for example, lead us to wonder whether they are subject to the right incentives. Levitt suggest himself as much toward the end of the Freakonomics movie: 'In some sense we're this peculiar beast, which actually has the right incentives to just seek the truth'. Now the only thing we hope is that in writing this paper we were not out to please either you as audience, or our Ph.D. supervisor, and that we just had the right incentives to seek the truth. Then really you have all the reason to believe that everything we claimed above is, well the truth, but about that we should perhaps let the market decide.

Notes

1. The genre perhaps taps into the same sentiment as the Dan Brown's bestseller 'The Da Vinci Code' (2003), which 'reveals' the biggest secret out of the Christian church's history. The fun of the rising Crime Scene Investigation (CSI) television series also seems stems from the same tree. In fact, one observer called Freakonomics 'CSI: Economics'.
2. Economics jokes circulate widely on the Internet. One source is http://www.jokes.net/economicsjokes.htm (accessed 5 March 2012).
3. The source of this joke is not (yet) known, but it apparently was heard at an evolutionary economists conference (IIASA). See http://www.gloge.com/jokeecon.html.
4. Economics has 'stand-up economist' Yoram Bauman, someone who by the way has quite serious ideals about economics education, the environment and the tax system. He has engaged Levitt for trying to debunk global warming.
5. See http://www.workjoke.com/ to see our point.
6. Dutch comedian Hans Teeuwen explained, when held accountable for his indecent remarks toward three Muslims TV presenters, that his jokes were funny because religion has power, but also because of the chastity of the presenters, saying: 'Issues that are sensitive or controversial are fun, exciting, there is the tension. As a comedian that is what you work with'. See Bimbo's and Boerka's, 30-08-2007, NPS (in Dutch).
7. Others think economists were not invited by other disciplines (Stigler 1984), that economists have rushed into other disciplines because they failed to solve their own problems (Coase 1978) or because they don't even have interesting questions themselves (Levitt and Dubner 2005).
8. The interview is available at Dubner's website: http://stephenjdubner.com/journalism/economist.html.
9. Harro Maas in his recent introduction to the philosophy of economics, also puts emphasis on the 'types' of economists, his chapter on Keynes and Tinbergen, for example, labels them dramatist and social engineer or model builder (2010).
10. Shapin distinguishes a fourth type, which for economists might be of special interest, although not for present purposes. That fourth type is the entrepreneur. For him, science is not just truth seeking, it is also big business. Shapin convincingly shows how modern scientists have turned more and more into successful managers.
11. Vromen (2009) tells a story about a mock paper by Oxoby, which was wrongfully understood by Levitt as a contribution to his field of research.

References

Bastiat, F. (1909), *Economic Sophisms*, New York: Putnam.
Brown, D. (2003), *The Da Vinci Code*, New York: Knopf Doubleday.
Becker, G. (1964), *Human Capital: A Theoretical and Empirical Analysis, with Special Reference to Education*, Chicago: University of Chicago Press.
———— (1990), 'Gary S. Becker', in *Economics and Sociology, Redefining Their Boundaries: Conversations with Economists and Sociologists*, ed. R. Swedberg, Princeton, NJ: Princeton University Press, pp. 27–46.

Beeman, W. (1999), 'Humor', *Journal of Linguistic Anthropology*, 9, 103–106.

Blinder, A.S. (1974), 'The Economics of Brushing Teeth', *The Journal of Political Economy*, 82, 887–891.

Coase, R. (1978), 'Economics and Contiguous Disciplines', *Journal of Legal Studies*, 7, 201–211.

Cowen, T. (2007), *Discover Your Inner Economist: Use Incentives to Fall in Love, Survive Your Next Meeting, and Motivate Your Dentist*, New York: Dutton Adult.

Dow, S. (2002), *Economic Methodology: An Inquiry*, Oxford: Oxford University Press.

Dubner, S.J. (2003), 'The Economist of Odd Questions: Inside the Astonishingly Curious Mind of Steven J. Levitt', *New York Times Magazine*.

Ewing, H., Gibney, A., Gordon, S., Grady, R., Jarecki, E., and Spurlock, M. (2010), 'Freakonomics, Chad Troutwine Films'.

Feynman, R.P. (1985), *Surely You're Joking, Mr. Feynman: Adventures of a Curious Character*, London: Unwin Paperbacks.

Fine, B. (2000), 'Economics Imperialism and Intellectual Progress: The Present as History of Economic Thought?' *History of Economics Review*, 32, 10–36.

Fine, B., and Milonakis, D. (2009), *From Economics Imperialism to Freakonomics: The Shifting Bounderies Between Economics and Other Social Sciences*, London: Routledge.

Frank, R.H. (2007), *The Economic Naturalist: In Search of Explanations for Everyday Enigmas*, New York: Perseus Books Group.

Harford, T. (2005), *The Undercover Economist: Exposing Why the Rich are Rich, the Poor are Poor – and Why You can Never Buy a Decent Used Car!* Oxford: Oxford University Press.

———— (2008), *The Logic of Life: The Rational Economics of an Irrational World*, New York: Random House.

Heilbroner, R.L., and Milberg, W.S. (1995), *The Crisis of Vision in Modern Economic Thought*, Cambridge: Cambridge University Press.

Klamer, A. (2007), *Speaking of Economics: How to Get into the Conversation*, London: Routledge.

Lazear, E.P. (2000), 'Economic Imperialism', *The Quarterly Journal of Economics*, 115, 99–146.

Leijonhufvud, A. (1973), 'Life among the Econ', *Western Economic Journal*, 11, 327–337.

Levitt, S.D., and Dubner, S.J. (2005), *Freakonomics: A Rogue Economist Explores the Hidden Side of Everything*, New York: William Morrow.

Levitt, S.D., and Dubner, S.J. (2009), *Superfreakonomics: Global Cooling, Patriotic Prostitutes, and Why Suicide Bombers Should Buy Life Insurance*, London: Allen Lane.

Maas, H. (2010), *Spelregels van Economen*, Amsterdam: Boom Lemma Uitgevers.

Meyer, J.C. (2000), 'Humor as a Double-Edged Sword: Four Functions of Humor in Communication', *Communication Theory*, 10, 310–331.

McCloskey, D.N. (1990), *If You're So Smart: The Narrative of Economic Expertise*, Chicago: University of Chicago Press.

———— (2001), *How to be Human, tough an Economist*, Ann Arbor: University of Michigan Press.

Rubinstein, A. (2006), 'Freak-Freakonomics', *Economists' Voice*, 3, Article 7.

Shapin, S. (2008), *The Scientific Life: A Moral History of a Late Modern Vocation*, Chicago: University of Chicago Press.

Souter, R.W. (1933), *Prolegomena to Relativity Economics*, New York: Columbia University Press.

Stigler, G. (1984), 'Economics – The Imperial Science?' *Scandinavian Journal of Economics*, 86, 301–313.

Veatch, T.C. (1998), 'A Theory of Humor', *Humor – International Journal of Humor Research*, 11, 161–215.

Vromen, J. (2009), 'The Booming Economics-Made-Fun Genre: More Than Having Fun, But Less Than Economics Imperialism', *Eramus Journal of Philosophy and Economics*, 2, 70–99.

Yergin, D., and Stanislaw, J. (1998), *The Commanding Heights: The Battle Between Government and the Marketplace That is Making the Modern World*, New York: Simon & Schuster.

Index

INDEX